TOBIT, JUDITH, AND ESTHER

THE IGNATIUS CATHOLIC STUDY BIBLE

REVISED STANDARD VERSION
SECOND CATHOLIC EDITION

TOBIT, JUDITH, AND ESTHER

With Introduction, Commentary, and Notes

by

Scott Hahn and Curtis Mitch

with

André Villeneuve

and

with Study Questions by

Dennis Walters

IGNATIUS PRESS   SAN FRANCISCO

Published with ecclesiastical approval
Original Bible text: Revised Standard Version, Catholic Edition
Nihil Obstat: Thomas Hanlon, S.T.L., L.S.S., Ph.L.
Imprimatur: +Peter W. Bartholome, D.D.
Bishop of Saint Cloud, Minnesota
May 11, 1966

Introduction, commentaries, and notes:
Nihil Obstat: Ruth Ohm Sutherland, Ph.D., Censor Deputatus
Imprimatur: +The Most Reverend Salvatore Cordileone
Archbishop of San Francisco
August 17, 2018

The *nihil obstat* and *imprimatur* are official declarations that a book or pamphlet is free of
doctrinal or moral error. No implication is contained therein that those who have granted
the *nihil obstat* and *imprimatur* agree with the contents, opinions, or statements expressed.

Second Catholic Edition approved by the
National Council of the Churches of Christ in the USA

Cover art: *Tobias Restoring His Father's Sight*
by Jan Sanders van Hemessen
(c. 1500–c. 1566)
RestoredTraditions.com

Cover design by Riz Boncan Marsella

Published by Ignatius Press in 2019

Introductions, commentaries, notes, headings, and study questions
© 2019 by Ignatius Press, San Francisco
All rights reserved
ISBN 978-1-62164-185-8 (PB)
ISBN 978-1-64229-080-6 (eBook)
Printed in the United States of America ∞

CONTENTS

INTRODUCTION TO
THE IGNATIUS STUDY BIBLE
by Scott Hahn, Ph.D.

You are approaching the "word of God". This is the title Christians most commonly give to the Bible, and the expression is rich in meaning. It is also the title given to the Second Person of the Blessed Trinity, God the Son. For Jesus Christ became flesh for our salvation, and "the name by which he is called is The Word of God" (Rev 19:13; cf. Jn 1:14).

The word of God is Scripture. The Word of God is Jesus. This close association between God's *written* word and his *eternal* Word is intentional and has been the custom of the Church since the first generation. "All Sacred Scripture is but one book, and this one book is Christ, 'because all divine Scripture speaks of Christ, and all divine Scripture is fulfilled in Christ'"[1] (CCC 134). This does not mean that the Scriptures are divine in the same way that Jesus is divine. They are, rather, divinely inspired and, as such, are unique in world literature, just as the Incarnation of the eternal Word is unique in human history.

Yet we can say that the inspired word resembles the incarnate Word in several important ways. Jesus Christ is the Word of God incarnate. In his humanity, he is like us in all things, except for sin. As a work of man, the Bible is like any other book, except without error. Both Christ and Scripture, says the Second Vatican Council, are given "for the sake of our salvation" (*Dei Verbum* 11), and both give us God's definitive revelation of himself. We cannot, therefore, conceive of one without the other: the Bible without Jesus, or Jesus without the Bible. Each is the interpretive key to the other. And because Christ is the subject of all the Scriptures, St. Jerome insists, "Ignorance of the Scriptures is ignorance of Christ"[2] (CCC 133).

When we approach the Bible, then, we approach Jesus, the Word of God; and in order to encounter Jesus, we must approach him in a prayerful study of the inspired word of God, the Sacred Scriptures.

Inspiration and Inerrancy The Catholic Church makes mighty claims for the Bible, and our acceptance of those claims is essential if we are to read the Scriptures and apply them to our lives as the Church intends. So it is not enough merely to nod at words like "inspired", "unique", or "inerrant". We

have to understand what the Church means by these terms, and we have to make that understanding our own. After all, what we believe about the Bible will inevitably influence the way we read the Bible. The way we read the Bible, in turn, will determine what we "get out" of its sacred pages.

These principles hold true no matter what we read: a news report, a search warrant, an advertisement, a paycheck, a doctor's prescription, an eviction notice. How (or whether) we read these things depends largely upon our preconceived notions about the reliability and authority of their sources—and the potential they have for affecting our lives. In some cases, to misunderstand a document's authority can lead to dire consequences. In others, it can keep us from enjoying rewards that are rightfully ours. In the case of the Bible, both the rewards and the consequences involved take on an ultimate value.

What does the Church mean, then, when she affirms the words of St. Paul: "All Scripture is inspired by God" (2 Tim 3:16)? Since the term "inspired" in this passage could be translated "God-breathed", it follows that God breathed forth his word in the Scriptures as you and I breathe forth air when we speak. This means that God is the primary author of the Bible. He certainly employed human authors in this task as well, but he did not merely assist them while they wrote or subsequently approve what they had written. God the Holy Spirit is the *principal* author of Scripture, while the human writers are *instrumental* authors. These human authors freely wrote everything, and only those things, that God wanted: the word of God in the very words of God. This miracle of dual authorship extends to the whole of Scripture, and to every one of its parts, so that whatever the human authors affirm, God likewise affirms through their words.

The principle of biblical inerrancy follows logically from this principle of divine authorship. After all, God cannot lie, and he cannot make mistakes. Since the Bible is divinely inspired, it must be without error in everything that its divine and human authors affirm to be true. This means that biblical inerrancy is a mystery even broader in scope than infallibility, which guarantees for us that the Church will always teach the truth concerning faith and morals. Of course the mantle of inerrancy likewise covers faith and morals, but it extends even farther to ensure that all the facts and events of salvation history are accurately presented for us in

---

[1] Hugh of St. Victor, *De arca Noe* 2, 8: PL 176, 642: cf. ibid. 2, 9: PL 176, 642–43.
[2] *DV* 25; cf. Phil 3:8 and St. Jerome, *Commentariorum in Isaiam libri xviii*, prol.: PL 24, 17b.

the Scriptures. Inerrancy is our guarantee that the words and deeds of God found in the Bible are unified and true, declaring with one voice the wonders of his saving love.

The guarantee of inerrancy does not mean, however, that the Bible is an all-purpose encyclopedia of information covering every field of study. The Bible is not, for example, a textbook in the empirical sciences, and it should not be treated as one. When biblical authors relate facts of the natural order, we can be sure they are speaking in a purely descriptive and "phenomenological" way, according to the way things appeared to their senses.

Biblical Authority Implicit in these doctrines is God's desire to make himself known to the world and to enter a loving relationship with every man, woman, and child he has created. God gave us the Scriptures not just to inform or motivate us; more than anything he wants to save us. This higher purpose underlies every page of the Bible, indeed every word of it.

In order to reveal himself, God used what theologians call "accommodation". Sometimes the Lord stoops down to communicate by "condescension"—that is, he speaks as humans speak, as if he had the same passions and weakness that we do (for example, God says he was "sorry" that he made man in Genesis 6:6). Other times he communicates by "elevation"—that is, by endowing human words with divine power (for example, through the Prophets). The numerous examples of divine accommodation in the Bible are an expression of God's wise and fatherly ways. For a sensitive father can speak with his children either by condescension, as in baby talk, or by elevation, by bringing a child's understanding up to a more mature level.

God's word is thus saving, fatherly, and personal. Because it speaks directly to us, we must never be indifferent to its content; after all, the word of God is at once the object, cause, and support of our faith. It is, in fact, a test of our faith, since we see in the Scriptures only what faith disposes us to see. If we believe what the Church believes, we will see in Scripture the saving, inerrant, and divinely authored revelation of the Father. If we believe otherwise, we see another book altogether.

This test applies not only to rank-and-file believers but also to the Church's theologians and hierarchy, and even the Magisterium. Vatican II has stressed in recent times that Scripture must be "the very soul of sacred theology" (*Dei Verbum* 24). As Joseph Cardinal Ratzinger, Pope Benedict XVI echoed this powerful teaching with his own, insisting that "the *normative theologians* are the authors of Holy Scripture" (emphasis added). He reminded us that Scripture and the Church's dogmatic teaching are tied tightly together, to the point of being inseparable: "Dogma is by definition nothing other than an interpretation of Scripture." The defined dogmas of our faith, then, encapsulate the Church's infallible interpretation of Scripture, and theology is a further reflection upon that work.

The Senses of Scripture Because the Bible has both divine and human authors, we are required to master a different sort of reading than we are used to. First, we must read Scripture according to its *literal* sense, as we read any other human literature. At this initial stage, we strive to discover the meaning of the words and expressions used by the biblical writers as they were understood in their original setting and by their original recipients. This means, among other things, that we do not interpret everything we read "literalistically", as though Scripture never speaks in a figurative or symbolic way (it often does!). Rather, we read it according to the rules that govern its different literary forms of writing, depending on whether we are reading a narrative, a poem, a letter, a parable, or an apocalyptic vision. The Church calls us to read the divine books in this way to ensure that we understand what the human authors were laboring to explain to God's people.

The literal sense, however, is not the only sense of Scripture, since we interpret its sacred pages according to the *spiritual* senses as well. In this way, we search out what the Holy Spirit is trying to tell us, beyond even what the human authors have consciously asserted. Whereas the literal sense of Scripture describes a historical reality—a fact, precept, or event—the spiritual senses disclose deeper mysteries revealed through the historical realities. What the soul is to the body, the spiritual senses are to the literal. You can distinguish them; but if you try to separate them, death immediately follows. St. Paul was the first to insist upon this and warn of its consequences: "God ... has qualified us to be ministers of a new covenant, not in a written code but in the Spirit; for the written code kills, but the Spirit gives life" (2 Cor 3:5–6).

Catholic tradition recognizes three spiritual senses that stand upon the foundation of the literal sense of Scripture (see CCC 115). **(1)** The first is the *allegorical* sense, which unveils the spiritual and prophetic meaning of biblical history. Allegorical interpretations thus reveal how persons, events, and institutions of Scripture can point beyond themselves toward greater mysteries yet to come (OT) or display the fruits of mysteries already revealed (NT). Christians have often read the Old Testament in this way to discover how the mystery of Christ in the New Covenant was once hidden in the Old and how the full significance of the Old Covenant was finally made manifest in the New. Allegorical significance is likewise latent in the New Testament, especially in the life and deeds of Jesus recorded in the Gospels. Because Christ is the Head of the Church and the source of her spiritual life, what was accomplished in Christ the Head during his earthly life prefigures what he continually produces in his members through grace. The allegorical sense builds up the virtue of faith. **(2)** The second is the *tropological* or *moral* sense, which reveals how the actions of God's people in the Old Testament and the life of Jesus in the New Testament prompt us to form virtuous habits in our own lives. It therefore draws from Scripture warnings against sin and vice as well as inspirations to pursue holiness and purity. The moral sense is intended to build up the virtue of charity. **(3)** The third is the *anagogical* sense, which points upward to heavenly glory. It shows us how countless events in the Bible prefigure our final union with God in eternity and how things that are "seen" on earth are figures of things "unseen" in heaven. Because the anagogical sense leads us to contemplate our destiny, it is meant to build up the virtue of hope. Together with the literal sense, then, these spiritual senses draw out the fullness of what God wants to give us through his Word and as such comprise what ancient tradition has called the "full sense" of Sacred Scripture.

All of this means that the deeds and events of the Bible are charged with meaning beyond what is immediately apparent to the reader. In essence, that meaning is Jesus Christ and the salvation he died to give us. This is especially true of the books of the New Testament, which proclaim Jesus explicitly; but it is also true of the Old Testament, which speaks of Jesus in more hidden and symbolic ways. The human authors of the Old Testament told us as much as they were able, but they could not clearly discern the shape of all future events standing at such a distance. It is the Bible's divine Author, the Holy Spirit, who could and did foretell the saving work of Christ, from the first page of the Book of Genesis onward.

The New Testament did not, therefore, abolish the Old. Rather, the New fulfilled the Old, and in doing so, it lifted the veil that kept hidden the face of the Lord's bride. Once the veil is removed, we suddenly see the world of the Old Covenant charged with grandeur. Water, fire, clouds, gardens, trees, hills, doves, lambs—all of these things are memorable details in the history and poetry of Israel. But now, seen in the light of Jesus Christ, they are much more. For the Christian with eyes to see, water symbolizes the saving power of Baptism; fire, the Holy Spirit; the spotless lamb, Christ crucified; Jerusalem, the city of heavenly glory.

The spiritual reading of Scripture is nothing new. Indeed, the very first Christians read the Bible this way. St. Paul describes Adam as a "type" that prefigured Jesus Christ (Rom 5:14). A "type" is a real person, place, thing, or event in the Old Testament that foreshadows something greater in the New. From this term we get the word "typology", referring to the study of how the Old Testament prefigures Christ (CCC 128–30). Elsewhere St. Paul draws deeper meanings out of the story of Abraham's sons, declaring, "This is an allegory" (Gal 4:24). He is not suggesting that these events of the distant past never really happened; he is saying that the events both happened *and* signified something more glorious yet to come.

The New Testament later describes the Tabernacle of ancient Israel as "a copy and shadow of the heavenly sanctuary" (Heb 8:5) and the Mosaic Law as a "shadow of the good things to come" (Heb 10:1). St. Peter, in turn, notes that Noah and his family were "saved through water" in a way that "corresponds" to sacramental Baptism, which "now saves you" (1 Pet 3:20–21). It is interesting to note that the expression translated as "corresponds" in this verse is a Greek term that denotes the fulfillment or counterpart of an ancient "type".

We need not look to the apostles, however, to justify a spiritual reading of the Bible. After all, Jesus himself read the Old Testament this way. He referred to Jonah (Mt 12:39), Solomon (Mt 12:42), the Temple (Jn 2:19), and the brazen serpent (Jn 3:14) as "signs" that pointed forward to him. We see in Luke's Gospel, as Christ comforted the disciples on the road to Emmaus, that "beginning with Moses and all the prophets, he interpreted to them in all the Scriptures the things concerning himself" (Lk 24:27). It was precisely this extensive spiritual interpretation of the Old Testament that made such an impact on these once-discouraged travelers, causing their hearts to "burn" within them (Lk 24:32).

Criteria for Biblical Interpretation We, too, must learn to discern the "full sense" of Scripture as it includes both the literal and spiritual senses together. Still, this does not mean we should "read into" the Bible meanings that are not really there. Spiritual exegesis is not an unrestrained flight of the imagination. Rather, it is a sacred science that proceeds according to certain principles and stands accountable to sacred tradition, the Magisterium, and the wider community of biblical interpreters (both living and deceased).

In searching out the full sense of a text, we should always avoid the extreme tendency to "over-spiritualize" in a way that minimizes or denies the Bible's literal truth. St. Thomas Aquinas was well aware of this danger and asserted that "all other senses of Sacred Scripture are based on the literal" (*STh* I, 1, 10, *ad* 1, quoted in CCC 116). On the other hand, we should never confine the meaning of a text to the literal, intended sense of its human author, as if the divine Author did not intend the passage to be read in the light of Christ's coming.

Fortunately the Church has given us guidelines in our study of Scripture. The unique character and divine authorship of the Bible call us to read it "in the Spirit" (*Dei Verbum* 12). Vatican II outlines this teaching in a practical way by directing us to read the Scriptures according to three specific criteria:

1. We must "[b]e especially attentive 'to the content and unity of the whole Scripture'" (CCC 112).

2. We must "[r]ead the Scripture within 'the living Tradition of the whole Church'" (CCC 113).

3. We must "[b]e attentive to the analogy of faith" (CCC 114; cf. Rom 12:6).

These criteria protect us from many of the dangers that ensnare readers of the Bible, from the newest inquirer to the most prestigious scholar. Reading Scripture out of context is one such pitfall, and probably the one most difficult to avoid. A memorable cartoon from the 1950s shows a young man poring over the pages of the Bible. He says to his sister: "Don't bother me now; I'm trying to find a Scripture verse to back up one of my preconceived notions." No doubt a biblical text pried from its context can be twisted to say something very different from what its author actually intended.

The Church's criteria guide us here by defining what constitutes the authentic "context" of a given biblical passage. The first criterion directs us to the literary context of every verse, including not only the words and paragraphs that surround it, but also the entire corpus of the biblical author's writings and, indeed, the span of the entire Bible. The *complete* literary context of any Scripture verse includes every text from Genesis to Revelation—because the Bible is a unified book, not just a library of different books. When the Church canonized the Book of Revelation, for example, she recognized it to be incomprehensible apart from the wider context of the entire Bible.

The second criterion places the Bible firmly within the context of a community that treasures a "living tradition". That community is the People of God down through the ages. Christians lived out their faith for well over a millennium before the printing press was invented. For centuries, few believers owned copies of the Gospels, and few people could read anyway. Yet they absorbed the gospel—through the sermons of their bishops and clergy, through prayer and meditation, through Christian art, through liturgical celebrations, and through oral tradition. These were expressions of the one "living tradition", a culture of living faith that stretches from ancient Israel to the contemporary Church. For the early Christians, the gospel could not be understood apart from that tradition. So it is with us. Reverence for the Church's tradition is what protects us from any sort of chronological or cultural provincialism, such as scholarly fads that arise and carry away a generation of interpreters before being dismissed by the next generation.

The third criterion places scriptural texts within the framework of faith. If we believe that the Scriptures are divinely inspired, we must also believe them to be internally coherent and consistent with all the doctrines that Christians believe. Remember, the Church's dogmas (such as the Real Presence, the papacy, the Immaculate Conception) are not something *added* to Scripture; rather, they are the Church's infallible interpretation *of* Scripture.

Using This Study Guide This volume is designed to lead the reader through Scripture according to the Church's guidelines—faithful to the canon, to the tradition, and to the creeds. The Church's interpretive principles have thus shaped the component parts of this book, and they are designed to make the reader's study as effective and rewarding as possible.

Introductions: We have introduced the biblical book with an essay covering issues such as authorship, date of composition, purpose, and leading themes. This background information will assist readers to approach and understand the text on its own terms.

Annotations: The basic notes at the bottom of every page help the user to read the Scriptures with understanding. They by no means exhaust the meaning of the sacred text but provide background material to help the reader make sense of what he reads. Often these notes make explicit what the sacred writers assumed or held to be implicit. They also provide a great deal of historical, cultural, geographical, and theological information pertinent to the inspired narratives—information that can help the reader bridge the distance between the biblical world and his own.

Cross-References: Between the biblical text at the top of each page and the annotations at the bottom, numerous references are listed to point readers to other scriptural passages related to the one being studied. This follow-up is an essential part of any serious study. It is also an excellent way to discover how the content of Scripture "hangs together" in a providential unity. Along with biblical cross-references, the annotations refer to select paragraphs from the *Catechism of the Catholic Church*. These are not doctrinal "proof texts" but are designed to help the reader interpret the Bible in accordance with the mind of the Church. The *Catechism* references listed either handle the biblical text directly or treat a broader doctrinal theme that sheds significant light on that text.

Topical Essays, Word Studies, Charts: These features bring readers to a deeper understanding of select details. The *topical essays* take up major themes and explain them more thoroughly and theologically than the annotations, often relating them to the doctrines of the Church. Occasionally the annotations are supplemented by *word studies* that put readers in touch with the ancient languages of Scripture. These should help readers to understand better and appreciate the inspired terminology that runs throughout the sacred books. Also included are various *charts* that summarize biblical information "at a glance".

Icon Annotations: Three distinctive icons are interspersed throughout the annotations, each one corresponding to one of the Church's three criteria for biblical interpretation. Bullets indicate the passage or passages to which these icons apply.

Notes marked by the book icon relate to the "content and unity" of Scripture, showing how particular passages of the Old Testament illuminate the mysteries of the New. Much of the information in these notes explains the original context of the citations and indicates how and why this has a direct bearing on Christ or the Church. Through these notes, the reader can develop a sensitivity to the beauty and unity of God's saving plan as it stretches across both Testaments.

Notes marked by the dove icon examine particular passages in light of the Church's "living tradition". Because the Holy Spirit both guides the Magisterium and inspires the spiritual senses of Scripture, these annotations supply information along both of these lines. On the one hand, they refer to the Church's doctrinal teaching as presented by various popes, creeds, and ecumenical councils; on the other, they draw from (and paraphrase) the spiritual interpretations of various Fathers, Doctors, and saints.

Notes marked by the keys icon pertain to the "analogy of faith". Here we spell out how the mysteries of our faith "unlock" and explain one another. This type of comparison between Christian beliefs displays the coherence and unity of defined dogmas, which are the Church's infallible interpretations of Scripture.

Putting It All in Perspective Perhaps the most important context of all we have saved for last: the interior life of the individual reader. What we get out of the Bible will largely depend on how we approach the Bible. Unless we are living a sustained and disciplined life of prayer, we will never have the reverence, the profound humility, or the grace we need to see the Scriptures for what they really are.

You are approaching the "word of God". But for thousands of years, since before he knit you in your mother's womb, the Word of God has been approaching you.

One Final Note. The volume you hold in your hands is only a small part of a much larger work still in production. Study helps similar to those printed in this booklet are being prepared for *all* the books of the Bible and will appear gradually as they are finished. Our ultimate goal is to publish a single, one-volume Study Bible that will include the entire text of Scripture, along with all the annotations, charts, cross-references, maps, and other features found in the following pages. Individual booklets will be published in the meantime, with the hope that God's people can begin to benefit from this labor before its full completion.

We have included a long list of Study Questions in the back to make this format as useful as possible, not only for individual study, but for group settings and discussions as well. The questions are designed to help readers both "understand" the Bible and "apply" it to their lives. We pray that God will make use of our efforts and yours to help renew the face of the earth! «

INTRODUCTION TO TOBIT

Author and Date Much uncertainty surrounds the origin of the Book of Tobit. Its author is unknown, and no clear signs of the time or place of its composition are indicated in the text. Tobit appears to have been written by a devout Israelite who wished to encourage faithful observance of the Torah among the dispersed community of Israel in exile. The author may have written from anywhere in the Near East, including the land of Israel, but the book's realistic depiction of life in exile suggests to many scholars that it originated in the eastern Diaspora, perhaps in Babylonia or Media.

As for the time of its composition, a handful of modern scholars have dated the Book of Tobit as early as the seventh century B.C., while a few others have suggested a date as late as the second century A.D. A majority of scholars, however, hold that the book was written in the third century or early second century B.C. Among the reasons for this, Tobit promotes distinctive expressions of Jewish piety such as almsgiving, burying the dead, and avoidance of Gentile foods that became prominent near the end of the Old Testament period. At the same time, the author expresses hope for the salvation of the nations (13:11), suggesting he was unaffected by the Jewish animosity toward Gentiles that rose sharply in the middle of the second century B.C. with the Seleucid persecution of Jews in Judea.

That said, the story of Tobit may be more ancient than the inspired Book of Tobit that appears in the Bible. This possibility is suggested by 12:20, where Tobit and his son are instructed to "write" about their experiences and give witness to the goodness of God in their lives. If the story is anchored in actual historical events, as traditionally held, one can reasonably imagine the account being passed down as oral or written tradition between the time of the events it describes, in the eighth and seventh centuries B.C., and the time when the biblical author set down his own account in writing. It is even possible that the writer mentions this detail because he made use of personal or family memoirs preserved among Tobit's descendants as a basis for the canonical book we have today. On the other hand, if the story was written as edifying historical fiction, as most contemporary scholars hold, it could still preserve authentic memories of persons and circumstances of the past. The command for Tobit and his son to "write" in 12:20 might then signal that the story was already a revered tradition before it reached the biblical author. Either way, the essential content of the book is likely to predate the composition of the book.

Title The book opens with the Greek expression *Biblos logōn Tōbith*, meaning "The Book of the Words of Tobit". The story thus takes its name from the character introduced in 1:3 as the narrator. His name, Tobit, is a shortened form of the Semitic name borne either by his father, Tobiel (*tobi'el*, meaning "God is my good") or by his son, Tobias (*tobiyah*, meaning "Yahweh is my good"). St. Jerome rendered the names of both father and son *Tobias* in the Latin Vulgate.

Place in the Canon There was some disagreement over the canonicity of Tobit in the early Christian centuries. Most of the Eastern Church Fathers were disinclined to accept the book as included in Scripture, with the exception of figures such as St. Clement of Alexandria and St. John Chrysostom. A majority of the Western Church Fathers, however, embraced it as an inspired book of the Old Testament, as did early Church synods held in Rome (A.D. 382), Hippo (A.D. 393), and Carthage (A.D. 397). Today the Book of Tobit is revered as biblical by Catholics and Eastern Orthodox. It may have been canonical in some Jewish communities as well, since it appears in surviving collections of the Greek Septuagint, the version of the Old Testament read in Greek-speaking synagogues of the ancient world, and several fragments of the book were discovered among the Dead Sea Scrolls, perhaps indicating that the Qumran community in Israel considered the book to be scriptural as well. At any rate, the Book of Tobit was not included in the canon of the Hebrew Bible accepted in later, rabbinic Judaism. Neither does Tobit appear as canonical in Protestant Bibles, although some editions include it in an appendix of writings designated "the Apocrypha".

Structure The Book of Tobit follows a conventional model of storytelling that moves from conflict to resolution. **(1)** The prologue sets the story in the Assyrian exile in the late eighth century B.C., where a faithful Israelite from the tribe of Naphtali named Tobit has been resettled as a captive (1:1–2). **(2)** The problem that sets the story in motion follows. Tobit, despite careful observance of the Torah, finds himself blinded, impoverished, and driven to the brink of despair (1:3—3:6). Meantime, in faraway Media, a relative named Sarah suffers the shame and disappointment of losing seven husbands, and she, too, reaches a point of personal breakdown (3:7–17). **(3)** In view of this family anguish, God sends the angel Raphael, disguised as the man Azariah, to help these individuals by lifting their burdens and restoring happiness to their homes. Central to the drama is a lengthy journey undertaken by Tobit's son, Tobias, who travels to Media with his angelic companion, marries the girl Sarah, and returns home to restore his father's sight (4:1—12:22). **(4)** The story reaches its climax with Tobit, his vision regained, praising the Lord for his goodness and foretelling future blessings for Israel and Jerusalem (13:1–18). In the end, Tobias follows his father's advice to move his family from Nineveh to Media in order to escape the Lord's coming judgment on Assyria (14:1–14).

Literary Background Tobit survives in its entirety only in Greek, although most scholars hold that the book was originally written in a Semitic language, probably Aramaic. In times past, this was inferred from linguistic features in the surviving Greek texts. But substantial support for this claim surfaced in the mid-twentieth century with the discovery of the Dead Sea Scrolls. Among these ancient manuscripts, scholars found portions of the Book of Tobit, four in Aramaic (4Q196–199) and one in Hebrew (4Q200).

As for Greek manuscripts, the book exists in a short form (preserved in *Codex Vaticanus* and *Codex Alexandrinus*) and a long form (preserved in *Codex Sinaiticus*). The story is substantially the same in both editions, although the two differ in matters of detail. An English translation of the short text appears in the RSVCE, while the long text appears in the NABRE, NJB, and NRSV. Most scholars today think the long text is closest to the original version of Tobit. The Latin translation of Tobit that appears in the Vulgate differs from both Greek and Semitic manuscripts. The reason for this difference is not entirely clear, although St. Jerome tells us that he worked from an Aramaic copy of the book that was first translated into Hebrew and then into Latin (*Preface to Tobit*). The Vulgate edition of Tobit, rendered into English in the Douay-Rheims translation, is shorter overall than the other ancient versions, yet it includes a number of passages not represented in any other editions of the book.

Literary Genre Besides the matter of Tobit's original language and length, the question of its literary genre must also be addressed. How should one classify the Book of Tobit? Is it a work of history or a work of historical fiction? On the one hand, the book features the kind of information one would expect from an account of the past, e.g., the story is situated in a known historical context (the Assyrian empire in the eighth and early seventh century B.C.) in known geographical locations (Nineveh, Media, Ecbatana, Rages), in relation to known historical figures (Shalmaneser, Sennacherib, Esarhaddon), and against the background of a known historical event (the Assyrian conquest of the Northern Kingdom of Israel). Given the presence of these genuinely historical elements, it is no surprise that Christian tradition has long considered Tobit one of the historical books of the Old Testament. On the other hand, this same information could be viewed as the author's attempt at creating a realistic setting for a work of historical fiction. Indeed, the book also displays several oddities in its presentation of history and geography that lead most modern scholars to classify Tobit as a religious folktale or novella rather than a strictly historical report of the past.

The Catholic Church has taken no official position on the literary genre of Tobit, and so scholars are free to adopt and defend different positions. For most of Christian history, the book was considered historical, and even modern times have seen a few interpreters argue for some degree of historical substance underlying the narrative. At the same time, contemporary scholarship within the Church has shown a new openness to reading books such as Tobit, Judith, and Esther as allegorical or moral narratives that deal with the history of Israel but are not books of history in the strict sense (e.g., John Paul II, Audience, May 8, 1985). In the end, regardless of how one classifies the Book of Tobit and its relationship to history, one can acknowledge that its literary depiction of characters and events is meant to impart lessons about religious faith and life. History and historical fiction are both capable of serving such a purpose.

Themes and Characteristics The Book of Tobit is a delightful example of ancient Israelite story-telling. It has a charm that speaks to the heart as well as the head. Some scholars trace its inspiration to ancient folktales such as the *Story of Ahikar* (a sage who counsels the kings of Assyria and leaves behind a treasury of wise sayings) and the *Dangerous Bride* (a man marries a wealthy woman afflicted by a curse). This may be true to a limited extent, but Tobit is much closer in spirit and sentiment to the biblical traditions of Israel, especially the patriarchal accounts in Genesis, the narrative portions of Job, and the exilic adventures of Esther and Daniel. It is a story, not about great heroes and their epic accomplishments, but about ordinary people of faith struggling to remain loyal to God and family through the difficult times of life. The teachings featured in Tobit also have links with the theology of retribution in Deuteronomy, the eschatological visions of Isaiah, and the ethical concerns of Sirach.

Tobit is nevertheless unique among the books of Scripture in one important respect. The Bible preserves several stories about the life of God's people in Babylonian Exile in the sixth century B.C., but only Tobit offers readers a glimpse into the Assyrian Exile that took place in the eighth century B.C. More than a century before the Southern Kingdom of Judah, formed around a nucleus of two tribes, was taken into captivity, the ten northern tribes of Israel, once forming the Northern Kingdom of Israel, were conquered by the Assyrians and scattered as exiles to various locations in Mesopotamia and Media (see

2 Kings 15:29; 17:6; 1 Chron 5:26). Tobit and his family, hailing from the tribe of Naphtali, were among those who suffered Assyrian deportation to these distant lands. The Book of Tobit thus adopts the viewpoint, not of a "Jewish" exile from Judea, but of an "Israelite" exile from Galilee.

Tobit's family story is further presented as a paradigm of Israel's national story. His own experience of hardship followed by healing offers a message of hope to the northern tribes awaiting restoration in the midst of exile. Just as divine mercy follows affliction in Tobit's personal life (11:15), so the dispersed children of Israel can expect to find the mercy of God as well (13:1–8), provided they heed the words and example of Tobit, who models an uncompromising commitment to the Lord, who shows kindness to the poor and to the dead, and who prayerfully accepts the trials that come with living in a foreign land. So too, just as the Lord brings healing to Tobit and Sarah through the angel Raphael, whose name means "God has healed", so Israel is encouraged to trust in the prophecies of Scripture that God will come to heal and restore them once again (see Is 30:26; 57:17–18; Hos 6:1, etc.). In these and other ways, the Book of Tobit reinforces the hope that all Israel will participate in the future restoration of God's people, including the northern tribes driven into exile by the Assyrians (Is 27:12–13; Jer 50:17–20; Obad 20–21).

Within this overarching framework, the Book of Tobit develops a number of themes related to God and his Providence, the spiritual life of the covenant people, and the future plans that God has for the world.

(1) *Theology.* The book presents God as a divine Father (13:4) whose loving concern extends to nations, families, and individuals alike. He is neither blind to human misery nor deaf to human prayers (3:16–17; 12:12). He may test his people to measure the strength of their faith (12:13), but his ultimate purpose is to heal and restore them with his mercy (12:14). The blessings he desires for them have been prepared from eternity (6:17; 7:12). Underlying all of these teachings is the conviction that God's Providence is the riverbed of history, the channel that guides all circumstances and events, fortunate and misfortunate alike, to the fulfillment of his gracious plan (13:1–18).

(2) *Spirituality.* Religious teachings are expressed in the prayers, speeches, and acts of charity that appear throughout the book. Prayers punctuate the story (4:19) from its lowest moments of anguish (3:2–6; 3:11–15) to its highest moments of joy (8:15–17; 11:14–15). Forms of prayer featured in the book include petitions, praises, blessings, and thanksgivings (see 8:4–6; 11:17; 12:6; 13:1–18). Acts of mercy and charity also stand in the foreground, most prominently in Tobit's personal example and fatherly advice to his son, which stresses the importance of almsgiving (4:7–11; 12:8–9; 14:11), burying the dead (1:18; 2:4; 14:10), and giving food and clothing to those who have none (1:16–17; 4:16). These are the pillars of Israelite piety in the lands of exile, where the Lord's people are challenged to preserve their religious heritage despite their loss of a homeland and their separation from worship in the Jerusalem Temple. The spiritual identity of the covenant community is also maintained by marrying within one's kinship group (4:12–13) and by resisting assimilation into the surrounding Gentile culture (1:10–12).

(3) *Angelology and Demonology.* Tobit sheds more light on the world of spirits than any other book of the Old Testament. Angels appear as servants of the Lord who can take human form to minister not just to nations or peoples but to individuals. Raphael, who is one of the holy angels who stand in God's presence (12:15), ministers in heaven by bringing the prayers of Tobit and Sarah before the Almighty (12:12) and on earth by directing the footsteps of Tobias (5:1–16), by binding the evil spirit that torments his bride-to-be (3:17; 8:3), and by revealing the cure for Tobit's blindness (6:4, 8; 11:7–8). Demons, which rarely appear in the Old Testament, are shown to have a perverse interest in human affairs and a real ability to inflict harm. The fallen spirit Asmodeus is a case in point. He causes great grief in the life of Sarah by killing her bridegrooms one by one (3:7–8), only to be driven away and bound by the authority of Raphael (8:1–3).

(4) *Eschatology.* Besides its primary focus on family history, the book also shows an interest in salvation history. This is mainly the subject of the final two chapters, where Tobit envisions the future restoration of Israel and the salvation of the Gentiles. Included in this vision of things to come is the restoration of the northern tribes of Israel (13:3–6), the exile and return of the southern tribes of Judah (14:4–5), and the rebuilding of Jerusalem and its Temple in the wake of conquest (13:9–18; 14:5). Not only will the twelve tribes of Israel be counted among the redeemed in these days, but Gentile nations will also come to embrace the God of Israel (13:11; 14:6–7).

Christian Perspective The Book of Tobit is never quoted directly in the New Testament, although its influence can still be felt, mainly at the level of moral instruction. For instance, Tobit utters an early version of the Golden Rule (4:15) that Jesus will later set forth in the Gospels (Mt 7:12; Lk 6:31). Tobit's example of feeding the hungry and clothing the naked (1:17; 4:16) sets a standard of charity that Jesus expects of all who hope for salvation (Mt 25:35–36). The threefold practice of prayer, fasting, and almsgiving, strongly encouraged in Tobit (12:8), is definitively endorsed by the teaching of Christ (Mt 6:1–18). Also common to Tobit and the New Testament is the teaching that charitable giving stores up treasure with God that is far more valuable than earthly wealth (compare 4:8–11 with Mt 6:19–21; Lk 12:33–34; 1 Tim 6:18–19), provided it comes from a cheerful giver and not from one who begrudges the gift (4:16; 2 Cor 9:7). Finally, the coming of Raphael, an angel appearing as a man, may be said to prefigure the Incarnation of God the Son, especially as this mystery is expressed in the Gospel of John. Neither Raphael nor Jesus comes down from heaven to do his own will, but, rather, both come to do the will of God (compare 12:18 with Jn 5:30; 6:38); and both, once their mission is complete, must ascend back to the One who sent him (compare 12:20 with Jn 16:5). In later Christian history, the Book of Tobit is invoked mainly for its exalted vision of marriage.

OUTLINE OF TOBIT

1. **Prologue (1:1–2)**

2. **Two Families in Exile (1:3—3:17)**
   A. The Plight of Tobit in Nineveh (1:3—3:6)
   B. The Plight of Sarah in Ecbatana (3:7–17)

3. **The Journey and Marriage of Tobias (4:1—12:22)**
   A. Tobit Counsels Tobias (4:1–21)
   B. Raphael Accompanies Tobias (5:1—6:17)
   C. The Marriage of Tobias and Sarah (7:1—8:21)
   D. Raphael Retrieves Tobit's Money (9:1–6)
   E. The Journey Home (10:1—11:19)
   F. Raphael Reveals His Identity (12:1–22)

4. **Tobit's Song of Thanksgiving (13:1–18)**
   A. The Greatness of the Lord (13:1–8)
   B. The Future Glory of Jerusalem (13:9–18)

5. **Epilogue (14:1–15)**

THE BOOK OF

TOBIT

1 The book of the acts[a] of Tobit the son of Tobi'el, son of Anan'iel, son of Adu'el, son of Gab'ael, of the descendants of As'i-el and the tribe of Naph'tali, ²who in the days of Shalmane'ser,[b] king of the Assyrians, was taken into captivity from Thisbe, which is to the south of Ke'desh Naph'tali in Galilee above Asher.

Tobit's Youth and Virtuous Life

3 I, Tobit, walked in the ways of truth and righteousness all the days of my life, and I performed many acts of charity to my brethren and countrymen who went with me into the land of the Assyrians, to Nin'eveh. ⁴Now when I was in my own country, in the land of Israel, while I was still a young man, the whole tribe of Naph'tali my forefather deserted the house of Jerusalem. This was the place which had been chosen from among all the tribes of Israel, where all the tribes should sacrifice and where the temple of the dwelling of the Most High was consecrated and established for all generations for ever.

5 All the tribes that joined in apostasy used to sacrifice to the calf[c] Ba'al, and so did the house of Naph'tali my forefather. ⁶But I alone went often to Jerusalem for the feasts, as it is ordained for all Israel by an everlasting decree. Taking the first fruits and the tithes of my produce and the first shearings, I would give these to the priests, the sons of Aaron,

---

1:1 Tobit: A Greek form of the Semitic name *ṭobî*, which is an abbreviation either of *ṭobi'el*, the name of his father ("God is my good"), or *ṭobiyah*, the name of his son ("Yahweh is my good"). **Tobiel ... Asiel:** Tobit's genealogy is traced back beyond four generations. **the tribe of Naphtali:** Occupied lands northwest of the Sea of Galilee (Josh 19:32–39).

1:2 Shalmaneser: Shalmaneser V, king of Assyria from 727 to 722 B.C. He is best known for initiating the siege of Samaria that led to the downfall of the Northern Kingdom of Israel (2 Kings 17:3–5). **captivity:** It is odd that Tobit, from the tribe of Naphtali, claims to have been exiled by Shalmaneser, since it was Tiglath-pileser III who conducted military campaigns in Galilee and Transjordan between 734 and 732 B.C. that resulted in the capture of Naphtali (2 Kings 15:29; 1 Chron 5:26). One possibility, from a historical standpoint, is that Tobit's family managed to escape the earlier deportations but not the latter, when Shalmaneser invaded "all the land" of northern Israel in ca. 725 B.C. and again took captives into exile (2 Kings 17:6). **Thisbe:** A town in Upper Galilee of uncertain location. **Kedesh Naphtali:** The town mentioned in Josh 20:7. **Asher:** Probably the city of Hazor.

1:3 I, Tobit: For reasons unclear, the story is narrated in the first person from 1:3 to 3:6, after which it shifts to the third person. **Nineveh:** The capital of Assyria on the east bank of the Tigris River near modern Mosul in Iraq. It was a sprawling metropolis in biblical times (Jon 3:3).

1:4 the house of Jerusalem: The Solomonic Temple, the only legitimate place of sacrifice in Israel under the Mosaic covenant (Deut 12:5, 10–11). **the Most High:** An ancient epithet for God the Creator (Gen 14:18–20; Deut 32:8).

1:5 apostasy: A reference to the rebellion of the northern tribes, who broke away from the Davidic monarchy in Judah and Jerusalem and established their own kingdom in ca. 930 B.C. (1 Kings 12:16–20). If the author means to say that Tobit was a young man at this time, then the detail is problematic, since the apostasy took place a full 200 years before Tobit's lifetime. On the other hand, the schism may be mentioned as background information only, so that Tobit's fidelity stands out starkly against several generations of infidelity among his own people. **the calf:** One of two golden calves that Jeroboam I placed in the cities of Bethel and Dan as the focus of his idolatrous state religion (1 Kings 12:25–30). **Baal:** The storm and fertility god of Canaanite religion. The name does not appear in the long text of Tobit preserved in *Codex Sinaiticus*. See introduction: *Literary Background*.

1:6 I alone went: Tobit is part of the remnant of northern Israelites who continue to offer sacrifice in Jerusalem in the time of the divided monarchy (cf. 2 Chron 11:16). Allowing for some exaggeration (see 5:13), the statement implies that the tribe of Naphtali was deeply involved in the Northern Kingdom's defection from the proper worship of God. The Mosaic Law requires adult males from all twelve tribes to sacrifice at the central sanctuary (= Temple) three times a year (Deut 16:16). **the first ... the tithes:** Offerings made to the sanctuary and its ministers. For various tithing laws observed by Tobit, see Ex 13:11–12; Lev 27:26–32; Num 18:21–30; Deut 14:22–29; 18:4.

The Books of Tobit, Judith and Esther
These three books appear together in the Greek Bible, usually after the historical books. The complete Aramaic original of Tobit and the Hebrew of Judith have not survived, and neither book was included in the Jewish canon at the end of the first century A.D. Existing as they did in the Greek Bible, they would have been used and recognized as Scripture by the first Christians. The Greek "Additions to Esther" were probably written two centuries after the Hebrew text. They were composed in Egypt and they exhibit a strictly Jewish doctrine. All three books have a literary form somewhat strange to the Western mind. They are, in effect, religious tales with the appearance of an historical narrative. They may have an historical basis, but the persons, places, events and dates are woven into the narrative in such a way as to have little resemblance to the actual historical record as we know it from other sources. It would seem, therefore, that the writers are intending, not to write history as we understand that term, but to use historical material to impart a religious message.

The Book of Tobit (The Book of Tobias)
The author relates the story of a family living among a pagan people yet trusting fully in God in spite of difficulties. Belief in one God is stressed; marriage between Jews is likewise emphasized and angels figure prominently in the narrative. The book has much to say, too, about the need for good works. It was written after the Exile at some time during the Persian period, though the story may be a good deal older than that. It shows signs of dependence on earlier writings such as the Story of Ahikar, a sixth-century work from Babylon. It also bears a likeness to Genesis in certain points, e.g., to his last injunctions to the family, the important role of angels, the son's search for a wife, and the care given to burial of the dead. It is interesting to note that fragments of the Hebrew and Aramaic texts have been found at Qumran, which favor the longer text of Codex Sinaiticus, the Old Latin and the Vulgate.

[a] Gk *words*.
[b] Gk *Enemessarus*.
[c] Other authorities read *heifer*.

at the altar. ⁷Of all my produce I would give a tenth to the sons of Levi who ministered at Jerusalem; a second tenth I would sell, and I would go and spend the proceeds each year at Jerusalem; ⁸the third tenth I would give to those to whom it was my duty, as Deborah my father's mother had commanded me, for I was left an orphan by my father. ⁹When I became a man I married Anna, a member of our family, and by her I became the father of Tobi′as.

Tobit Taken Captive to Nineveh

10 Now when I was carried away captive to Nin′eveh, all my brethren and my relatives ate the food of the Gentiles; ¹¹but I kept myself from eating it, ¹²because I remembered God with all my heart. ¹³Then the Most High gave me favor and good appearance in the sight of Shalmane′ser,ᵇ and I was his buyer of provisions. ¹⁴So I used to go into Med′ia, and once at Ra′ges in Med′ia I left ten talents of silver in trust with Gab′ael, the brother of Ga′brias. ¹⁵But when Shalmane′serᵇ died, Sennach′-erib his son reigned in his place; and under him the highways were unsafe, so that I could no longer go into Med′ia.

Courage in Burying the Dead

16 In the days of Shalmane′serᵇ I performed many acts of charity to my brethren. ¹⁷I would

---

1:8 Deborah: Tobit's grandmother and guardian in his early life. She was probably named after the famous judge and prophetess of Judg 4:4. Her name in Hebrew means "honey bee".

1:9 Anna: Her Semitic name means "favor" or "grace". **member of our family:** An example of endogamy, the practice of marrying members of the same clan or tribe. This is a central concern in the Book of Tobit (3:15; 4:12; 6:10, 15; 7:9–10). It was expected that Israelites were not to intermarry with Gentiles for religious reasons (Deut 7:1–4), and the example of the Genesis Patriarchs shows that marriage within one's kinship group was the norm (Gen 20:12; 24:3–4; 28:1–5). Mosaic inheritance law took a step beyond this by recommending marriages within one's tribe, lest ancestral lands pass into the possession of other tribes (Num 36:5–9). In the exile, marrying within one's kinship group was a way of preserving Israel's ethnic and religious identity in the midst of a pagan world, where the pressure to assimilate into the dominant culture was great. The threats posed by mixed marriages between Jews and Gentiles remained a concern for the community in Judea after the return from Babylonian Exile (Ezra 9–10; Neh 13:23–27) (CCC 1633–37). **Tobias:** A Greek spelling of the Semitic name Tobiah. See note on 1:1.

1:10 the food of the Gentiles: Avoided by the pious of Israel, either because the food was legally unclean (Lev 14:1–47), improperly prepared with respect to blood (Ex 23:19; Lev 17:10–14), or linked in some way to rites of idolatrous worship (Ex 34:15). • Refusal to eat Gentile foods was also the practice of Daniel (Dan 1:8; 10:3), Esther (Esther 14:17), and Judith (Jud 10:5; 12:2).

1:13 buyer of provisions: Tobit serves as a purchasing agent for the Assyrian government.

1:14 Media: The region east of the Zagros Mountains in the northern part of modern Iran. **Rages:** Located at modern Rai, a few miles southeast of Tehran, the capital of Iran. **ten talents of silver:** A substantial sum of money, although its equivalence in modern terms cannot be determined accurately. The decision to retrieve this family fortune, left in Media for safekeeping, prompts the adventure that lies at the heart of the book (4:1–2, 20–21). The deposit of the silver is a providential event, setting the stage for Tobit's financial recovery. **Gabael:** Probably Tobit's kinsman, since the name appears in his genealogy (1:1) and the man attends the wedding celebration for Tobit's son (9:5–6).

1:15 Shalmaneser died: 722 B.C. He was succeeded by his brother Sargon II. **Sennacherib:** King of Assyria from 705 to 681 B.C. Tobit abbreviates the story of succession by omitting mention of Sennacherib's father, Sargon II, who ruled Assyria from 722 to 705 B.C. **his son:** Sennacherib was actually Shalmaneser's nephew, not his biological son. It may have been customary in popular speech, however, to regard a king and his successor on the throne as "father" and "son", regardless of their exact relationship. See note on Dan 5:2.

1:17 I would bury him: Burial of the dead is portrayed as a sacred duty in the Bible, not least in the Book of Tobit (1:19; 2:4; 4:3–4; 6:14; 8:9–12; 14:10–11, 13). Although burial is not mandated in the Mosaic Law (except in Deut 21:22–23), it was the venerable practice of the Genesis Patriarchs (Gen 23:19; 25:9; 35:29; etc.) and was considered a moral obligation in later Judaism (Josephus, *Against Apion* 2, 211; Mishnah *Nazir* 7, 1). To be left unburied so that one's remains became food for animals was considered a great indignity, even a curse (Deut 28:26; Jer 7:33). Interment in

ᵇGk *Enemessarus.*

WORD STUDY

Acts of Charity (1:16)

eleēmosynē (Gk.): mercy or compassion expressed in acts of "charity" and "almsgiving". The term is almost a one-word summary of the piety commended in the Book of Tobit, where it appears more than a dozen times. Twice it refers to the Lord's "mercy" toward mankind (Tob 3:2; 13:6), but most often it refers to charitable works of mercy, especially almsgiving, that are done for a person in need of necessities (Tob 1:3; 2:14; 4:7–8, 16; 14:2, 10–11). Charitable giving is set alongside prayer (Tob 12:8) as a path leading to the fullness of life (Tob 12:9). It is a form of religious service tailored to life in exile: despite being cut off from the Temple and its ministries, Israelites can make almsgiving an offering to the Lord (Tob 4:11) and thus obtain the benefits normally acquired through sacrifice, namely, purgation from sin (Tob 12:9) and deliverance from death (Tob 4:10). Use of the word *eleēmosynē* in the Book of Sirach coheres with this theological outlook: almsgiving joined with prayer (Sir 7:10) is an acceptable sacrifice (Sir 35:2) that atones for sin (Sir 3:30) and rescues the giver from adversity (Sir 29:12; 40:24). The NT shares this perspective and promotes almsgiving as a Christian work of mercy (Mt 6:2–4; Lk 12:33; Acts 9:36).

give my bread to the hungry and my clothing to the naked; and if I saw any one of my people dead and thrown out behind the wall of Nin'eveh, I would bury him. [18]And if Sennach'erib the king put to death any who came fleeing from Judea, I buried them secretly. For in his anger he put many to death. When the bodies were sought by the king, they were not found. [19]Then one of the men of Nin'eveh went and informed the king about me, that I was burying them; so I hid myself. When I learned that I was being searched for, to be put to death, I left home in fear. [20]Then all my property was confiscated and nothing was left to me except my wife Anna and my son Tobi'as.

21 But not fifty[d] days passed before two of Sennach'erib's[e] sons killed him, and they fled to the mountains of Ar'arat. Then E'sar-had'don,[f] his son, reigned in his place; and he appointed Ahi'kar, the son of my brother An'ael, over all the accounts of his kingdom and over the entire administration. [22]Ahi'kar interceded for me, and I returned to Nin'eveh. Now Ahikar was cupbearer, keeper of the signet, and in charge of administration of the accounts, for E'sar-had'don[f] had appointed him second to himself.[g] He was my nephew.

2 When I arrived home and my wife Anna and my son Tobi'as were restored to me, at the feast of Pentecost, which is the sacred festival of the seven weeks, a good dinner was prepared for me and I sat down to eat. [2]Upon seeing the abundance of food I said to my son, "Go and bring whatever poor man of our brethren you may find among the exiles in Nineveh, who is mindful of the Lord, and he shall eat together with me. I will wait for you until you come back." [3]So Tobias went out to look for some poor person of our people. When he came back, he said, "Father!" And I replied, "Here I am, my child." And he went on to say, "Look, Father, one of our own people has been murdered and thrown into the market place, and now he lies there strangled." [4]So before I tasted anything I sprang up and removed the body[h] to a place of shelter until sunset when I might bury it. [5]And when I returned I washed myself and ate my food in sorrow. [6]Then I remembered the prophecy of Amos, how he said against Bethel,

"Your feasts shall be turned into mourning,
    and all your songs into lamentation."
And I wept.

Tobit Becomes Blind

7 When the sun had set I went and dug a grave and buried the body.[h] [8]And my neighbors laughed at me and said, "He is still not afraid; he has already been hunted down to be put to death for

---

a grave remained the funeral custom of the covenant people into NT times (Mt 27:59–60; Jn 11:17). • In Catholic tradition, burying the dead is a corporal work of mercy, along with feeding the hungry and clothing the naked (CCC 2300, 2447). • Let those who fear God and are mindful of divine things offer the Lord obedience with all faith, devoted minds, and frequent good works. Let us give earthly clothing that we may receive heavenly garments, earthly food and drink that we may come to the heavenly banquet. Lest we reap little, let us sow much. While our time remains, let us be concerned for eternal salvation (St. Cyprian of Carthage, *Works and Almsgiving* 24).

1:19 I left home: Tobit is forced to flee Nineveh and go into hiding at an unknown location.

1:20 nothing was left to me: Tobit resembles Job in being an upright man who is deprived of honor and possessions in spite of his righteousness.

1:21 sons killed him: For Sennacherib's assassination, see 2 Kings 19:36–37; Is 37:37–38. **Ararat:** North of Upper Mesopotamia in modern Armenia (Gen 8:4). **Esar-haddon:** King of Assyria from 681 to 669 B.C. **Ahikar:** Identified as Tobit's nephew and the highest ranking official in the Assyrian government under the king (1:22). He plays a pivotal role in interceding for Tobit and facilitating his return to Nineveh. This is the first of four allusions in the Book of Tobit to a popular Near Eastern folktale called the *Story of Ahikar* (also 2:10; 11:18; 14:10). In the nonbiblical account, an Aramaic version of which survives from the fifth century B.C., Ahikar (or Ahiqar) is a court sage who counseled Assyrian kings, groomed his nephew Nadin to be his successor, and left behind a treasury of wise sayings. In Tobit, Ahikar appears as an Israelite rather than a Gentile, a fact that some scholars take as a sign that the book was intended to be historical fiction.

2:1 Pentecost: The Greek name for a spring harvest festival known in Hebrew as *Shavu'ot*, "the feast of weeks" (Deut 16:10). It was celebrated 50 days (= seven weeks) after the feast of Passover (Lev 23:15–21). Tobit's desire to share his meal with a poor kinsman (2:2) may be inspired by Deut 16:11, which indicates that the festival should be a time of joy for all in Israel, including the less fortunate.

2:2 Nineveh: See note on 1:3.

2:5 I washed myself: It is uncertain whether Tobit's action was hygienic (washing before a meal) or religious (a cleansing from corpse defilement). The latter seems more probable. In the Torah, uncleanness incurred by contact with the dead lasted seven days, during which time one was required to undergo a series of ritual washings before entering the sanctuary (Num 19:11–22). However, since Tobit is living in exile and is separated from the Temple and its ministries, he is prevented from following the letter of the Torah. He thus appears to improvise a cleansing rite to rid himself of uncleanness. The longer text of Tobit states that he washed himself again after burying the body (2:9 in *Codex Sinaiticus*).

2:6 Your feasts: A quotation from Amos 8:10. • The prophet pronounces doom on the Northern Kingdom of Israel, mainly because of the idolatrous worship that took place at the shrines in Bethel (central Israel) and Dan (northern Galilee). Tobit sees its fulfillment with the northern tribes being thrust into exile and reduced to mourning. The passage probably comes to mind, not only because Tobit grieves on a religious feast day, but because Amos foresaw that God's judgments included "dead bodies" being "cast out" in every place (Amos 8:3). Despite his own fidelity, Tobit accepts that he must suffer and weep in solidarity with his captive people.

---

[d]Other authorities read *fifty-five*.
[e]Gk *his*.
[f]Gk *Sacherdonus*.
[g]Or *a second time*.
[h]Gk *him*.

doing this, and he ran away, yet here he is burying the dead again!" ⁹On the same night after I, Tobit, returned from burying the dead, I went into my courtyard and slept by the wall of the courtyard, and my face was uncovered because of the heat. ¹⁰I did not know that there were sparrows on the wall and their fresh droppings fell into my open eyes and white films formed on my eyes. I went to physicians to be healed, but the more they treated me with ointments, the more my vision was obscured by the white films, until I became completely blind. For four years I remained unable to see. All my kindred were sorry for me, and Ahi′-kar took care of me for two years until he¹ went to El″yma′is.

Tobit's Wife Earns Their Livelihood

11 Then my wife Anna earned money at women's work. ¹²She used to send the product to the owners, and they paid her wages. One day, the seventh of Dystrus, when she cut off a piece she had woven and sent it to the owners, they paid her full wages and they also gave her a kid. ¹³When she returned to me it began to bleat. So I called her and said to her, "Where did you get the kid? It is not stolen, is it? Return it to the owners; for it is not right to eat what is stolen." ¹⁴And she said, "It was given to me as a gift in addition to my wages." But I did not believe her, and told her to return it to the owners; and I blushed for her. Then she replied to me, "Where are your charities and your righteous deeds? You seem to know everything!"

Tobit's Prayer

3 Then in my grief I wept, and I prayed in anguish, saying, ²"Righteous are you, O Lord; all your deeds are just and all your ways are mercy and truth, and you render true and righteous judgment for ever. ³And now, O Lord, remember me and look favorably upon me; do not punish me for my sins and for my unwitting offenses and those which my fathers committed before you. ⁴For we disobeyed your commandments, and you gave us over to plunder, captivity, and death; you made us the talk, the byword, and an object of reproach in all the nations among which you have dispersed us. ⁵And now your many judgments are true in exacting penalty from me for my sins and those of my fathers, because we did not keep your commandments. For we did not walk in truth before you. ⁶And now deal with me according to your pleasure; command my spirit to be taken up, that I may be released from the face of the earth and become dust. For it is better for me to die than to live, because I have heard false reproaches, and great is the sorrow within me. Command that I now be released from my distress; release me to go to the eternal abode; and do not, O Lord, turn your face away from me. For it is better

---

2:9 my courtyard: See note on 2:5.
2:10 blind: Once again Tobit's religious commitments bring him suffering (as in 1:16–20). He will later learn that God is testing him (12:13). For Christian readers, the "films" that formed over Tobit's eyes call to mind the "scales" that temporarily blinded the apostle Paul (Acts 9:18). **Ahikar:** Tobit's nephew. See note on 1:21. **Elymais:** The Greek name for the region of Elam (southern Iran; see 1 Mac 6:1).
2:11 earned money: Anna, a skilled weaver, becomes the family breadwinner two years after her husband's disability left him unable to work (2:10).
2:12 Dystrus: The month corresponding to January-February in the Macedonian calendar. **a kid:** The young goat is a bonus from one of Anna's clients.
2:14 I did not believe her: Anna is greeted with distrust and unfounded accusation. Little wonder her response comes out as a stinging rebuke. **Where are your charities …?:** Anna seems to question the genuineness of Tobit's pious acts. At this point in the story, his generosity appears to have gone unrewarded by God; instead of health and prosperity, he is left with blindness, poverty, and misery.
• The spousal tension evident in Anna's retort recalls how Job's wife reproached her agonizing husband (Job 2:9). The difference is that Job "did not sin with his lips" (Job 2:10), while Tobit speaks foolishly in his frustration, thus provoking his wife's irritated reply.
3:1–15 Alongside the initial plot (Tobit's distress), a second plot develops over 300 miles away (Sarah's distress). Neither is aware of the other's situation. However, both Tobit and Sarah are members of the same clan; both are suffering despite their uprightness; both are buffeted by verbal rebuke; and both pray to God for release from the painful burdens of

life. Resolution of these twin tragedies is the subject of the rest of the book.
3:1–6 Tobit's prayer, which (1) affirms God's righteousness, mercy, and truth, (2) appeals to God for the forgiveness of his and his people's sins, and (3) petitions God to end his suffering by taking his life.
3:2 Righteous: For the Hebrew background of this, see word study: *Righteous* at Neh 9:8.
3:4 we disobeyed: An acknowledgment that Israel's afflictions in exile are God's just punishment for national disobedience to the covenant. Tobit himself is a saintly man but not a sinless man, as admitted in 3:3. He was never a brazen idolater like others of his tribe, but neither does he pretend to be innocent of all wrongdoing. Consequently, he recognizes that his personal suffering is partly deserved and partly endured in solidarity with the rest of his unfaithful kinsmen. For similar confessions of national sin, see Ezra 9:6–15 and Dan 9:4–19. **Plunder, captivity … death … byword:** Curses of the Mosaic covenant delineated in Deut 28:20, 30–33, 37, 41, 51.
3:6 my spirit: Separated from the body at death (Ps 104:29). **dust:** The corpses of the dead dissolve into the dust of the ground (Gen 3:19; Eccles 12:7). **better for me to die:** Tobit is not the first righteous man to pray for death. Others include Moses (Num 11:15), Elijah (1 Kings 19:4), Job (Job 7:13–21), and Jonah (Jon 4:3). **reproaches:** The taunting words of his neighbors (2:8). **the eternal abode:** Not heaven, a place of everlasting happiness, but the netherworld of Sheol or Hades, a place of rest for the dead that was separated from the miseries of this life (Sir 30:17). Before the revelation of eternal life in the Book of Wisdom and more fully in the NT, it was thought that Sheol was the permanent destination of the dead, a realm from which no one returns (Job 7:9; 10:20–21; Eccles 12:5). See word study: *Sheol* at Num 16:30.

---

¹Other authorities read *I.*

for me to die than to see so much distress in my life and listen to such insults."

Sarah Falsely Accused

7 On the same day, at Ecbat'ana in Med'ia, it also happened that Sarah, the daughter of Rag'uel, was reproached by her father's maids, [8]because she had been given to seven husbands, and the evil demon As"mode'us had slain each of them before he had been with her as his wife. So the maids[j] said to her, "You are the one who kills your husbands! See, you already have had seven and have had no benefit from[k] any of them. [9]Why do you beat us? Because your husbands are dead? Go with them! May we never see a son or daughter of yours!"

Sarah's Prayer for Death

10 On that day she was deeply grieved in spirit and wept. When she had gone up to her father's upper room, she intended to hang herself. But she thought it over and said, "Never shall they reproach my father, saying to him, 'You only had one beloved daughter but she hanged herself because of her distress.' And I shall bring his old age down in sorrow to the grave.[l] It is better for me not to hang myself, but to pray the Lord that I may die and not listen to these reproaches any more." [11]At that same time, with hands outstretched toward the window, she prayed and said, "Blessed are you, O Lord, merciful God, and blessed is your holy and honored name for ever. May all your works praise you for ever. [12]And now, O Lord, I have turned my eyes and my face toward you. [13]Command that I be released from the earth and that I hear reproach no more. [14]You know, O Lord, that I am innocent of any sin with man, [15]and that I did not stain my name or the name of my father in the land of my captivity. I am my father's only child, and he has no child to be his heir, no near kinsman or kinsman's[m] son for whom I should keep myself as wife. Already seven husbands of mine are dead. Why should I live? But if it be not pleasing to you to take my life, command that respect be shown to me and pity be taken upon me, and that I hear reproach no more."

An Answer to Prayer

16 At that very moment the prayer of both was heard in the presence of the glory of the great God. [17]And Ra'phael[n] was sent to heal the two of them: to scale away the white films of Tobit's eyes; to give Sarah the daughter of Rag'uel in marriage to Tobi'as the son of Tobit, and to bind As"mode'us the evil demon, because Tobias was entitled to possess her. At that very moment Tobit returned and entered his house and Sarah the daughter of Raguel came down from her upper room.

3:7 On the same day: The coincidence of events occurring at the same time hints that God's Providence is at work in the lives of Tobit and Sarah (see 3:10, 16; 4:1). From this point forward, the author shifts from first-person narration, begun at 1:3, to third-person narration. **Ecbatana:** Located at Hamadan in Media (northern Iran). **Sarah:** The name in Hebrew means "princess"—probably an instance of irony, given her miserable situation in life. Besides having the same name, the matriarch Sarah likewise endured the contempt of a housemaid for being childless through no fault of her own (Gen 16:4-6). **Raguel:** The name in Aramaic means "friend of God".

3:8 seven husbands: Seven kinsmen suitors acting on the levirate law of Deut 25:5-10. A similar scenario is envisioned in Mk 12:18-22. Some take the number seven as symbolic of "many" husbands (cf. Is 4:1). **Asmodeus:** The evil spirit who loves Sarah (6:14). The name is derived either from Hebrew and means "the destroyer" or from the Persian expression *aeshma daeva*, meaning "demon of wrath". Asmodeus is mentioned in ancient texts outside the Bible (*Testament of Solomon* 5, 1-13) and is known in later rabbinic texts as Ashmedai. Violently jealous for Sarah, he watches over the girl and kills any man who approaches her in the bridal chamber on their wedding night. Demons are rarely mentioned in the OT, but see Deut 32:17 and Ps 106:37.

3:9 Why do you beat us?: Points to a mutual animosity between Sarah and the housemaids. Their open wish for her death pushes Sarah to the brink of despair.

3:10 hang herself: Suicide by hanging is contemplated but not committed, in contrast to 2 Sam 17:23 and Mt 27:5. **down in sorrow to the grave:** Similar to the sentiment expressed in Gen 42:38; 44:29, 31.

3:11-15 Rejecting suicide, Sarah turns to prayer. Like Tobit, she asks the Lord to take her life; but, unlike Tobit, she maintains her innocence from sin.

3:11 hands outstretched: A traditional posture for prayer in biblical times (Ex 9:29; Ezra 9:5). **the window:** Probably opens in the direction of Jerusalem (Ps 28:2; 134:2; Dan 6:10). See note on 1 Kings 8:29.

3:13 released ... reproach no more: The same petitions made in Tobit's prayer (3:6).

3:14 I am innocent: Sarah, unlike Tobit in 3:3, considers her suffering undeserved.

3:15 no near kinsman: Sarah despairs of finding a husband from among her kinsmen. She is unaware of Tobias, a family relative who is eligible to claim her hand in marriage (6:10). For the practice of endogamous marriage, see note on 1:9.

3:17 Raphael: The name in Hebrew means "God has healed". It announces his mission to heal the physical and emotional wounds of Tobit and Sarah (12:14). Raphael is one of the seven holy angels who bring the prayers of the saints before the throne of God (12:15; Rev 8:2-3). He is only mentioned by name in the OT in the Book of Tobit. In Jewish tradition, Raphael binds demons, has authority over human illness and injury (*1 Enoch* 10, 4; 40, 9), and fights on behalf of God's people (Dead Sea Scrolls: 1QM 9, 15-16). See note on 5:12. • Christian tradition honors Raphael as an archangel alongside Michael (Dan 12:1; Jude 9; Rev 12:7) and Gabriel (Dan 8:16; 9:21; Lk 1:19) (CCC 335). • The Lord's holy angel Raphael was sent to deliver both Tobit from blindness and Sarah from the demon. This signifies how the Lord was sent into the world to redeem both the Jews from the darkness of unbelief and the Gentiles from the bonds of idolatry (St. Bede, *On Tobit* 7).

---

[j] Gk *they.*
[k] Other authorities read *have not borne the name of.*
[l] Gk *to Hades.*
[m] Gk *his.*
[n] Other authorities read *the great Raphael. And he.*

Tobit Gives Instructions to His Son

4 On that day Tobit remembered the money which he had left in trust with Gab'ael at Ra'ges in Med'ia, and he said to himself: ²"I have asked for death. Why do I not call my son Tobi'as so that I may explain to him about the money° before I die?" ³So he called him and said, "My son, when I die, bury me, and do not neglect your mother. Honor her all the days of your life; do what is pleasing to her, and do not grieve her. ⁴Remember, my son, that she faced many dangers for you while you were yet unborn. When she dies, bury her beside me in the same grave.

5 "Remember the Lord our God all your days, my son, and refuse to sin or to transgress his commandments. Live uprightly all the days of your life, and do not walk in the ways of wrongdoing. ⁶For if you do what is true, your ways will prosper through your deeds. ⁷Give alms from your possessions to all who live uprightly, and do not let your eye begrudge the gift when you make it. Do not turn your face away from any poor man, and the face of God will not be turned away from you. ⁸If you have many possessions, make your gift from them in proportion; if few, do not be afraid to give according to the little you have. ⁹So you will be laying up a good treasure for yourself against the day of necessity. ¹⁰For charity* delivers from death and keeps you from entering the darkness; ¹¹and for all who practice it charity is an excellent offering in the presence of the Most High.

12 "Beware, my son, of all immorality.† First of all take a wife from among the descendants of your fathers and do not marry a foreign woman, who is not of your father's tribe; for we are the sons of the prophets. Remember, my son, that Noah, Abraham, Isaac, and Jacob, our fathers of old, all took wives from among their brethren. They were blessed in their children, and their posterity will inherit the land. ¹³So now, my son, love your brethren, and in your heart do not disdain your brethren and the sons and daughters of your people by refusing to take a wife for yourself from among them. For in pride there is ruin and great confusion; and in shiftlessness there is loss and great want, because shiftlessness is the mother of famine. ¹⁴Do not hold over till the next day the wages of any man who works for you, but pay him at once; and if you serve God you will receive payment.

"Watch yourself, my son, in everything you do, and be disciplined in all your conduct. ¹⁵And what you hate, do not do to any one. Do not drink wine to excess or let drunkenness go with you on your way. ¹⁶Give of your bread to the hungry, and of your clothing to the naked. Give all your surplus to

---

4:1–21 A farewell discourse following Tobit's prayer for death (3:6). It summarizes the moral and religious instruction of the book, its maxims resembling those in the Wisdom Books of the OT, especially Proverbs and Sirach. It is no coincidence that Tobit's instruction is largely concerned with the proper use of material wealth, since he is sending his son to retrieve his family's fortune. The young Tobias must understand that true prosperity comes from living wisely, that is, observing the Lord's commandments (4:5–6) and being generous in giving alms (4:7–11, 16–17). Ironically, Tobit has a clear vision of life's most important duties in spite of his blindness. • Besides the eyes of the flesh, there is an inner eye. Tobit, while blinded in the eyes of his body, was not without sight when he gave rules of life to his son and counseled him to follow the way of righteousness. These are the eyes of the understanding (St. Augustine, *Tractates on John* 13, 3).

4:1 the money: The ten silver talents left in Media. Gabael: See note on 1:14.

4:3 bury me: The injunction is fulfilled at the funeral in 14:11. On the importance of burial in the book, see note on 1:17. Honor her: A sacred obligation commanded by the Torah (Ex 20:12) and echoed in later books (Sir 7:27–28). It remains a solemn duty for Christians (Mt 19:19; Eph 6:2; CCC 2214–18).

4:4 the same grave: Follows the example of the Patriarchs, all of whom were buried with their wives in the same family cave (Gen 25:10; 49:29–32).

4:7 your eye: In biblical language, the eye can symbolize generosity or a lack thereof (Deut 15:9; Sir 14:8–10; Mt 6:22–23).

4:8 in proportion: The duty to give alms corresponds to financial means: the more wealth one possesses, the more one is urged to help those who are less fortunate (Sir 35:10; 2 Cor 8:12–15).

4:9 laying up a good treasure: Jesus uses nearly identical language to speak about charitable giving in the Sermon on the Mount (Mt 6:19–21).

4:10 charity: Almsgiving is primarily in view. See word study: *Acts of Charity* at 1:16 and note on 12:9. the darkness: Refers to the realm of the dead, pictured as a place of shadow and gloom (Job 17:13; 38:17; Ps 88:11–12).

4:11 an excellent offering: Giving alms to the poor is accorded the value that a sacrificial offering would have in the Temple, its effect being the purgation of sin (12:9; Sir 3:30).

4:12 immorality: The Greek *porneia* means "sexual misconduct" specifically. your father's tribe: On marriage within one's kinship group, see note on 1:9. the prophets: Here refers to the Patriarchs, as in 1 Chron 16:22. Abraham is designated a prophet in Gen 20:7.

4:13 pride: Often a prelude to personal humiliation (Prov 16:18; Sir 10:12–13; Mt 23:12). shiftlessness: The word can also be translated "worthlessness" or "idleness". The lesson is that hunger awaits those who are unwilling to work for a living (Prov 19:15).

4:14 the wages: Agrees with the law of prompt payment in Deut 24:14–15.

4:15 what you hate: An ancient version of the Golden Rule, here stated in negative terms. • Jesus urges the same moral standard but formulates it in positive terms: "Whatever you wish that men would do to you, do so to them" (Mt 7:12; Lk 6:31; CCC 1789). Do not drink wine to excess: Tobit, in concert with other biblical passages, advocates moderation in the consumption of alcohol (Sir 31:28–29; Eph 5:18).

4:16 bread ... clothing: Tobit himself practices the charity that he preaches to his son (1:17). • The prophet Isaiah calls for these same works of mercy (Is 58:7), as does Jesus, who heightens their importance by making them conditions for salvation (Mt 25:34–36). On the corporal works of mercy, see note on 1:17 and CCC 2447.

°Other authorities omit *about the money.*
*4:10, *charity:* i.e., almsgiving; cf. also verses 11 and 16.
†4:12, *immorality:* i.e., impurity, fornication.

0008066049E3

charity, and do not let your eye begrudge the gift when you make it. [17]Place your bread* on the grave of the righteous, but give none to sinners. [18]Seek advice from every wise man, and do not despise any useful counsel. [19]Bless the Lord God on every occasion; ask him that your ways may be made straight and that all your paths and plans may prosper. For none of the nations has understanding; but the Lord himself gives all good things, and according to his will he humbles whomever he wishes.

"So, my son, remember my commands, and do not let them be blotted out of your mind. [20]And now let me explain to you about the ten talents of silver which I left in trust with Gab'ael the son of Ga'brias at Ra'ges in Med'ia. [21]Do not be afraid, my son, because we have become poor. You have great wealth if you fear God and refrain from every sin and do what is pleasing in his sight."

The Angel Raphael

5 Then Tobi'as answered him, "Father, I will do everything that you have commanded me; [2]but how can I obtain the money when I do not know the man?" [3]Then Tobit gave him the receipt, and said to him, "Find a man to go with you and I will pay him wages as long as I live; and go and get the money." [4]So he went to look for a man; and he found Ra'phael, who was an angel, [5]but Tobi'as[p] did not know it. Tobias[p] said to him, "Can you go with me to Ra'ges in Med'ia? Are you acquainted with that region?" [6]The angel replied, "I will go with you; I am familiar with the way, and I have stayed with our brother Gab'ael." [7]Then Tobi'as said to him, "Wait for me, and I shall tell my father." [8]And he said to him, "Go, and do not delay." So he went in and said to his father, "I have found some one to go with me." He said, "Call him to me, so that I may learn to what tribe he belongs, and whether he is a reliable man to go with you."

9 So Tobi'as[p] invited him in; he entered and they greeted each other. [10]Then Tobit said to him, "My brother, to what tribe and family do you belong? Tell me." [11]But he answered, "Are you looking for a tribe and a family or for a man whom you will pay to go with your son?" And Tobit said to him, "I should like to know, my brother, your people and your name." [12]He replied, "I am Azari'as the son of the great Anani'as, one of your relatives." [13]Then Tobit said to him, "You are welcome, my brother. Do not be angry with me because I tried to learn your tribe and family. You are a relative of mine, of a good and noble lineage. For I used to know Anani'as and Ja'than, the sons of the great Shemai'ah, when we went together to Jerusalem to worship and offered the first-born of our flocks and the tithes of our produce. They did not go astray in the error of our brethren. My brother, you come of good stock. [14]But tell me, what wages am I to pay you—a drachma a day, and expenses for yourself as for my son? [15]And besides, I will add to your wages if you both return safe and sound." So they agreed to these terms.

16 Then he said to Tobi'as, "Get ready for the journey, and good success to you both." So his son made the preparations for the journey. And his father said to him, "Go with this man; God who dwells in heaven will prosper your way, and may

---

4:17 place your bread: Literally, "pour out your bread", suggesting that the original text of Tobit included a reference to wine, as in the Latin Vulgate. Scholars have noticed a parallel between this verse and the *Story of Ahikar* 2, 10 (in the Syriac version). The purpose of the rite remains obscure, although food offerings placed on gravesites is clearly frowned upon in Scripture (Deut 26:14; Sir 30:18). Alternatively, it is possible that Tobit recommends the charitable practice of bringing meals to families mourning the loss of a loved one (Jer 16:7; Ezek 24:17). See note on 1:21.

4:19 ask him: The moral life must be supported by a vibrant prayer life, since the help of grace is necessary to walk the straight and narrow way of the Lord.

4:20 Gabael ... Rages: See note on 1:14.

4:21 You have great wealth if you fear God: Summarizes the whole of Tobit's exhortation to his son. See note on 4:1–21.

📖 **5:1–22** Arrangements are made to retrieve Tobit's fortune from Media. Unbeknownst to father and son, the traveler hired to accompany Tobias is the angel Raphael disguised as a family relative. The story is entertaining in part because the reader knows information that the main characters do not (cf. 3:16–17). • In several passages of the Bible, angels take on a human appearance to disguise their heavenly identity (Gen 18:1–8; Judg 6:11–24; Heb 13:2).

5:3 receipt: A document that matches a certificate kept with the deposit of money.

5:4 Raphael: Sent from heaven to heal Tobit's blindness and to bring Tobias and Sarah together in marriage. See note on 3:17.

5:5 Rages: See note on 1:14.

5:12 Azarias: The name in Hebrew means "Yahweh has helped", which reveals the aim of Raphael's mission even as it conceals his angelic identity. Presenting himself as a kinsman is a strategy to gain Tobit's complete trust as the guide and caretaker of his son. The intent is not to deceive in a permanent or injurious way that undermines Tobit's understanding of reality, but to assume a human identity until his mission to heal and restore is complete, at which point a full disclosure of his identity is made and Tobit is brought to a clearer understanding of reality (see 12:11–15). Concealing a truth that another is not entitled to know can be legitimate under certain circumstances (CCC 2488–89). **Ananias:** The name in Hebrew means "Yahweh has shown mercy", alluding to the fact that God will be gracious to Tobit and his family. Like Tobit (1:5–8), the relative in question was a faithful participant in the Temple worship of Jerusalem even in times of national apostasy (5:13).

5:14 a drachma: Equivalent to a laborer's daily wage.

5:16 may his angel attend you: An obvious instance of irony. See note on 5:21.

---

[p]Gk *he.*
*4:17, *place your bread:* The Greek verb means literally "pour out." The Latin, with its "your bread and your wine," preserves better the original text, cf. the *Story of Ahikar:* "Pour out your wine on the graves of the righteous and drink it not with evil men."

his angel attend you." So they both went out and departed, and the young man's dog was with them.

17 But Anna,[q] his mother, began to weep, and said to Tobit, "Why have you sent our child away? Is he not the staff of our hands as he goes in and out before us? [18]Do not add money to money, but consider it rubbish as compared to our child. [19]For the life that is given to us by the Lord is enough for us." [20]And Tobit said to her, "Do not worry, my sister; he will return safe and sound, and your eyes will see him. [21]For a good angel will go with him; his journey will be successful, and he will come back safe and sound." [22]So she stopped weeping.

A Miraculous Fish

6 Now as they proceeded on their way they came at evening to the Tigris river and camped there. [2]Then the young man went down to wash himself. A fish leaped up from the river and would have swallowed the young man; [3]and the angel said to him, "Catch the fish." So the young man seized the fish and threw it up on the land. [4]Then the angel said to him, "Cut open the fish and take the heart and liver and gall and put them away safely." [5]So the young man did as the angel told him; and they roasted and ate the fish.

And they both continued on their way until they came near to Ecbat′ana.[r] [6]Then the young man said to the angel, "Brother Azari′as, of what use is the liver and heart and gall of the fish?" [7]He replied, "As for the heart and liver, if a demon or evil spirit gives trouble to any one, you make a smoke from these before the man or woman, and that person will

never be troubled again. [8]And as for the gall, anoint with it a man who has white films in his eyes, and he will be cured."

Raphael's Instructions

9 When he entered Med′ia and was already approaching Ecbat′ana, [10]Ra′phael said to the young man, "Brother Tobi′as!" "Here I am," he answered. Then Raphael said to him, "We must stay this night in the home of Ra′guel. He is your relative, and he has a daughter named Sarah. He has no male heir and no daughter except Sarah only, and you, as next of kin to her, have before all other men a hereditary claim on her. [11]Also, it is right for you to inherit her father's possessions. [12]Moreover, the girl is sensible, brave, and very beautiful, and her father is a good man."

13 Then the young man said to the angel, "Brother Azari′as, I have heard that the girl has been given to seven husbands and that each died in the bridal chamber. [14]Now I am the only son my father has, and I am afraid that if I go in I will die as those before me did, for a demon is in love with her, and he harms no one except those who approach her. So now I fear that I may die and bring the lives of my father and mother to the grave in sorrow on my account. And they have no other son to bury them."

15 But the angel said to him, "Do you not remember the words with which your father commanded you to take a wife from among your own people? Now listen to me, brother, for she will become your wife; and do not worry about the demon, for this very night she will be given to you in marriage.

5:20 your eyes: These words will be fulfilled when Anna lays eyes on Tobias in 11:9. The blind Tobit has no idea that he, too, will see his son at his return (11:10–15).

5:21 good angel: Tobit accepts on faith (5:16) what the reader has already learned as a fact, namely, that Tobias will be traveling with an angel sent from God (3:17; 5:4–5; CCC 336). • Tobit's words echo Gen 24:7, 40, where Abraham declares that an angel will go with his servant as he travels to find a wife for Isaac, his son. • Through the archangel, the divinity of Christ our Savior is signified, just as his humanity is signified by Tobias. By two persons, an angel and a man, the one person who is the Mediator between God and man is prefigured (St. Bede, *On Tobit* 6).

6:1 the Tigris: Flows along the western side of Nineveh. That Tobias should camp beside the Tigris on a journey to Media is often thought to be problematic, since a direct route from Nineveh to Media is an eastward journey that neither crosses the river nor runs parallel with it. Some infer from the oddity of Tobias' route that the author lacked reliable information about the geography of Mesopotamia. But this is not necessarily so. It is plausible that such a journey could have taken him along the river for a short time before turning directly east, depending on the travel routes chosen for the trip. Moreover, one might reasonably expect travelers to take an indirect route from Nineveh to Media at a time when major highways could be "unsafe" (1:15).

6:2 swallowed: Other versions of Tobit say the fish tried to swallow, not Tobias himself, but only his "foot".

6:4 heart and liver: To be used in an exorcistic rite. The procedure involves burning the organs of the fish on coals to create a vile-smelling smoke, while the effect is deliverance from demonic harassment (see 6:16–17 and 8:2–3). **gall:** Considered a medicinal remedy for various eye problems in ancient times (11:8; Pliny, *Natural History* 32, 14, and 32, 24).

6:5 Ecbatana: See note on 3:7.

6:8 white films: A type of infection that caused Tobit's blindness (2:10).

6:10 Here I am: The response of someone ready to listen and act on command (Gen 22:1; Ex 3:4; 1 Sam 3:4; Is 6:8). **Raguel:** His name in Aramaic means "friend of God". **no male heir:** Moses made provision for a daughter to inherit her father's estate in the event that he has no sons (Num 27:1–8). This makes Sarah the legal heir, but because she remains unmarried and childless, a solution must be found so that Raguel's property can be passed down to future generations within his family line. **claim on her:** The angel reveals another purpose of his mission: Tobias should return, not just with his family's wealth, but with a suitable wife.

6:13 I have heard: Sarah's marital misfortunes were evidently known in Nineveh among her relatives.

6:14 the only son: Sarah, too, is an "only child" (3:15). Both she and Tobias are anxious not to endanger themselves out of filial devotion to their parents (compare 6:14 with 3:10). **a demon:** Asmodeus. See note on 3:8. **in love with her:** The demon's actions are motivated by a violent jealousy.

6:15 take a wife: For Tobit's counsel on marriage, see 4:12. **she will be given to you:** The angel knows the marriage of Tobias and Sarah is divinely predestined (6:17).

---

[q]Other authorities omit *Anna*.
[r]Other authorities read *Rages*.

¹⁶When you enter the bridal chamber, you shall take live ashes of incense and lay upon them some of the heart and liver of the fish so as to make a smoke. ¹⁷Then the demon will smell it and flee away, and will never again return. And when you approach her, rise up, both of you, and cry out to the merciful God, and he will save you and have mercy on you. Do not be afraid, for she was destined for you from eternity. You will save her, and she will go with you, and I suppose that you will have children by her." When Tobi'as heard these things, he fell in love with her and yearned deeply for her.

Arrival at Raguel's Home; and a Marriage Contract

7 Now when they reached Ecbat'ana, Tobi'as said to him, "Brother Azari'ah, take me straight to our brother Rag'uel." So he took him to the house of Raguel, and they found Raguel sitting beside the courtyard door. They greeted him first, and he replied, "Joyous greetings, brothers; welcome and good health!" Then he brought them into his house. ²Then Rag'uel said to his wife Edna, "How much the young man resembles my cousin Tobit!" ³And Rag'uel asked them, "Where are you from, brethren?" They answered him, "We belong to the sons of Naph'tali, who are captives in Nin'eveh." ⁴So he said to them, "Do you know our brother Tobit?" And they said, "Yes, we do." And he asked them, "Is he in good health?" ⁵They replied, "He is alive and in good health." And Tobi'as said, "He is my father." ⁶Then Rag'uel sprang up and kissed him and wept. ⁷And he blessed him and exclaimed, "Son of that good and noble man!" When he heard that Tobit had lost his sight, he was stricken with grief and wept. ⁸And his wife Edna and his daughter Sarah wept.

9 Then Rag'uel killed a ram from the flock and received them very warmly. When they had bathed and washed themselves and had reclined to dine, Tobi'as said to Ra'phael, "Brother Azari'as, ask Raguel to give me my kinswoman Sarah." ¹⁰But Rag'uel overheard it and said to Tobi'as, "Eat, drink, and be merry; for no one except you, brother, has the right to marry my daughter Sarah. Likewise, I am not at liberty to give her to any other man than yourself, because you are my nearest relative. ¹¹But let me explain the true situation to you. I have given my daughter to seven men of our kinsmen, and when each came to her he died in the night. But for the present, my child, eat and drink, and the Lord will act on behalf of you both." But Tobi'as said, "I will eat nothing here unless you make a binding agreement with me." ¹²So Rag'uel

---

6:16–17 The Latin Vulgate supplies a longer ending for chap. 6 in which Raphael enjoins the newlyweds to spend the first three nights of their married life in prayer before consummating the union with sexual intercourse. The lesson is that couples should be animated by a pure love for one another rather than a selfish desire for carnal pleasure.

6:17 cry out to ... God: Prayer is an essential part of the exorcistic rite (8:2–4). **destined for you:** Tobias and Sarah are a match made in heaven (7:12). That God foreordains marriage partners, see also Gen 24:14, 51. **he fell in love with her:** Shows that the divine decree is effective even before Tobias first meets Sarah.

7:1–18 Tobias proposes and arranges his marriage with Sarah. The importance of kinship relations that underlies much of the book moves into the foreground in this chapter, where familial language is especially prominent (brother, 7:1; cousin, 7:2; brethren, 7:3; father, 7:5; son, 7:7; daughter, 7:8; kinswoman, 7:9; nearest relative, 7:10; kinsmen, 7:11; sister, 7:12).

7:1–8 Similarities between Tobias' encounter with Raguel and Jacob's encounter with the shepherds of Haran and Laban in Gen 29:1–28 hints that a marriage between kinsfolk is about to take place. Tobias is thus following in the footsteps of Jacob, the revered father of the nation of Israel. For another link to this story, see note on 10:10–12.

7:1 greetings, brothers: The travelers are recognized as kin, although Raguel is unaware until 7:5 that Tobias is a close relative.

7:2 Edna: The name in Hebrew is related to the word *Eden* and is translated as "pleasure" or "delight". **Naphtali:** Tobit is a member of this tribe (1:1), and presumably Raguel is as well (7:10).

7:9 very warmly: Lavish hospitality was and remains a sacred obligation in Middle Eastern culture. • Welcoming the visitors, one of whom is an angel in disguise, recalls the story of Abraham hosting messengers from heaven with water for washing and a feast for refreshment (Gen 18:1–8).

7:10 eat, drink, and be merry: An attempt to ease the impatience of Tobias about negotiating the marriage (7:11). • Some detect an allusion to Is 22:13, where those who die tomorrow indulge themselves in life's pleasures today (cf. Lk 12:19–20). If Raguel meant to evoke this passage, it would suggest he had little confidence that Tobias, like Sarah's seven previous bridegrooms, would survive the night (8:9–10). **nearest relative:** On the practice of kinship marriages, see note on 1:9.

7:12 the book of Moses: The Torah provides, not the rubrics of a marriage ceremony, but a vision of marriage as a divine institution (Gen 1:27–28; 2:21–24) that is subject to

---

WORD STUDY

Brother, Sister (7:12)

adelphos, adelphē (Gk.): the nouns for "brother" and "sister". Modern Western culture tends to restrict these terms to siblings born of the same parents. Semitic culture, however, tends to apply them more broadly to include one's kin in a more general sense. This can be seen in the Book of Tobit, where the words appear more than 20 times and not once in the sense of a blood brother or sister. The masculine *adelphos* is used as a reference to kindred (2:10) or brethren within the tribal family of Israel (1:16; 2:2; 4:12–13; 5:11, 13; 7:1). It embraces Israelites of the northern (1:3) and southern tribes (14:4). It can also designate a relative or kinsman within one's own tribe or clan (3:15; 7:4, 10–11; 10:12). In one passage, the word "brother" is an affectionate address for a husband (7:12). The feminine *adelphē* is applied to a similar range of familial relations. A "sister" can be a kinswoman (7:9; 8:7) or a term of endearment for a man's bride (5:20; 7:12, 16; 8:4; cf. Song 4:9–10; 5:1). For additional considerations, see word study: *My Sister* at Song 4:9.

said, "I will do so. She is given to you in accordance with the decree in the book of Moses, and it has been decreed from heaven that she be given to you. Take your kinswoman; from now on you are her brother and she is your sister. She is given to you from today and for ever. May the Lord of heaven, my child, guide and prosper you both this night and grant you mercy and peace." ¹³Then he called his daughter Sarah, and taking her by the hand he gave her to Tobi′as to be his wife, saying, "Here she is; take her to be your wife in accordance with the law and the decree written in the book of Moses. Take her and bring her safely to your father. And may the God of heaven prosper your journey with his peace." ¹⁴Then he called her mother and told her to bring writing material; and he wrote out a copy of the marriage contract, to the effect that he gave her to him as wife according to the law of Moses. ¹⁵Then they began to eat and drink.

16 And Rag′uel called his wife Edna and said to her, "Sister, make up the other room, and take her into it." ¹⁷So she did as he said, and took her there; and the girl**ˢ** began to weep. But the mother**ˢ** comforted her daughter in her tears, and said to her, ¹⁸"Be brave, my child; the Lord of heaven and earth grant you joy**ᵗ** in place of this sorrow of yours. Be brave, my daughter."

Tobias Routs the Demon and Prays with Sarah

8 When they had finished eating and drinking, they wanted to retire; so they took the young man and brought him into the bedroom. ²As he went he remembered the words of Ra′phael, and he took the live ashes of incense and put the heart and liver of the fish upon them and made a smoke. ³And when the demon smelled the odor he fled to the remotest parts of Egypt, and the angel bound him. ⁴When the door was shut and the two were alone, Tobi′as got up from the bed and said, "Sister, get up, and let us pray and implore our Lord that he grant us mercy and safety." ⁵And they began to say,

"Blessed are you, O God of our fathers,
    and blessed be your holy and glorious name
        for ever.
Let the heavens and all your creatures bless
    you.
⁶You made Adam and gave him Eve his wife
    as a helper and support.
From them the race of mankind has sprung.
You said, 'It is not good that the man should be
    alone;
    let us make a helper for him like himself.'
⁷And now, O Lord, I am not taking this sister of mine because of lust, but with sincerity. Grant that I may find mercy and may grow old together with her." ⁸And they both said, "Amen, amen." ⁹Then they both went to sleep for the night.

But Rag′uel arose and went and dug a grave, ¹⁰with the thought, "Perhaps he too will die." ¹¹Then Rag′uel went into his house ¹²and said to his wife Edna, "Send one of the maids to see whether he

---

the laws of God (Lev 18:6–23; Deut 24:1–4). **decreed from heaven:** Reiterates the point made in 6:17 that the marriage of Tobias and Sarah was predestined by God.

7:14 marriage contract: A legal document that came to be called a *ketubbah* in rabbinic Judaism, in which the groom-to-be set forth in writing his financial and marital obligations toward his future spouse. Since the document here is written by the bride's father instead of the bridegroom, it may be a certificate of betrothal rather than a marriage contract (see Mishnah, *Kiddushin* 1, 1).

7:16 the other room: Prepared as a bridal chamber for the newlyweds.

7:17 the girl began to weep: Sarah expects that Tobias will not survive the wedding night.

8:2 words of Raphael: Recorded in 6:7–8. For the fumigation rite, see note on 6:4.

8:3 the demon: Asmodeus (3:8). **remotest parts of Egypt:** The lifeless expanse of desert beyond the fertile Nile Valley. Demons were believed to lurk in desolate (Is 13:21; 34:14) and arid places (Mt 12:43; Lk 11:24). **bound:** To bind a demon is to overpower and subdue the spirit with divine authority (Mt 12:29; Rev 20:2). Raphael was known to exercise the power of binding evil spirits in Jewish tradition (e.g., *1 Enoch* 10, 4).

8:4–8 The wedding night prayer of Tobias and Sarah in 8:4b–8 is often read at Nuptial Masses.

8:4 Sister: See word study: *Brother, Sister* at 7:12. **let us pray:** Tobias follows the angel's instruction to "cry out" to the Lord for "mercy" (6:17).

8:5–6 A traditional form of prayer called a *berakhah* (Hebrew, "blessing"). Tobias' prayer of praise on his wedding night is mirrored by Raguel's prayer of praise the next morning (8:15–17). The expression "Blessed are you" is the signature feature of such prayers (8:5, 15, 16, 17).

8:6 Adam . . . Eve: The first marriage, as presented in Genesis, reveals God's will for all marriages. Here it is stressed that man and woman are brought together for mutual help and benefit (CCC 2361). • Tobias refers to the creation of the marriage covenant in Gen 2:18–24. Moreover, Tobias may be viewed as a new and more faithful Adam, a bridegroom who acts to protect his bride from the treachery of an evil spirit, unlike the first Adam. **the race of mankind:** An assertion of monogenism, the notion that all human beings descend from a single couple, whom the Bible calls Adam and Eve. As a result of having a common origin, men and women of all times, places, and races share a common nature and condition (CCC 360). • Pope Pius XII affirmed a form of monogenism in 1950 when he denied certain forms of polygenism that supposed some human beings did not descend from Adam or that Adam was not an individual but a plurality of ancestors (*Humani Generis* 37). For Pius XII, it was unclear how such an understanding of human origins could be reconciled with the doctrine of Original Sin, which entails the transgression of an individual man whose action impacted all his descendants, resulting in mankind's universal need for redemption (CCC 403–5). This doctrine rests on the Church's view of the human person as a bodily creature with a spiritual and rational soul. The Church, as the custodian and interpreter of God's word, neither affirms nor denies the past existence of pre-rational ancestors with physical and genetic features similar to our own (i.e., what natural scientists call "anatomically human ancestors").

8:9 dug a grave: A precautionary step that reveals the growing pessimism of Raguel.

8:12 without any one knowing: A secret burial would spare the family still more shame than it had already endured.

---

is alive; and if he is not, let us bury him without any one knowing about it." [13]So the maid opened the door and went in, and found them both asleep. [14]And she came out and told them that he was alive. [15]Then Rag'uel blessed God and said,

"Blessed are you, O God, with every pure and holy blessing.
Let your saints and all your creatures bless you;
let all your angels and your chosen people bless you for ever.

[16]Blessed are you, because you have made me glad.
It has not happened to me as I expected;
but you have treated us according to your great mercy.

[17]Blessed are you, because you have had compassion on two only children.
Show them mercy, O Lord;
and bring their lives to fulfilment in health and happiness and mercy."

[18]Then he ordered his servants to fill in the grave.

The Wedding Feast

19 After this he gave a wedding feast for them which lasted fourteen days. [20]And before the days of the feast were over, Rag'uel declared by oath to Tobi'as[u] that he should not leave until the fourteen days of the wedding feast were ended, [21]that then he should take half of Rag'uel's[v] property and return in safety to his father, and that the rest would be his "when my wife and I die."

The Money Recovered from Gabael

9 Then Tobi'as called Ra'phael and said to him, [2]"Brother Azari'as, take a servant and two camels with you and go to Gab'ael at Ra'ges in Med'ia and get the money for me; and bring him to the wedding feast. [3]For Rag'uel has sworn that I should not leave; [4]but my father is counting the days, and if I delay

long he will be greatly distressed." [5]So Ra'phael made the journey and stayed overnight with Gab'-ael. He gave him the receipt, and Gabael[w] brought out the money bags with their seals intact and gave them to him. [6]In the morning they both got up early and came to the wedding feast. And Gab'ael blessed Tobi'as and his wife.[x]

Tobias and Sarah Journey Home to Tobit and Anna

10 Now his father Tobit was counting each day, and when the days for the journey had expired and they did not arrive, [2]he said, "Is it possible that he has been detained?[y] Or is it possible that Gab'ael has died and there is no one to give him the money?" [3]And he was greatly distressed. [4]And his wife said to him, "The lad has perished; his long delay proves it." Then she began to mourn for him, and said, [5]"Am I not distressed, my child, that I let you go, you who are the light of my eyes?" [6]But Tobit said to her, "Be still and stop worrying; he is well." [7]And she answered him, "Be still and stop deceiving me; my child has perished." And she went out every day to the road by which they had left; she ate nothing in the daytime, and throughout the nights she never stopped mourning for her son Tobi'as, until the fourteen days of the wedding feast had expired which Rag'uel had sworn that he should spend there.

At that time Tobias said to Raguel, "Send me back, for my father and mother have given up hope of ever seeing me again." [8]But his father-in-law said to him, "Stay with me, and I will send messengers to your father, and they will inform him how things are with you." [9]Tobi'as replied, "No, send me back to my father." [10]So Rag'uel arose and gave him his wife Sarah and half of his property in slaves, cattle, and money. [11]And when he had blessed them he sent them away, saying, "The God of heaven will prosper you, my children,

---

8:15–17 Raguel blessed God: See note on 8:5–6.

8:19 fourteen days: Double the typical length of a marriage feast in Israel (Judg 14:12).

8:21 half: Sarah, being an only child, is the sole heiress of her family's belongings (3:15). The first half of the inheritance is given on her wedding day (6:10–11; 10:10); the second half will come when her parents pass away (14:13).

9:2 Gabael: A kinsman of Tobit (5:6) entrusted with his deposit of silver (1:14). **Rages:** See note on 1:14.

9:5 the receipt: A certificate of ownership (5:3). **seals intact:** Verifies that the deposit has not been tampered with.

9:6 came to the wedding feast: The journey from Ecbatana to Rages is about 180 miles one way, and traveling there and back again would take at least three weeks with camels (9:2). This creates a chronological problem: the wedding celebration lasted only fourteen days (8:19), which allows too

little time for Raphael to make the round trip and return with Gabael to Ecbatana before the festivities ended (9:5–6). Since no indication is given that the journey involved a miracle, it is reasonable to suppose that the wedding night in 8:1–9 was followed by several days of preparation before the start of the two-week celebration. Some of these preparations are mentioned in the longer text of Tobit (8:19 in *Codex Sinaiticus*). See introduction: *Literary Background*.

10:1–12 Anxiety mounts in Nineveh regarding the whereabouts of Tobias (10:1–7) and in Ecbatana regarding the welfare of Tobias' parents (10:7–12). Tobit is becoming distressed (10:3), Anna is next to despair (10:7), and Tobias is unwilling to delay his return any longer (10:8–9).

10:5 the light of my eyes: An idiom meaning "the joy of my life" (11:14; cf. Ps 38:10).

10:7 stop deceiving me: Fearing that Tobias has perished, Anna mourns and refuses consolation, much like Jacob, who mistakenly thinks his son dead in Gen 37:35.

10:10–12 Raguel sends off Tobias and Sarah with a blessing. The account resembles Laban's farewell to his daughters Rachel and Leah, who departed for the land of Canaan with their husband, Jacob (Gen 31:43–55). See note on 7:1–8.

---

[u]Gk *him.*
[v]Gk *his.*
[w]Gk *he.*
[x]Cn: Gk *And Tobias blessed his wife.*
[y]One Gk Ms Lat: Gk *they are put to shame* or *they are disappointed.*

before I die." ¹²He said also to his daughter, "Honor your father-in-law and your mother-in-law; they are now your parents. Let me hear a good report of you." And he kissed her. And Edna said to Tobi′as, "The Lord of heaven bring you back safely, dear brother, and grant me to see your children by my daughter Sarah, that I may rejoice before the Lord. See, I am entrusting my daughter to you; do nothing to grieve her."

The Return

11 After this Tobi′as went on his way, praising God because he had made his journey a success. And he blessed Rag′uel and his wife Edna.

So he continued on his way until they came near to Nin′eveh. ²Then Ra′phael said to Tobi′as, "Are you not aware, brother, of how you left your father? ³Let us run ahead of your wife and prepare the house. ⁴And take the gall of the fish with you." So they went their way, and the dog went along behind them.

5 Now Anna sat looking intently down the road for her son. ⁶And she caught sight of him coming, and said to his father, "Behold, your son is coming, and so is the man who went with him!"

Tobit's Sight Restored

7 Ra′phael said to Tobi′as, before they approached his father, "I know that his eyes will be opened. ⁸Smear the gall of the fish on his eyes, and the medicine will cause the white films to fall away. And your father will regain his sight and see the light."

9 Then Anna ran to meet them, and embraced her son, and said to him, "I have seen you, my child; now I am ready to die." And she wept. ¹⁰Tobit got up, and came stumbling out through the courtyard door. But his son ran to him ¹¹with the gall of the fish in his hand, and holding him firmly, he blew into his eyes, saying, "Take courage, Father." ¹²With this he applied the medicine on his eyes. ¹³Next, with both his hands, he peeled off the white films from the corners of his eyes. ¹⁴Then he saw his son and embraced him, and he wept and said, "Here I see my son, the light of my eyes!" Then he said, "Blessed be God, and blessed be his great name, and blessed be all his holy angels. May his holy name be blessed throughout all the ages. ¹⁵Though he afflicted me, he has had mercy on me. Now I see my son Tobi′as!"

16 And his son went in rejoicing, and he reported to his father the great things that had happened to him in Med′ia. Then Tobit went out to meet his daughter-in-law at the gate of Nin′eveh, rejoicing and praising God. Those who saw him as he went were amazed because he could see. ¹⁷And Tobit gave thanks before them that God had been merciful to him. When Tobit came near to Sarah his daughter-in-law, he blessed her, saying, "Welcome, daughter! Blessed is God who has brought you to us, and blessed are your father and your mother." So there was rejoicing among all his brethren in Nin′eveh. ¹⁸Ahi′kar and his nephew Na′dab² came, ¹⁹and Tobi′as' marriage was celebrated for seven days with great festivity.

Raphael's Wages

12 Tobit then called his son Tobi′as and said to him, "My son, see to the wages of the man

---

10:12 Honor: A reference to the fourth commandment, here applied to Sarah's new in-laws (Ex 20:12). **brother:** In this context, the word refers to a kinsman recently become a son-in-law. See word study: *Brother, Sister* at 7:12. **nothing to grieve:** Edna's farewell speech is a plea to give Sarah a happy life. Her words are especially poignant in view of her daughter's long history of sorrows (3:7–15; 7:17–18).

11:1 Nineveh: The capital of Assyria. See note on 1:3.

11:4 the dog: Appears at the end of the journey as well as the beginning (5:16).

11:5 Anna sat looking: Despite fearing the worst, Tobias' mother has not lost all hope of seeing him again (10:7).

11:7–19 The highpoint of the book is the happy ending of the journey. Tobias returns to restore his father's sight; and he brings back, not only his family's wealth, but a new and beautiful wife. The twofold mission of Raphael, sent from heaven to deliver Tobit and Sarah from their distress, is now complete (3:16–17; 12:14).

11:8 the gall: An ancient eye ointment. See note on 6:4. **see the light:** After four years of living in darkness (2:10). • Healing from blindness is a personal experience of Tobit that anticipates one of the great messianic blessings awaited by Israel as a whole (Is 35:5; 42:7, 19). Isaiah even prophesied that the tribes of Zebulun and Naphtali, who walked for a time in darkness, will see "a great light" (Is 9:1–2). Tobit is from the tribe of Naphtali (1:1).

11:9 ready to die: Anna is relieved to know she will not die a bereaved mother (10:4–7).

11:10 courtyard: A significant detail, showing that Tobit is healed in the same place where he was blinded (2:9–10).

11:14 Then he saw: The instantaneous effect of the application suggests a miracle is being described. **the light of my eyes:** An idiom meaning "the joy of my life" (10:5; cf. Ps 38:10). The expression has a deeper significance for Tobit, whose son has just restored his ability to see "the light" of day (11:8). **Blessed be God:** Tobit offers a *berakhah* of thanksgiving to the Lord. See note on 8:5–6.

11:15 afflicted ... mercy: The same word pair is used in chap. 13 in reference to Israel and Jerusalem (13:2, 5, 9). The storyteller thus implies that Tobit represents his people, so that his personal plight foreshadows the national plight of Israel as a whole. Specifically, the suffering and healing experienced by Tobit stand as a sign of hope for the twelve tribes in exile, who await restoration and healing. See introduction: *Themes and Characteristics*. • Tobit's words are an allusion to Deut 32:39, where the Lord declares: "I wound and I heal."

11:18 Ahikar: Tobit's nephew. See note on 1:21. **Nadab:** His name appears differently in several ancient versions of the book (e.g., Nasbas in some Greek manuscripts; Nadin in the Aramaic fragment 4Q199; Nabath in the Latin Vulgate).

11:19 seven days: It was customary for wedding feasts to last a full week in biblical times (Judg 14:12). The reception in Nineveh follows the fourteen days of celebration that took place previously in Ecbatana (8:19).

12:1–5 Tobit follows his own counsel on the prompt payment of hired workers (see 4:14). Both he and his son show themselves generous beyond the strict requirements of justice: Tobit proposes adding a bonus to Azariah's wages (12:1), and

---

²Other authorities read *Nasbas.*

who went with you; and he must also be given more." [2]He replied, "Father, it would do me no harm to give him half of what I have brought back. [3]For he has led me back to you safely, he cured my wife, he obtained the money for me, and he also healed you." [4]The old man said, "He deserves it." [5]So he called the angel and said to him, "Take for your wages half of all that you two have brought back, and farewell."

Raphael's Exhortation

6 Then the angel[a] called the two of them privately and said to them: "Praise God and give thanks to him; exalt him and give thanks to him in the presence of all the living for what he has done for you. It is good to praise God and to exalt his name, worthily declaring the works of God, and with fitting honor to acknowledge him. Do not be slow to give him thanks. [7]It is good to guard the secret of a king, but gloriously to reveal the works of God, and with fitting honor to acknowledge him. Do good, and evil will not overtake you. [8]Prayer is good when accompanied by fasting, almsgiving, and righteousness. A little with righteousness is better than much with wrongdoing. It is better to give alms than to treasure up gold. [9]For almsgiving delivers from death, and it will purge away every sin. Those who perform deeds of charity* and of righteousness will have fulness of life; [10]but those who commit sin are the enemies of their own lives.

Raphael Reveals His Identity

11 "I will now declare the whole truth to you and I will not conceal anything from you. I have said, 'It is good to guard the secret of a king, but gloriously to reveal the works of God.' [12]And so, when you and your daughter-in-law Sarah prayed, I brought a reminder of your prayer before the Holy One; and when you buried the dead, I was likewise present with you. [13]When you did not hesitate to rise and leave your dinner in order to go and lay out the dead, I was sent to test you. [14]So now God sent me to heal you and your daughter-in-law Sarah. [15]I am Ra'phael, one of the seven holy angels who present the prayers of the saints and enter into the presence of the glory of the Lord."

16 They were both alarmed; and they fell upon their faces, for they were afraid. [17]But he said to them, "Do not be afraid; you will be safe. But praise God for ever. [18]For I did not come as a favor on my part, but by the will of our God. Therefore praise him for ever. [19]All these days I merely appeared to you and did not eat or drink, but you were seeing a vision. [20]And now bless the Lord upon the earth and give thanks to God, for I am ascending to him who sent me. Write in a book everything that has happened to you." [21]Then they stood up; but they saw him no more. [22]So they confessed the great and wonderful works of God, and acknowledged that the angel of the Lord had appeared to them.

Tobias is ready to offer him 50 percent of everything acquired on the trip (12:2).

12:6–10 Raphael's words echo Tobit's address in 4:3–19. Note how the angel, who was directly involved in the miracles of recent days, takes no credit for any of them. He gives all praise and thanksgiving to the Lord, who sent him to "heal" Tobit's family of their afflictions (3:17; 12:14).

12:8 Prayer . . . fasting, almsgiving: Pillars of Jewish piety in the final centuries of the OT period (4:8–11; Sir 7:10). • Jesus endorsed this triad of religious practices in the Sermon on the Mount (Mt 6:1–18); and, like Raphael, he added a warning about treasuring up earthly wealth (Mt 6:19–21). • The Church promotes the practice of prayer, fasting, and almsgiving, especially during the penitential season of Lent (CCC 1434). • There are three things supremely related to religious observance: prayer, fasting, and the giving of alms. By prayer, we aim to propitiate God; by fasting, we extinguish the desires of the flesh; and by almsgiving, we redeem sins. This threefold duty brings all the virtues into action (St. Leo the Great, *Sermons* 12).

12:9 almsgiving: A practical expression of mercy toward persons in need. See word study: *Acts of Charity* at 1:16. **purge away:** Charitable giving is a means of expiating sin (Sir 3:30). See note on Dan 4:27.

12:11–12 Raphael discloses his true identity, informing Tobit and Tobias about things the reader has known since 3:16–17 and 5:4.

12:12 reminder: The Greek *mnēmosynon* is used for the "memorial portion" of a Levitical offering (Lev 2:2; 5:12; Sir 38:11; 45:16). Prayer is thus accorded a value equivalent to an acceptable sacrifice made to the Lord in the sanctuary (cf. Acts 10:4). **before the Holy One:** Angels bring the prayers of the saints before God according to Scripture (Rev 8:2–3) as well as Jewish tradition (*1 Enoch* 9, 1–3; 99, 3).

12:13 sent to test you: God tests his people, not to tempt them into sin (Jas 1:13), but to strengthen them through suffering and lead them to a more perfect faith (Gen 22:1; 1 Mac 2:52; Jas 1:2–4; 1 Pet 1:6–7).

12:15 I am Raphael: See note on 3:17. **the seven holy angels:** Only mentioned here in the Bible, although the tradition is assumed in Lk 1:19. • The angels are prompt in doing God's will and appear in whatever location the divine pleasure commands them to be. They are set over nations and places as determined by the Creator. They give us help and take whatever form the Lord commands. Thus they appear to men and reveal divine mysteries (St. John of Damascus, *Orthodox Faith* 2, 3).

12:16 fell upon their faces: Falling prostrate is a common reaction to angelic apparitions in the Bible (Josh 5:14; Judg 13:20; Rev 22:8).

12:17 Do not be afraid: Words of reassurance often given to those who are visited by an angel (Mt 1:20; 28:5; Lk 1:13, 30).

12:19 did not eat: Evidence that Raphael is a spirit who only appears to be a flesh-and-blood man (contrast with Lk 24:36–42).

12:20 ascending to him who sent me: Similar to Jesus' words in Jn 16:5. That the angels of God ascend and descend between heaven and earth, see Gen 28:12 and Jn 1:51. **Write in a book:** Tobit's family story must be recorded as a witness to the mighty works of God (in fulfillment of 12:6–7). Perhaps the canonical Book of Tobit is based on this ancient memoir. See introduction: *Author and Date*.

---

[a]Gk *he*.
* 12:9, *charity:* See note on 4:10.

Tobit's Prayer of Thanksgiving

13 Then Tobit wrote a prayer of rejoicing, and said:

"Blessed is God who lives for ever,
 and blessed is his kingdom.
²For he afflicts, and he shows mercy;
 he leads down to Hades, and brings up
 again,
 and there is no one who can escape his
 hand.
³Acknowledge him before the nations, O sons of
 Israel;
 for he has scattered us among them.
⁴Make his greatness known there,
 and exalt him in the presence of all the living;
 because he is our Lord and God,
 he is our Father for ever.
⁵He will afflict us for our iniquities;
 and again he will show mercy,
 and will gather us from all the nations
 among whom youᵇ have been scattered.
⁶If you turn to him with all your heart and with
 all your soul,
 to do what is true before him,
 then he will turn to you
 and will not hide his face from you.
But see what he will do with you;
 give thanks to him with your full voice.
Praise the Lord of righteousness,
 and exalt the King of the ages.
I give him thanks in the land of my captivity,
 and I show his power and majesty to a nation
 of sinners.
Turn back, you sinners, and do right before
 him;
 who knows if he will accept you and have
 mercy on you?

⁷I exalt my God;
 my soul exalts the King of heaven,
 and will rejoice in his majesty.
⁸Bless the Lord, all you his chosen ones,
 all of you, praise his glory.
Celebrate days of joy, and give thanks to him.
⁹O Jerusalem, the holy city,
 he will afflict you for the deeds of your
 sons,
 but again he will show mercy to the sons
 of the righteous.
¹⁰Give thanks worthily to the Lord,
 and praise the King of the ages,
 that his tent may be raised for you again with
 joy.
May he cheer those within you who are captives,
 and love those within you who are distressed,
 to all generations for ever.
¹¹Many nations will come from afar to the name of
 the Lord God,
 bearing gifts in their hands, gifts for the King
 of heaven.
Generations of generations will give you joyful
 praise.
¹²Cursed are all who hate you;
 blessed for ever will be all who love you.
¹³Rejoice and be glad for the sons of the righteous;
 for they will be gathered together,
 and will praise the Lord of the righteous.
¹⁴How blessed are those who love you!
 They will rejoice in your peace.
Blessed are those who grieved over all your
 afflictions;
 for they will rejoice for you upon seeing all
 your glory,
 and they will be made glad for ever.
¹⁵Let my soul praise God the great King.

13:1–18 A hymn of praise and thanksgiving. Its focus is twofold: verses 1–8 speak of the exile and restoration of the tribes of Israel; and verses 9–13 foretell the destruction and glorification of Jerusalem. The Lord is praised throughout the hymn for his *justice*, which is manifest in past and present history, and his *mercy*, which Israel hopes to experience in the future. • The opening of the hymn alludes to the latter chapters of Deuteronomy (compare 13:2 with Deut 32:39 and 13:5–6 with Deut 30:1–5), and the second part uses imagery from the latter chapters of Isaiah (compare 13:11 with Is 60:1–6, 13:14 with Is 66:10, and 13:16 with Is 54:11–12).

13:2 afflicts ... shows mercy: God's response to sin and repentance, respectively (13:5, 9). See note on 11:15. **Hades:** The Greek equivalent of Sheol, the Hebrew name for the netherworld of the dead. See note on 3:6.

13:3–4 The exile is an opportunity for Israel to offer witness to the Gentiles by making known the mighty works of the Lord (13:6). For this missionary vocation of God's people, see note on Ex 19:6.

13:3 sons of Israel: A reference to the tribes of Israel, most of which are scattered abroad in exile (1:1–2; 2 Kings 15:29; 17:6).

13:4 our Father: Yahweh is the divine Father of the covenant people (Is 63:16; Jer 31:9).

13:6 nation of sinners: The Assyrians.

13:8 chosen ones: The Israelites, who are the Lord's elect people (Deut 7:6; Ps 33:12).

13:9 Jerusalem: Tobit, prophesying in the seventh century B.C., foresees the destruction of the holy city in the sixth century B.C. along with its eventual restoration. Some take this as evidence that the Book of Tobit was written after the ruin and rebuilding of Jerusalem, i.e., in the fifth century B.C. or later; however, this conclusion is only necessary if one denies the possibility of predictive prophecy. **the holy city:** Another name for Jerusalem (Neh 11:1).

13:10 his tent: The Temple was destroyed by the Babylonians in 586 B.C. (2 Kings 25:8–9) and rebuilt by Jewish returnees ca. 520–515 B.C. (Ezra 6:13–15).

13:11 nations will come: A vision of messianic times, when non-Jewish peoples will come from the ends of the earth to worship the God of Israel. This is a prominent prophetic hope in the OT (Is 2:2–3; 60:3; Jer 3:17; Zech 2:11; 8:23). **bearing gifts:** That the nations will bring their wealth to Jerusalem, see Ps 72:10–11; Is 45:14; 60:5–6.

13:12 Cursed ... blessed: A reference to God's promise to Abraham in Gen 12:3, which was further applied to his descendants in Num 24:9.

ᵇ Other authorities read *we*.

¹⁶For Jerusalem will be built with sapphires and
> emeralds,
> her ᶜ walls with precious stones,
> and her towers and battlements with pure
> gold.
¹⁷The streets of Jerusalem will be paved ᵈ with
> beryl and ruby and stones of O'phir;
¹⁸ all her lanes will cry 'Hallelujah!' and will give
> praise,
> saying, 'Blessed is God, who has exalted you
> for ever.'"

Tobit's Final Counsel and Death

14 Here Tobit ended his words of praise. ²He was fifty-eight years old when he lost his sight, and after eight years he regained it. He gave alms, and he continued to fear the Lord God and to praise him. ³When he had grown very old he called his son and grandsons, and said to him, "My son, take your sons; behold, I have grown old and am about to depart this life. ⁴Go to Med'ia, my son, for I fully believe what Jonah the prophet said about Nin'eveh, that it will be overthrown. But in Media there will be peace for a time. Our brethren will be scattered over the earth from the good land, and Jerusalem will be desolate. The house of God in it will be burned down and will be in ruins for a time. ⁵But God will again have mercy on them, and bring them back into their land; and they will rebuild the house of God, ᵉ though it will not be like the former one until the times of the age are completed. After this they will return from the places of their captivity, and will rebuild Jerusalem in splendor. And the house of God will be rebuilt there with a glorious building for all generations for ever, just as the prophets said of it. ⁶Then all the Gentiles will turn to fear the Lord God in truth, and will bury their idols. ⁷All the Gentiles will praise the Lord, and his people will give thanks to God, and the Lord will exalt his people. And all who love the Lord God in truth and righteousness will rejoice, showing mercy to our brethren.

8 "So now, my son, leave Nin'eveh, because what the prophet Jonah said will surely happen. ⁹But keep the law and the commandments, and be merciful and just, so that it may be well with you. ¹⁰Bury

---

13:16–18 Building with precious metals and stones points to a glorified Jerusalem that outshines in splendor the metropolis known to history, as in Is 54:11–12. • In the Book of Revelation, it is the heavenly Jerusalem that shines with pure gold and has gemstones set in its walls, gates, and foundations (Rev 21:10–21).

13:18 Blessed is God: The final *berakhah* of the book is pronounced by a personified and glorified Jerusalem. For this type of prayer, see note on 8:5–6.

14:2 eight years: It is unclear how this figure relates to the "four years" in 2:10. It may be a later addition to the story, since several ancient versions of the book omit the number.

14:3–11 Tobit's farewell speech delivered on his deathbed. Like other testaments in the Bible and related Jewish literature, the elderly man's counsel is full of exhortations and predictions (e.g., the testament of Jacob in Gen 49:1–33). • In particular, like Moses, who foresaw at the end of his life the curses of the covenant that would come upon Israel for its transgressions (Deut 28:15–68; 30:1), the elderly Tobit foresees the curses of desolation, destruction, and dispersion coming upon the Judeans still living in the land of Israel (14:4).

14:4 Media: The home of Tobias' in-laws, Raguel and Edna, in northern Iran. **Jonah:** The name that appears in the short text of Tobit. In the long text, this prophet is identified as Nahum, which is more likely the correct reading, since Nahum delivered oracles of doom against the wicked city of Nineveh (Nah 1:1; 2:8–10; 3:18–19). Jonah, by contrast, preached repentance to a generation of Ninevites, whose acceptance of his words delayed the divine judgment on the city (Jon 3:1–10). For the short and long texts of Tobit, see introduction: *Literary Background*. **overthrown:** Tobit foresees the fall of Nineveh in 612 B.C. at the hands of the Babylonians and Medes. **Our brethren:** The tribes of the Southern Kingdom of Judah, who will be carried off as exiles to Babylon in the sixth century B.C. See word study: *Brother, Sister* at 7:12. **the good land:** A description of Canaan often used in the Book of Deuteronomy (Deut 1:35; 3:25; 4:21; etc.). **desolate:** Envisions the destruction of Jerusalem in 586 B.C. (Is 64:10).

14:5 again have mercy: As stated in 13:5–6. The hope for God's mercy in exile can be traced back to Deut 30:1–6. **they will rebuild:** Three different sanctuaries are mentioned in this verse: the Solomonic Temple, finished ca. 959 B.C. (**the former one**), the Second Temple, built after the return from Babylonian Exile and finished ca. 515 B.C. (**the house of God**), and a future Temple (**a glorious building**) that coincides with the conversion of "all the Gentiles" (14:6). • According to the NT, the glorious sanctuary to come is the universal Church, built from believers of every nation into a living Temple of the Spirit (1 Cor 3:16; 2 Cor 6:16; Eph 2:19–22; 1 Pet 2:4–5). **Not . . . like the former:** The Second Temple was not nearly as impressive as Solomon's (Ezra 3:12; Hag 2:3). **the times of the age:** The time of eschatological and messianic fulfillment (cf. 1 Cor 10:11). **they will return:** The restoration and reunion of all the tribes of Israel and Judah from exile is a prominent expectation in the OT (Sir 48:10; Is 11:11–12; 49:3–7; Jer 3:18; 16:14–15; Ezek 37:19–22). See essay: *The Salvation of All Israel* at Rom 11. **splendor:** As indicated in 13:16–18.

14:6–7 Tobit urges his son both to **fear** God and to **love** God. Fearing and loving are two ways of speaking about obedience to the covenant in the Book of Deuteronomy (Deut 6:5, 13; 8:6; 10:12; 11:1; 28:58; etc.).

14:6 all the Gentiles: According to the NT, the conversion of all nations takes place through the spread of the gospel (Mt 28:19; Rom 1:16; Eph 3:1–6). As a result, Gentiles no less than Jews are incorporated into the Temple of Christ's Body, which is the Church. See note on 14:5. **bury their idols:** As the household of Jacob did in Gen 35:2–4. Gentiles repudiate idolatry when they come to faith in the living and true God (Jer 16:19–20; 1 Thess 1:9).

14:7 our brethren: Fellow Israelite exiles.

14:8 Jonah: Or, better, "Nahum". See note on 14:4.

14:10 Nadab: Ahikar's nephew (called Nadin) in the ancient folktale known as the *Story of Ahikar*. Nadab betrayed Ahikar and plotted his demise, despite his uncle's numerous acts of kindness on his behalf. In the end, the tables were turned: Ahikar was brought out of hiding and cleared of charges, while Nadab was found out and left to die in a dungeon. See notes on 1:21 and 11:18. **Ahikar was saved:** Because of his almsgiving. Recall that he supported Tobit at his own expense for two years (2:10).

ᶜ Gk *your*.
ᵈ Or *inlaid*.
ᵉ Gk *house*.

me properly, and your mother with me. And do not live in Nin'eveh any longer. See, my son, what Na'dab[f] did to Ahi'kar who had reared him, how he brought him from light into darkness, and with what he repaid him. But Ahikar was saved, and the other received repayment as he himself went down into the darkness. Ahikar[g] gave alms and escaped the deathtrap which Nadab[h] had set for him; but Nadab[f] fell into the trap and perished. [11]So now, my children, consider what almsgiving accomplishes and how righteousness delivers." As he said this he died in his bed. He was a hundred and fifty-eight years old; and Tobi'as[h] gave him a magnificent funeral. [12]And when Anna died he buried her with his father.

Then Tobi'as returned with his wife and his sons to Ecbat'ana, to Rag'uel his father-in-law. [13]He grew old with honor, and he gave his father-in-law and mother-in-law magnificent funerals. He inherited their property and that of his father Tobit. [14]He died in Ecbat'ana of Med'ia at the age of a hundred and twenty-seven years. [15]But before he died he heard of the destruction of Nin'eveh, which Nebuchadnez'zar and Ahas'u-erus had captured. Before his death he rejoiced over Nineveh.

14:11 almsgiving: A towering theme in the book. See word study: *Acts of Charity* at 1:16. **a hundred and fifty-eight:** Other ancient editions of the book give Tobit's age at death as 102 years old (Latin Vulgate) and 112 years old (14:2 in *Codex Sinaiticus*). **funeral:** On the duty of burial, see note on 1:17.

14:12 Tobias returned: In obedience to his father's exhortation in 14:4.

14:14 a hundred and twenty-seven: Other ancient editions of the book give Tobias' age at death as 99 years old (Latin Vulgate) and 117 years (*Codex Sinaiticus*).

14:15 Nineveh: Conquered in 612 B.C. through the combined efforts of Nabopolassar, king of Babylon (625 to 605 B.C.), and Cyaxares, king of Media (625 to 585 B.C.). The Greek text translated by the RSVCE is not likely original, as it lists its captors as **Nebuchadnezzar** of Babylon, whose reign began in 605, and **Ahasuerus** of Persia, whose reign began in 486 B.C. No mention is made of these later kings in the longer text of the Book of Tobit (on which, see introduction: *Literary Background*).

---

[f] Other authorities read *Aman*.
[g] Other authorities read *Manasses*.
[h] Gk *he*.

Study Questions
Tobit

Chapter 1

For understanding

1. **1:6.** As part of the remnant of northern Israelites in the time of the divided monarchy, what did Tobit continue to do? Allowing for some rhetorical exaggeration, what does Tobit's statement imply? What does the Torah require of adult males from all twelve tribes? What are the first fruits and the tithes?
2. **1:9.** What does the Semitic name Anna mean? What is endogamy? What was generally expected that Israelites were not to do among Gentiles? What was the accepted norm, and how did the Mosaic inheritance law go beyond it? In the lands of exile, what purpose did marrying within one's kinship group serve?
3. **Word Study: Acts of Charity (1:16).** What does the Greek word *eleēmosynē* mean? Of what is the term almost a one-word summary? Though it twice refers to the Lord's "mercy" toward humanity, to what does it most often refer? How is it a form of religious service tailored to life in exile? How does use of the word *eleēmosynē* in the Book of Sirach cohere with this theological outlook?
4. **1:17.** Although burial of the dead is not mandated in the Torah (except in Deut 21:22–23), why did Israelites practice it? What was being left unburied considered to be? In Catholic tradition, what kind of work is burying the dead regarded to be? What does St. Cyprian of Carthage have to say about such works?

For application

1. **1:3.** For whom does Tobit perform many acts of charity? According to Gal 6:10, to whom should Christians be especially careful to do good? Why especially to them?
2. **1:6.** Have you ever made a pilgrimage of any sort, whether locally or to another country? What prompted you to make the pilgrimage? What spiritual benefits did you derive from it?
3. **1:7–8.** How much of Tobit's income did he give away? What percentage of your income do you give away?
4. **1:9.** Why does the Catholic Church strongly recommend that Catholics marry within the Catholic faith? According to CCC 1633–37, what is required if a Catholic wishes to marry a baptized Christian from another tradition or someone who is not baptized ("disparity of cult")? Why do you think these requirements are necessary?

Chapter 2

For understanding

1. **2:1.** For what feast is *Pentecost* the Greek name, and as what is it known in Hebrew? When was it celebrated? By what may Tobit's desire to share his meal with a poor kinsman be inspired?
2. **2:5.** What is uncertain about Tobit's action of washing himself? Which motive is more probable? In the Torah, how long did the period of uncleanness from contact with the dead last, and what was one required to undergo? Why could Tobit not follow the letter of the Mosaic Law? What does he thus appear to be doing?
3. **2:6.** What does the quotation from Amos 8:10 pronounce on the Northern Kingdom of Israel, and why? How does Tobit see its fulfillment? Why does the passage probably come to mind? Despite his own fidelity, what does Tobit accept?
4. **2:14.** How is Anna greeted by Tobit? What does she seem to question? At this point in the story, what appears to have happened to his generosity? What does the spousal tension evident in Anna's retort recall about Job and his wife's reproach, and what is the difference between them and Tobit and Anna?

For application

1. **2:2.** Jesus recommends inviting the poor, maimed, lame, and blind to dinner rather than relatives or rich neighbors (Lk 14:12–14). How literally do you think he means that? Have you ever opened your home to other Christians or to those less fortunate than yourself?
2. **2:7–8.** What are the spiritual and corporal works of mercy (CCC 2447)? Which of these works have you had occasion to perform? Which is the hardest for you? Although civil laws regulate funerals and burials, how might the work of burying the dead still be something you could perform?
3. **2:7.** When would you consider an individual's religious devotion to be scrupulously excessive? What do you think Jesus' standard of judgment would be? How might a church community become divided by differing devotional practices?
4. **2:13–14.** How closely does the disagreement between Tobit and Anna match your own experience of home life? How are admissions of fault and the giving and receiving of forgiveness practiced in your home? What effects do these behaviors have on family relationships?

Chapter 3

For understanding

1. **3:4.** Of what is Tobit's prayer an acknowledgment? Though Tobit is a saintly man, how does he show himself not to be a sinless one? Consequently, what does he recognize about himself?
2. **3:6.** If Tobit is not the first righteous man to wish for death in Scripture, who else desired it? What is "the eternal abode"? Before the revelation of eternal life in Scripture, what was Sheol thought to be?
3. **3:8.** Who are the seven husbands of Sarah? What is Asmodeus? From what two languages is the name derived, and what is their meaning? Where else is Asmodeus mentioned?
4. **3:17.** What does the name Raphael in Hebrew mean? What does it announce here? What is Raphael's role in heaven, and where in the Old Testament is he mentioned by name? In Jewish tradition, what does Raphael do? In Christian tradition, who is often honored along with Raphael? According to St. Bede, what does Raphael's mission to Tobit and Sarah signify?

Study Questions: Tobit

For application

1. **3:4–5.** How do you feel about the moral deterioration of society? Do you pray about it? Do you, like Tobit, include yourself among the morally or spiritually disobedient? What is the spiritual value of doing so?
2. **3:7–9.** Have you ever been falsely accused over a situation beyond your control? How serious were the accusations? What did you do about them? Given what Jesus says about dealing with anger and revenge (e.g., Mt 5:21–24, 38–48), how might such accusations be handled?
3. **3:10.** The *Catechism* calls suicide a grave offense against love of self, of neighbor, and of God (CCC 2281–82). How does it violate each of these three relationships? Why should Christians pray for the soul of one who has killed himself?
4. **3:11.** In the midst of near despair, why does Sarah begin with a prayer of praise? How might imitating her approach to prayer help you when you pray about difficulties?

Chapter 4

For understanding

1. **4:1–21.** Of what is the farewell discourse following Tobit's prayer for death a synopsis? Why is it no coincidence that Tobit's instruction is largely concerned with the proper use of material wealth? What must the young Tobias understand? What is ironic about Tobit's vision? According to St. Augustine, what eyes was Tobit using?
2. **4:11.** What value is accorded to giving alms to the poor, and what is its effect?
3. **4:13.** To what is pride often the prelude? How can the word translated "shiftlessness" also be translated? What is the lesson here?
4. **4:17.** What does the literal translation "pour out your bread" suggest about the original text of Tobit? What parallel have scholars noticed? What is the purpose of the rite of placing bread on gravesites? What is a possible alternative that Tobit may be recommending?

For application

1. **4:6.** Does your experience match Tobit's words in this verse? Although Tobit is thinking of material prosperity, what other kinds of prosperity might result from obeying his injunction?
2. **4:7–11.** What is the difference between philanthropy and almsgiving? Why do you think Tobit regards almsgiving as protective? How do you practice almsgiving, and what limits if any do you place on it?
3. **4:12.** Read the note for this verse. How does Tobit's caution regarding immorality stand in opposition to today's prevailing culture? What personal and social benefits can result from steering clear of sexual immorality?
4. **4:16.** What would you consider to be your surplus income, and how would you calculate it? How much of it does Tobit think you should give away? What do you think of his advice?

Chapter 5

For understanding

1. **5:1–22.** What arrangements are made? Unbeknownst to father and son, who is the traveler hired to accompany Tobias? Why is the story entertaining?
2. **5:12.** What does the name Azarias mean in Hebrew, and what aim does it reveal? What is the cover story of posing as a near kinsman designed to gain? What does the name Ananias mean in Hebrew, and to what does it allude? How is the relative in question like Tobit?
3. **5:21.** What does Tobit accept on faith that the reader has already learned as a fact? What do Tobit's words echo? According to St. Bede, what do the two persons, the angel and the man, prefigure?

For application

1. **5:1–3.** If you were to be entrusted with an important family or business project that you had no idea how to accomplish, how would you decide what to do? What part would prayer play in your decision making?
2. **5:9–11.** How would you verify the honesty and reliability of someone you had just met? What sorts of questions would you ask? In an age of distrust like ours, what difference would it make if the person claimed to be a relative of yours?
3. **5:12.** Read the note for this verse. What is the importance of a person's name? What does your name mean, and why did your parents select that name for you? If you wanted to change your name, what would you select, and why?
4. **5:16.** Tobias' dog appears only here and in 11:4. Since ancient Israelites were generally contemptuous of dogs, what use might a dog have had in the home of an exiled Jewish family? What is the point of adding this detail to the Tobit story? To what uses do modern families put dogs?

Chapter 6

For understanding

1. **6:1.** Where does the Tigris River flow? Of what geographical error do some insist that the author is guilty? Why is the allegation lacking force? What is perfectly plausible about their travel route?
2. **6:4.** For what rite are the fish's heart and liver to be used? What does the procedure involve, and what is its effect? For what was gall considered a medicinal remedy?
3. **6:10.** What does the name Raguel mean in Aramaic? What inheritance provision did Moses make for a daughter? While Sarah is Raguel's legal heir, what solution must be found for her? What other purpose of his mission does the angel reveal?
4. **6:16–17.** In the Vulgate's longer ending for chap. 6, what does Raphael enjoin the newlyweds to do? What is the lesson?

For application
1. **6:7.** In addition to prayer, what physical objects (sacramentals) might be used in delivering someone from demonic harassment? Since a demon is a spirit, what is it about such physical objects that would cause the demon to depart?
2. **6:10–12.** What are some of the advantages and disadvantages of arranging a marriage with someone you have never met? On what basis are marriages contracted in our culture? What are some of the advantages and disadvantages of this approach?
3. **6:13.** Read the note for this verse. Are there any stories of misfortune that have passed around your family? If so, how have they affected family relationships? At what point does intrafamily gossip become sinful?
4. **6:17.** Raphael reassures Tobias that Sarah was chosen from the beginning to be his wife and that he will save her from the demon. What part do you think destiny plays in the selection of one's marriage partner? How might destiny and free will interact here?

Chapter 7

For understanding
1. **7:1–18.** What does Tobias propose and arrange? How does the importance of kinship relations that underlies much of the book move into the foreground in this chapter?
2. **7:10.** What is Raguel's request that Tobias eat, drink, and be merry an attempt to do? What allusion to Isaiah do some detect? If Raguel meant to evoke this passage, what would it suggest?
3. **Word Study: Brother, Sister (7:12).** To what does modern Western culture tend to restrict these terms? How does Semitic culture apply them? How can this be seen in the Book of Tobit? How is the masculine *adelphos* used, and what does it embrace? What else can it also designate? How is the feminine *adelphē* applied? What can a "sister" be?
4. **7:14.** What is the marriage contract? How might the document here be considered a certificate of betrothal rather than of marriage?

For application
1. **7:9.** Read the note for this verse. In what ways might hospitality be described as a virtue? According to the *Catechism* (CCC 1971), from which of the theological virtues does it flow? Which of them animates it? How would you characterize your practice of hospitality within the Christian community?
2. **7:12.** What is the difference between treating one's spouse as an intimate friend and treating him or her as a brother or sister? Under normal circumstances, how might siblings of the opposite sex treat each other? How might such a relationship strengthen the "one flesh" bond between husband and wife?
3. **7:14.** In a Christian environment, what is the purpose of the period of engagement? What should be taking place between prospective spouses during that period? Why is sexual intimacy during engagement a grave offense against the dignity of marriage (CCC 2391)?

Chapter 8

For understanding
1. **8:3.** What is the name of the demon? Why would the demon flee to the lifeless expanse of desert beyond the fertile Nile Valley? What does it mean to bind a demon? In Jewish tradition, what power is Raphael known to exercise?
2. **8:5–6.** What type of prayer is the traditional form called a *berakhah*? What is the signature feature of such prayer?
3. **8:6.** What does the first marriage, as presented in Genesis, reveal? What is stressed here? How may Tobias be viewed as a more faithful Adam? What is *monogenism*, and what is the result of having a common origin? When Pope Pius XII affirmed the biblical doctrine of monogenism in 1950, what theory of human origins did he deny?

For application
1. **8:2–3.** Whether you are married or not, why might you consider a prayer of consecration over your bedroom? How would it contribute to the virtue of chastity for yourself and in spousal relationships?
2. **8:7.** How might Jesus' warning in Mt 5:28 against lustful looks apply to the sexual relationship of husband and wife? On the other hand, how does sexual intimacy within marriage contribute to the holiness of the partners?
3. **8:9–12.** According to the note for v. 9, Raguel is taking precautions by digging a grave. As a reader, how do you react to what he is doing? What is the point of comic relief in a story like this?
4. **8:16.** Has God ever dealt with you more mercifully than you expected? How have you thanked him for the mercy he has shown you?

Chapter 9

For understanding
1. **9:5.** What is the receipt that Tobias gives Gabael? Why is it important that the seals on the money bags are intact?
2. **9:6.** Given the distance between Ecbatana and Rages, how long would a journey there and back again take? Why does this create a chronological problem in Tobit? Since no indication is given that the journey involved a miracle, what is it reasonable to suppose?

For application
1. **9:2–4.** Since Tobias cannot leave Raguel's home to retrieve Tobit's fortune from Gabael, what does it say about Tobias' relationship to Azarias/Raphael that he commissions someone he has only recently met to retrieve it? Whom would you trust with such an assignment?

Chapter 10

For understanding

1. **10:1–12.** Where is anxiety mounting in these verses, and about what?
2. **10:10–12.** How does Raguel send off Tobias and Sarah? What other sendoff does the account resemble?
3. **10:12.** In this context, to whom does the word "brother" refer? For what is Edna's farewell speech a plea? How are her words especially poignant?

For application

1. **10:1–6.** What sorts of things cause you to worry? What do you do to calm your fears and concerns? How might you apply to yourself Jesus' and St. Paul's injunctions not to be anxious (Mt 6:25–34; Phil 4:6)?
2. **10:12a.** If you are married, what is your relationship with your in-laws? Despite any tensions that may exist between you and them, how do you show honor to them?
3. **10:12b.** Read the note for this verse, particularly about Edna's concern for her daughter's treatment. According to St. Paul's exhortation in Eph 5:21–32, how is the husband to treat his wife? What real-life models of that kind of treatment can you recall or have you met? If you have adult children, what have you taught them about how to treat their spouses?

Chapter 11

For understanding

1. **11:8.** How long has Tobit been living in darkness? What does Tobit's personal experience of being healed of blindness anticipate? What did Isaiah prophesy about Zebulun and Naphtali? From which tribe is Tobit?
2. **11:10.** Why is the courtyard a significant detail in the story?
3. **11:14.** What does the instantaneous effect of the application of gall suggest? What does the idiom "the light of my eyes" mean? Why does the expression have a deeper meaning for Tobit? What does Tobit offer to the Lord?
4. **11:15.** Of whom is the word pair "afflicted ... mercy" used in chap. 13? What does the storyteller thus imply? Specifically, of what does the suffering and healing experienced by Tobit stand as a sign? To what passage are Tobit's words an allusion?

For application

1. **11:6.** Notice the words "your son" that Anna uses in this verse. Why does she not say "our son"? Given the tension between Tobit and herself in 10:4–7 and elsewhere, what do you think her attitude is toward her husband at this point? When couples quarrel, how might the language they use place emotional distance between each other?
2. **11:14–17.** Think of a significant favor that you believe God has done for you or your family. How did you give thanks for it? Did you keep your gratitude to yourself or tell others about the favor? Why make it known to others?
3. **11:18.** Given your ethnic background, how long should a wedding celebration ideally last? Why hold a celebration, regardless of whether it be long or short? Why is eternal life in heaven often compared to a wedding celebration?

Chapter 12

For understanding

1. **12:1–5.** What counsel does Tobit follow? How do he and his son show themselves generous beyond the strict requirements of justice?
2. **12:8.** What are the pillars of Jewish piety in the final centuries of the OT period? When did Jesus endorse this triad of religious practices, and what warning did he, like Raphael, add? According to St. Leo the Great, how are these three things supremely related to religious observance?
3. **12:12.** For what is the Greek word *mnēmosynon* used? What value is prayer thus accorded? Who bring the prayers of the saints before God?
4. **12:15.** Where in the Bible are the seven holy angels mentioned, and where is the tradition assumed? According to St. John of Damascus, what are the angels prompt in doing; where do they appear; and what are their functions?

For application

1. **12:1–5.** What constitutes a just, fair, or appropriate wage? How might an employer determine a just wage for an employee? According to the *Catechism* (CCC 2434), why is agreement between employer and employee not enough to justify morally the amount received in a wage?
2. **12:6–10.** What does the expression "preaching to the choir" mean? Why, at this point in the story, does Raphael speak about thanksgiving and almsgiving to characters who have a reputation for practicing it? To whom might his exhortation really be addressed?
3. **12:12.** Read the note for this verse. How does prayer operate as a *reminder* before God? Since God knows everything and forgets nothing, what does a reminder accomplish, and for whom?
4. **12:15.** According to the *Catechism* (CCC 329–36), what is the role of angels? For Christians, what is the appropriate attitude toward them? Why are some angels given the title of Saint, even though they are not human?

Chapter 13

For understanding

1. **13:1–18.** What is the twofold focus of Tobit's hymn of praise and thanksgiving? Throughout the hymn, for what is the Lord praised? To what two books of Scripture does the hymn allude?
2. **13:9.** What does Tobit, prophesying in the seventh century B.C., foresee? For what do some take this as evidence, and what response can one make to this conclusion?
3. **13:11.** What vision of messianic times does Tobit see? What gifts will the non-Jewish peoples bring to Jerusalem?

4.   **13:16–18.** What activity points to a glorified Jerusalem, and what does it outshine? In the Book of Revelation, what city shines in this way?

For application
1.   **13:5.** When you suffer affliction in this life for wrongs done, what is the proper attitude to take as a Christian? By contrast, when you suffer affliction for doing right, what attitude should you adopt (cf. 1 Pet 4:12–19)?
2.   **13:10.** Tobit writes to exiles, encouraging them to give thanks and praise to the Lord. When you are undergoing suffering of any sort, what benefit comes to you for giving God thanks and praise? How does a thankful attitude alleviate suffering?
3.   **13:14.** What blessing comes to you from rejoicing over another's good fortune or from grieving over another's sufferings? How does this contribute to the building up of the Body of Christ (as in 1 Cor 12:25–27)?

Chapter 14

For understanding
1.   **14:3–11.** Like other testaments in the Bible and related Jewish literature, with what is the elderly Tobit's speech on his deathbed filled? In particular, like Moses, what does the elderly Tobit foresee?
2.   **14:4.** Where is Media? Although Jonah is the name that appears in the short text of Tobit, in the long text, as whom is this prophet identified, and why is it more likely the correct reading? When was Nineveh overthrown, and by whom? Who are the brethren to whom Tobit refers? In which book of Scripture is the description of Canaan as "the good land" often used?
3.   **14:6–7.** What does Tobit urge his son to do? To what do these two ways of speaking refer in the Book of Deuteronomy?
4.   **14:10.** Who is Nadab? In the *Story of Ahikar*, what did Nadab do to Ahikar, and how were the tables turned in the end? Why was Ahikar saved?

For application
1.   **14:6–7.** Read the note for these verses. What does "fear of the Lord" mean to you? In what ways is this a virtue, and how does it fulfill the New Covenant?
2.   **14:10.** What concern or involvement have you had in your parents' burial plans or in the execution of those plans? What planning have you done for your own? How can planning your own funeral in advance become an act of charity to the rest of the family?
3.   **14:13.** What is the purpose of a funeral? How does the deceased benefit from it? How do those who attend a funeral benefit from it? In the Christian dispensation, what expressions of hope should be evident at a funeral?

INTRODUCTION TO JUDITH

Author and Date Little is known with certainty about the origin of the Book of Judith. The story was written anonymously, and scholars can sketch only a basic profile of the author by making inferences from its contents. Scholars attribute the book to a Jew who was deeply devoted to the nation and faith of Israel. The blend of piety and patriotism that runs through the book suggests to some that its author shared the outlook of early Pharisaism. Others find this judgment to be overly specific, arguing that concern for Israel's national security and fidelity to the covenant was not confined to a single sectarian group in postexilic Judaism. Familiarity with the geography of central Palestine further suggests that its author lived in the land of Israel.

Establishing a date of composition for the Book of Judith involves a similar degree of educated guesswork. The main story is set in the Persian period, not long after the exiles of Judah returned from captivity in Babylon (beginning in 538 B.C.) and rebuilt the Temple in Jerusalem (ca. 520–515 B.C.). These are events of recent memory according to 4:3 and 5:19. Reinforcing this historical setting are references to Persian customs (preparing earth and water, 2:7) as well as the appearance of Persian loanwords ("turbans", 4:15; "governors", 5:2; "sword", 13:6; etc.) and Persian names ("Holofernes", 2:4; "Bagoas", 12:11). However, the book mentions distinctively Greek customs as well, such as celebrating with garlands (3:7) and reclining at table (12:15), leading most scholars to conclude that the book comes from the Hellenistic period between 331 and 63 B.C. Narrowing down a more specific date depends on issues of interpretation. Some interpret the book as an allegorical retelling of the Maccabean revolt against the Seleucid regime that outlawed the practice of Judaism in the 160s B.C. Others, noting the friendly relations between Judith's hometown of Bethulia, located on the outskirts of Samaritan territory, and the religious authorities in Jerusalem, prefer a date after 107 B.C., when John Hyrcanus I, the Hasmonean high priest, incorporated Samaria into the expanding Judean state.

The coexistence of Persian and Hellenistic features in the same book may be accounted for by tracing the original story of Judith to the fifth or fourth century B.C., while acknowledging that the canonical Book of Judith we possess today may have been written or last edited in the second century B.C. A degree of speculation is unavoidable at this point. Perhaps the story of Judith circulated as oral or written tradition in Israel well before the Maccabean uprising, but it assumed a heightened importance in the midst of this national crisis, when the covenant people faced grave dangers of foreign intrusion and religious oppression. Since the Judith story exemplifies a valiant response to these types of threats, one might conclude that the book reached its canonical form about this time, regardless of when the story may have originated.

Title The book is named after Judith, a widow of the tribe of Simeon, who emerges as the brave and beautiful heroine of chapters 8–16. This is the case in the Greek Septuagint, which gives the heading *Ioudith*, and in the Latin Vulgate, which titles the work *Liber Iudith*. The name Judith represents the Hebrew *Yehudith*, meaning "Jewish woman" or "Jewess".

Place in the Canon Judith is revered as an inspired book of the Old Testament by Catholics and Eastern Orthodox but is not accepted as biblical in the Jewish and Protestant traditions. Debate over its canonicity stretches back into ancient times. It is possible that Jews living in the Diaspora considered it scriptural, since the book appears in surviving collections of the Greek Septuagint. Judith was not included in the Jewish canon of the Bible, however. Judith was also considered non-canonical by a few of the Church Fathers, such as St. Athanasius of Alexandria and St. Cyril of Jerusalem, while St. Jerome seems to have accepted and rejected its canonicity at different times in his life. That said, most early Christian writers cited the Book of Judith as inspired Scripture, including St. Clement of Rome, St. Clement of Alexandria, St. Ambrose of Milan, St. Basil of Caesarea, St. John Chrysostom, and St. Augustine. It was also judged canonical by early Church synods held in Rome (A.D. 382), Hippo (A.D. 393), and Carthage (A.D. 397).

Structure The Book of Judith is a literary work of art. The story is arranged in symmetrical fashion so that its two halves parallel each other, sometimes by sharing common themes and sometimes by setting up sharp contrasts. In addition, each half of the book shares a similar internal structure outlined according to a mirroring technique called *chiasmus* (the pattern A, B, C, B′, A′). The two major panels of the story may be summarized as follows. **(1)** Chapters 1–7 highlight *the fear of the nations* as the Assyrian army marches west on a campaign to punish states who refuse to support Nebuchadnezzar in his fight against Media. Powerful men stand at the center of the action, while Nebuchadnezzar is hailed as a god and lord over the world. **(2)** Chapters 8–16 highlight *the fearlessness of Judith* in taking a stand against the Assyrian superpower. It is now a pious woman who stands at the center of the drama, and through her courageous action, the God of Israel is revealed as the true Lord of the world before whom no earthly enemy can stand.

Literary Background The oldest form of the Book of Judith that survives today is written in Greek, although scholars have long suspected it was originally composed in Hebrew. But, unlike the Book of Tobit, of which Hebrew and Aramaic copies were discovered among the Dead Sea Scrolls, scholars have yet to uncover a Semitic version of Judith that predates the Greek Septuagint. Moreover, there are differences among the extant Greek editions, making it difficult to determine the precise length and wording of the original book. Saint Jerome's translation of Judith for the Latin Vulgate differs in several ways from modern translations of the book, presumably because he paraphrased an Aramaic copy of Judith that no longer survives. English translations based on the Latin Vulgate (Douay-Rheims) therefore exhibit differences from those based on the Greek texts of the Septuagint (RSVCE, NABRE, JB, NJB).

Literary Genre One of the most challenging issues surrounding the Book of Judith is the question of its literary genre. For centuries Christians read Judith as a book of history that speaks about real people and real events of the past. Modern times, however, have seen a dramatic swing of the pendulum, with most scholars now holding that Judith is either a work of historical fiction, written to inspire Jewish resistance to the pressures of Gentile rule, or an allegory of a well-known historical incident using coded language. The question, then, is whether the Book of Judith is intended to be (1) a historical account, (2) a fictional account situated in a historical setting, or (3) an allegorical account that retells a significant event of history in a symbolic way.

(1) *Judith as History*. In the eyes of some interpreters, the author of Judith gives the distinct impression of writing about events of the past. Features typical of other historical books in the Bible are also present in Judith. The heroine is given a lengthy genealogy and tribal affiliation (8:1). Chronological notations specifying regnal years (1:1), calendar dates (2:1), and agricultural seasons (2:27; 8:2) are interspersed throughout. The author makes reference to real places of the biblical world (Nineveh, Ecbatana, Damascus, Jerusalem), real peoples of the biblical world (Assyrians, Ammonites, Midianites), real events of the biblical world (Judah's exile and return from Babylon), and real names used in the biblical world (Nebuchadnezzar, Holofernes, Bagoas, Uzziah). Furthermore, the story takes place during the high priesthood of a certain Joakim (4:6), which is elsewhere the name borne by the second high priest of the postexilic period (Neh 12:10). It was his father, the high priest Jeshua, who reinstituted sacrificial services in Jerusalem after the return of the exiles from Babylon (Ezra 3:2) and who led the effort to rebuild the Temple (Ezra 4:3). These features could be taken to support the essential historicity of the book. For other considerations, see note on 1:1.

(2) *Judith as Historical Fiction*. Many scholars today classify Judith as a work of fiction that was given a broadly historical setting. On this reading, the author made use of historical elements and figures in order to underscore the story's relevance to Jewish life in the postexilic period. At the same time, it seems to display blatant historical inaccuracies as well as confusion regarding details of eastern Mediterranean geography. For instance, the first verse identifies Nebuchadnezzar as king of Assyria rather than Babylonia; it identifies his capital city as Nineveh, which was conquered and destroyed in 612 B.C., several years before Nebuchadnezzar came to the throne; and it speaks of his military campaign against Arphaxad, although no king of Media bearing this name is known to history. Furthermore, Nebuchadnezzar of Babylon reigned from 605 to 562 B.C., yet the story of Judith takes place after the return of the Jewish exiles from Babylon and the rebuilding of the Temple, which was completed about 515 B.C. As for the book's geographical difficulties, the itinerary of conquest delineated in 2:21–27 seems illogical, beginning with the remarkable claim that Nebuchadnezzar's troops advanced three hundred miles on foot from Nineveh to Upper Cilicia in a mere three days. Many who read the Book of Judith as a historical novella interpret such glaring oddities as the author's way of signaling his intent to write historical fiction rather than history.

(3) *Judith as Allegory*. Other scholars interpret the Book of Judith as an allegorical representation of an actual historical crisis. For instance, Nebuchadnezzar has been taken as a pseudonym for King Artaxerxes III Ochus of Persia, who reigned from 358 to 338 B.C. Not only did this king conduct military campaigns in the west, as Nebuchadnezzar is said to have done, but he had a general named Holofernes (as in 2:4) and a courtier named Bagoas (as in 12:11). More popular is the view that Judith offers a coded or cryptic retelling of the Maccabean revolt against the Seleucid assault on Palestinian Judaism. According to this interpretation, Nebuchadnezzar represents Antiochus IV Epiphanes, the Seleucid ruler who proclaimed himself a god and threatened the people of Israel with annihilation in the second century B.C. Judith corresponds to the Jewish resistance fighters who refused to compromise their loyalty to God in the face of this onslaught, and the general Holofernes stands for the Seleucid prince Nicanor, whose demise in 1 Mac 7:39–50 exhibits parallels with the events surrounding Holofernes' death in chapters 13–14. Read in this way, the Book of Judith is not historical in the usual sense of the term; nevertheless, it deals with actual historical events under the guise of a fictional crisis and cast of characters set in a different period of history.

Deciding among these options is a delicate task. None of the approaches outlined above is without difficulties, and the Catholic Church has never made an official ruling on the book's literary form. Reading Judith as history falls in line with centuries of Christian interpretation and establishes a historical basis for patristic and medieval typology, which often viewed Judith as an OT type of the Church as well as of the Blessed Virgin Mary. At the same time, the book's historical and geographical inconsistencies have yet to be resolved. Reading Judith as historical fiction offers an explanation for these inconsistencies and likewise accounts for Christian interpretive tradition by viewing the heroine of the story as a literary type of Mary and the Church. For that matter, the use of a nonhistorical genre does not rule out the possibility that Judith was a historical person. However, this approach must confront the problem of why the author was inconsistent in the use of historical and geographical data, sometimes constructing his story on sound information and other times introducing obvious anachronisms. One would have to suppose the author wished to make his narrative historically plausible without feeling compelled to ensure factual accuracy throughout. Reading the book as an allegory of another historical event likewise has the appeal of eliminating its tensions with documented history, but this approach leaves the great majority of the story's details unaccounted for. The narrative can be shown to have parallels with other historical crises of the biblical period, but only in broad outline, and even then the points of correspondence are only partial and imperfect. Moreover, the allegorical reading requires the story to operate on two levels—as an edifying tale set in a roughly historical context, with multiple details intended for that purpose only, and as a cryptic retelling of a historical incident by means of a fictional narrative. In the final analysis, the literary genre of the Book of Judith remains a debated question.

Themes and Characteristics Regardless of the book's genre and relationship to history, interpreters generally agree that the Book of Judith is a story well told. Its genius lies in many things. For one, the author took obvious delight in the use of irony, offering readers insight into the meaning of sayings and situations that passed undetected by individuals in the story. For another, the author added depth and dimension to his portrait of Judith by drawing extensively on the Old Testament. Rather than cutting and pasting quotations from earlier biblical books into his narrative, his preference was to evoke the Scriptures of Israel in more subtle ways. Indeed,

the whole account of Judith's bravery is presented in a way that invites comparison with some of the greatest figures and feats of biblical history. Furthermore, one could say that the author of the book had a flair for the dramatic. He was skilled at creating tension and suspense as well as portraying the main characters with believable realism.

The theological message of the Book of Judith centers on a clash between the beliefs of Israel and the rival claims of the Gentile world. On one side stands Nebuchadnezzar, the warrior-king whose army marches invincibly over much of the Near East, giving a measure of credence to his self-description as "the Great King, the lord of the whole earth" (2:5). Nebuchadnezzar boasts that nothing can prevent his "hand" from accomplishing all that he intends, including his oath to exact revenge from all nations who refuse his lordship (2:12). To demonstrate this power, he authorizes his general Holofernes to abolish the religious practices of rebel nations by destroying their temples and imposing a "ruler cult" in which Nebuchadnezzar alone is worshiped as god (3:8). Opposing him in this contest is the God of Israel, who is truly "invincible" (16:13). The people of Israel are right to acknowledge no god except the Lord of hosts, for he alone wields the power to protect or destroy the chosen people according to his purposes (8:15). To demonstrate this truth, God gives strength to a widow named Judith to deliver his people from annihilation, to defend his sanctuary in Jerusalem from desecration, and to decapitate the enemy threat "by the hand of a woman" (13:15). In the end, this theological contest is decisively won by the Lord. To him belongs worship and praise (16:1–17) for destroying (13:14) and humiliating the adversaries of the covenant people (13:17). To Nebuchadnezzar belongs only a legacy of disgrace (14:18).

In addition to its validation of Israel's belief in God, the book has a spiritual message that is arrestingly simple: courageous faith can accomplish great things for God. Judith is a living embodiment of this lesson. Because of her unwavering trust in the Lord, she turned away a massive fighting force with two strokes of a sword (13:6–8) and became "the great glory of Israel" (15:9). On the one hand, she is endowed with all the natural qualities of a woman destined for greatness, for she is described as uncommonly beautiful (8:7), wealthy (8:7), wise (8:29), and respected in her community (8:8). Yet these are mere accessories to the real character of Judith. More important, she appears as a deeply spiritual woman who "feared God with great devotion" (8:8). Judith was committed to a life of chaste widowhood (16:22) and careful observance of Jewish purity and dietary norms (10:5; 12:1–2). Beyond this, she embraced a life of asceticism: fasting frequently, wearing penitential garments, and living detached from the comforts of her home (8:5–6). None of this is mere ritualism, for the depths of

Judith's convictions are revealed through the many prayers and speeches that punctuate the storyline (see 8:11–27; 9:2–14; 13:4–5, 15–16; 16:2–17). From these texts, it is clear that Judith's most outstanding virtue is faith. It is her absolute trust in the Lord that sustains the daring adventure that unfolds at the climax of the book. Judith's dangerous game of deception with Holofernes (11:5–23), which ends with his beheading (13:1–10), is undertaken in the belief that the Lord opposes the proud but shows mercy to those who fear him (16:15; cf. Lk 1:51–52). Judith's confidence rests secure in a God who defends the weak and lowly (9:11). Having acted on this conviction, she was hailed with the grandest of all compliments: "O daughter, you are blessed by the Most High God above all women on earth" (13:18).

Finally, Judith overturns the stereotype of a devout widow from biblical times. In ancient Semitic culture, women played a behind-the-scenes role that was crucial to family life but was more or less removed from the stage of public life. Judith, however, steps confidently into the spotlight to provide steady leadership for her people during a time of national emergency. Indeed, the author highlights Judith's bravery and bold initiative over against the timidity and weakness of various male figures in the story, such as the cowardly leaders of Bethulia and the licentious Holofernes. The lesson is partly that women are no less capable than men of becoming instruments of salvation and partly that God can choose the least powerful of the world to show himself mighty beyond measure. Being a woman, Judith would not have been asked to take up arms against an invader; and being a widow, she could not rely on a husband to be her defender. Yet she ventures out to face the enemy, while the fighting men of Bethulia remain huddled behind the safety of the city walls.

Christian Perspective Judith is never quoted in the New Testament. Allusions to passages in the book have been detected, however, as when Elizabeth honors Mary with the words, "Blessed are you among women" (Lk 1:42, compare with 13:18) and when Paul contends that the "depths" and "thoughts of God" are beyond the reach of the human mind (1 Cor 2:10–11, compare with 8:14). One might even say that Paul's assertion in 1 Cor 1:27 that God uses "the weak" of the world to shame "the strong" is a compact summary of the lesson illustrated by Judith. Over the centuries, Christian theologians have looked to Judith as a model of heroic chastity and bravery. Beyond that, Judith is seen as an image of Mary, the Mother of God, as well as a type of the Church, which cuts off the head of the devil (St. Jerome, *Letters* 79, 10).

OUTLINE OF JUDITH

1. Assyria Intimidates and Invades the West (chaps. 1–7)
   A. Nebuchadnezzar's Campaign against Media (1:1–16)
   B. Nebuchadnezzar's Campaign against Vassal Nations (2:1—3:9)
   C. Israel Prepares for Invasion (4:1–15)
   D. Holofernes' Council against Israel (5:1—6:21)
   E. Holofernes Lays Siege to Bethulia (7:1–32)

2. Judith Deceives and Defeats Assyria (chaps. 8–16)
   A. Introduction of Judith (8:1–8)
   B. Judith Plans and Prays for Her Mission (8:9—10:10)
   C. Judith in the Assyrian Camp (10:11—12:20)
   D. Judith Assassinates Holofernes (13:1–11)
   E. Judith Returns, and Assyria Is Routed (13:12—15:7)
   F. Celebration and Song of Triumph (15:8—16:17)
   G. The Legacy of Judith (16:18–25)

THE BOOK OF

JUDITH

Arphaxad Fortifies Ecbatana

1 In the twelfth year of the reign of Nebuchadnez'-zar, who ruled over the Assyrians in the great city of Nin'eveh, in the days of Arpha'xad, who ruled over the Medes in Ecbat'ana—²he is the king who built walls about Ecbat'ana with hewn stones three cubits thick and six cubits long; he made the walls seventy cubits high and fifty cubits wide; ³at the gates he built towers a hundred cubits high and sixty cubits wide at the foundations; ⁴and he made its gates, which were seventy cubits high and forty cubits wide, so that his armies could march out in force and his infantry form their ranks—⁵it was in those days that King Nebuchadnez'zar made war against King Arpha'xad in the great plain which is on the borders of Ragae. ⁶He was joined by all the people of the hill country and all those who lived along the Euphrates and the Tigris and the Hydas'pes and in the plain where Ar'ioch ruled the El"ymae'ans. Many nations joined the forces of the Chalde'ans.

Nebuchadnezzar's Orders Disregarded

7 Then Nebuchadnez'zar king of the Assyrians sent to all who lived in Persia and to all who lived in the west, those who lived in Cili'cia and Damascus and Lebanon and An"ti-leb'anon and all who lived along the seacoast, ⁸and those among the nations of Carmel and Gilead, and Upper Galilee and the great

---

1:1 Nebuchadnezzar: Usually identified as Nebuchadnezzar II, who reigned from 605 to 562 B.C. as the mightiest king of the Neo-Babylonian Empire. The identification poses a problem, however, because the story of Judith is set after the rebuilding of the Temple in Jerusalem, a task completed about 515 B.C. Various explanations of this historical discrepancy have been proposed. **(1)** According to some, the storyteller was either confused about the chronology of the sixth century B.C., or he placed an obvious historical inaccuracy at the outset of the story to signal his intention to write fiction and to advance the particular narrative he intended. Regarding the last point, one can surmise that he made his antagonist one of the most infamous historical enemies of Israel, as this would increase the dramatic tension of the narrative. **(2)** According to others, the name Nebuchadnezzar is used as a pseudonym for a king of earlier or later times, such as Ashurbanipal of Assyria (668–627 B.C.), Artaxerxes III Ochus of Persia (358–338 B.C.), or Antiochus IV Epiphanes of Seleucia (175–164 B.C.). **(3)** A small number of others have tried to square the information in Judith with documented history outside the Bible. One theory contends that the king in 1:1 is an Aramean usurper, Arakha, who led the people of Babylon in revolt against Persia in 521 B.C. The *Behistun Inscription* of Darius I, discovered in Iran, relates that Arakha called himself "Nebuchadnezzar, son of Nabonidus" (= Nebuchadnezzar IV). Little is known about this political figure, but the presence of another individual who styled himself Nebuchadnezzar in the late sixth century may allow for a possible historical solution. Efforts to support this possibility have drawn attention to other ancient evidence to explain "Nebuchadnezzar's" link with Assyria, e.g., the Arameans/Syrians were sometimes still called Assyrians in the Persian period (Herodotus, *Histories* 7, 63); at least one ancient writer located the city of Babylon in Assyria, even after the demise of the Assyrian Empire in the seventh century (Herodotus, *Histories* 1, 178); and in popular speech, rulers of post-Assyrian empires such as Babylon and Persia were sometimes called kings of Assyria (2 Chron

33:11; Ezra 6:22). **Nineveh:** Capital of the Assyrian Empire located on the east bank of the Tigris River. It was destroyed in 612 B.C. and left in ruins thereafter. Given the setting of the Book of Judith after 515 B.C., it is possible the author is attaching the infamous reputation of Nineveh as a wicked metropolis to another capital city (possibly Babylon). **Arphaxad:** No king of this name is known to have ruled over Media, the region south of the Caspian Sea. However, it may be a Median throne name rather than a personal name, i.e., a royal title assumed by the king at his coronation. **Ecbatana:** The capital of Media, about 300 miles northeast of Babylon (Ezra 6:2; Tob 3:7). Its ancient ruins lie beneath the city of Hamadan in modern Iran.

1:2 built walls: History knows of fortifications built at Ecbatana at a much earlier time but not of this enhancement to the city's defenses (Herodotus, *Histories* 1, 98). The purpose of the detailed description in 1:2–4 is to make Nebuchadnezzar's army appear unstoppable. If the mighty fortress of Ecbatana could not withstand the king's forces, the small town of Bethulia where Judith lives can expect certain destruction—apart from a miracle of God. **cubits:** A single cubit measured about 18 inches, the average length of a man's arm from elbow to fingertips.

1:5 Ragae: The town of Rai, a few miles southeast of modern Tehran, the capital of Iran. It was also known as Rages (Tob 1:14).

1:6 the hill country: The Zagros Mountains, stretching across Iran, Iraq, and southeastern Turkey. **Hydaspes:** Identification uncertain. The name of the river appears differently in Greek, Syriac, and Latin versions of Judith. A river of this name is located in India, but here a river in Mesopotamia is meant. **Arioch:** Otherwise unknown. **Elymaeans:** Peoples of the Persian district of Elyma. **Chaldeans:** Literally "sons of Cheleoud". Their identity remains uncertain.

1:7 the west: The western half of the Fertile Crescent, formed by Syria, Israel, and Egypt (1:7–10). The inhabitants of these lands are portrayed as vassals of Nebuchadnezzar who are obligated to supply him with auxiliary troops in times of war. The king's eastern vassals did precisely this when they supported his campaign against Media (1:6). **Cilicia:** The region of southeastern Asia Minor (modern Turkey).

1:8 Carmel … Gilead … Galilee: Regions of northern Israel on both sides of the Jordan River. **Esdraelon:** The fertile valley that forms a natural border between Galilee (northern Israel) and Samaria (central Israel). The confrontation between Nebuchadnezzar's army and the town of Bethulia will take place at this location (3:9). Esdraelon is a Greek spelling of the Hebrew name Jezreel.

This is an account of the routing of an army and the freeing of the people of God through a stratagem devised and carried out by a woman (cf. Esther). The story is strongly nationalist in sentiment, especially the victory song in chapter 16. The writer stresses that Judith's strength comes from God in response to her trust in him, and because she faithfully keeps all the prescriptions of the law. The Greek version of the book (the basis of this translation) was made from a Hebrew original, now lost. The Latin version was made from an Aramaic text, almost a paraphrase, which is not now extant and which apparently omitted about a fifth of the book.

Plain of Esdrae'lon, ⁹and all who were in Samar'ia and its surrounding towns, and beyond the Jordan as far as Jerusalem and Beth'any and Chelous and Ka'desh and the river of Egypt, and Tah'panhes and Ra-am'ses and the whole land of Go'shen, ¹⁰even beyond Tanis and Memphis, and all who lived in Egypt as far as the borders of Ethiopia. ¹¹But all who lived in the whole region disregarded the orders of Nebuchadnez'zar king of the Assyrians, and refused to join him in the war; for they were not afraid of him, but looked upon him as only one man,ᵃ and they sent back his messengers empty-handed and shamefaced.

Arphaxad Is Defeated

12 Then Nebuchadnez'zar was very angry with this whole region, and swore by his throne and kingdom that he would surely take revenge on the whole territory of Cili'cia and Damascus and Syria, that he would kill by the sword all the inhabitants of the land of Moab, and the people of Ammon, and all Jude'a, and every one in Egypt, as far as the coasts of the two seas. ¹³In the seventeenth year he led his forces against King Arpha'xad, and defeated him in battle, and overthrew the whole army of Arphaxad, and all his cavalry and all his chariots. ¹⁴Thus he took possession of his cities, and came to Ecbat'ana, captured its towers, plundered its markets, and turned its beauty into shame. ¹⁵He captured Arpha'xad in the mountains of Ragae and struck him down with hunting spears;

and he utterly destroyed him, to this day. ¹⁶Then he returned with them to Nin'eveh, he and all his combined forces, a vast body of troops; and there he and his forces rested and feasted for one hundred and twenty days.

Revenge against the West

2 In the eighteenth year, on the twenty-second day of the first month, there was talk in the palace of Nebuchadnez'zar king of the Assyrians about carrying out his revenge on the whole region, just as he said. ²He called together all his officers and all his nobles and set forth to them his secret plan and recounted fully, with his own lips, all the wickedness of the region;ᵇ ³and it was decided that every one who had not obeyed his command should be destroyed. ⁴When he had finished setting forth his plan, Nebuchadnez'zar king of the Assyrians called Hol"ofer'nes, the chief general of his army, second only to himself, and said to him,

5 "Thus says the Great King, the lord of the whole earth: When you leave my presence, take with you men confident in their strength, to the number of one hundred and twenty thousand foot soldiers and twelve thousand cavalry. ⁶Go and attack the whole west country, because they disobeyed my orders. ⁷Tell them to prepare earth and water, for I am coming against them in my anger, and will cover the whole face of the earth with the feet of my armies, and will hand them over to be plundered by my troops,ᶜ ⁸till their wounded shall fill their valleys,

---

1:9 Samaria: The central hill country of Israel. **Jerusalem ... Chelous:** Locations in southern Israel or Judea. **Kadesh:** Kadesh-barnea, directly south of Israel on the Sinai Peninsula. **the river of Egypt:** The seasonal stream that juts across the northern Sinai Peninsula (modern Wadi el-Arish). It is also called "the Brook of Egypt" and marks the southwestern border of the Promised Land (Num 34:5). **Tahpanhes ... Raamses ... Goshen:** All three are locations in northern Egypt. See notes on Gen 45:10 and Ex 1:11.
1:10 the borders of Ethiopia: The southernmost lands of Egypt.
1:11 refused to join him: An act of political rebellion that throws Nebuchadnezzar into a fit of rage (1:12). **as only one man:** Or, according to one Greek manuscript: "as a man of equal stature".
1:12 Moab ... Ammon: Nations east of the Dead Sea and the lower Jordan River. Both will assist the Assyrians in the attempt to conquer Israel (5:2; 7:8, 17–18). **two seas:** Meaning obscure. Possible references include (1) the white and blue branches of the Nile, (2) the Mediterranean Sea and the Persian Gulf, and (3) the Red Sea and the Persian Gulf.
1:13 seventeenth year: Suggests that Nebuchadnezzar warred against Arphaxad and the Medes for five years (see 1:1, 5).
1:14 Ecbatana: The city was captured by Cyrus II of Persia about 554 B.C. The event related here is unknown outside the Bible. See note on 1:1.

2:1–28 Nebuchadnezzar's campaign of revenge against western nations who snubbed his call for military aid against Media (1:7–11). These peoples will pay an awful price for their insubordination (2:21–27).
2:1 the eighteenth year: The year following Arphaxad's defeat (1:13). Perhaps the timing is mentioned in order to sound an ominous note, bringing to mind how Nebuchadnezzar II demolished Jerusalem and its Temple in his nineteenth year (2 Kings 25:8–9). In the Latin Vulgate, the king reveals his plans in "the thirteenth year" of his reign. **the first month:** Nisan, formerly called Abib, which corresponds to March-April. Nisan 22 is the day after the weeklong festival of Passover/Unleavened Bread (Ex 12:18; Lev 23:5–8).
2:2 his secret plan: An instance of irony, in which king's hidden intentions are publicized before an assembly of the royal court.
2:4 Holofernes: A form of the Persian name "Orophernes". As commander of the Assyrian forces, Holofernes will serve as the instrument of Nebuchadnezzar's wrath and will assume center stage as the principal antagonist throughout the rest of the book.
2:5 the Great King: A traditional title used by Near Eastern monarchs who conquered and ruled other nations (2 Kings 18:19). **the lord of the whole earth:** A grandiose claim often made by Persian kings. It points ahead to the contest that unfolds hereafter: the question to be resolved is whether Nebuchadnezzar or the God of Israel is truly worthy of such a title.
2:7 earth and water: Tokens of surrender in Persian times, probably signifying that one's city and homeland are made an offering to the conquering king (see Herodotus, *Histories* 6, 48). **cover the whole face of the earth:** Language used in Num 22:5 to describe Israel after the exodus from Egypt.

ᵃ Or *a man.*
ᵇ The meaning of the Greek of the last clause of this verse is uncertain.
ᶜ Gk *them.*

and every brook and river shall be filled with their dead, and overflow; ⁹and I will lead them away captive to the ends of the whole earth. ¹⁰You shall go and seize all their territory for me in advance. They will yield themselves to you, and you shall hold them for me till the day of their punishment. ¹¹But if they refuse, your eye shall not spare and you shall hand them over to slaughter and plunder throughout your whole region. ¹²For as I live, and by the power of my kingdom, what I have spoken my hand will execute. ¹³And you—take care not to transgress any of your sovereign's commands, but be sure to carry them out just as I have ordered you; and do not delay about it."

Campaign of Holofernes

14 So Hol″ofer′nes left the presence of his master, and called together all the commanders, generals, and officers of the Assyrian army, ¹⁵and mustered the picked troops by divisions as his lord had ordered him to do, one hundred and twenty thousand of them, together with twelve thousand archers on horseback, ¹⁶and he organized them as a great army is marshaled for a campaign. ¹⁷He collected a vast number of camels and donkeys and mules for transport, and innumerable sheep and oxen and goats for provision; ¹⁸also plenty of food for every man, and a huge amount of gold and silver from the royal palace. ¹⁹So he set out with his whole army, to go ahead of King Nebuchadnez′zar and to cover the whole face of the earth to the west with their chariots and horsemen and picked troops of infantry. ²⁰Along with them went a mixed crowd like a swarm of locusts, like the dust of the earth—a multitude that could not be counted.

21 They marched for three days from Nin′eveh to the plain of Bec′tileth, and camped opposite Bectileth near the mountain which is to the north of Upper Cili′cia. ²²From there Hol″ofer′nes ᵈ took his whole army, his infantry, cavalry, and chariots, and went up into the hill country ²³and ravaged Put and Lud, and plundered all the people of Rassis and the Ish′maelites who lived along the desert, south of the country of the Chel′leans. ²⁴Then he followed ᵉ the Euphrates and passed through Mesopota′mia and destroyed all the hilltop cities along the brook Abron, as far as the sea. ²⁵He also seized the territory of Cili′cia, and killed every one who resisted him, and came to the southern borders of Ja′pheth, fronting toward Arabia. ²⁶He surrounded all the Mid′ianites, and burned their tents and plundered their sheepfolds. ²⁷Then he went down into the plain of Damascus during the wheat harvest, and burned all their fields and destroyed their flocks and herds and sacked their

---

2:9 lead them away captive: The forcible deportation and exile of conquered peoples was a common practice in Near Eastern warfare (2 Kings 17:6; 25:11; Is 20:4). **to the ends of the whole earth:** Another pompous claim by Nebuchadnezzar, who thinks that his power and dominion equal that of God, who is the Creator, Lord, and Judge of the ends of the earth (1 Sam 2:10; Job 28:24; Ps 2:8; Is 40:28).

2:11 your eye shall not spare: A Hebrew idiom meaning "you shall show no mercy" (cf. Deut 7:16).

2:12 as I live: An oath formula in which a person swears to forfeit his life should he fail to carry out his pledge. Ancient Jewish readers probably heard Nebuchadnezzar's words as a blasphemous claim to deity, since the God of Israel swears by his own life to execute his revenge on those who oppose him (Deut 32:40–42; cf. Num 14:20–23). The Bible knows of several Near Eastern kings who considered themselves divine (Is 14:13–14; Ezek 28:2; Dan 11:36). The proclamation of Nebuchadnezzar as a god is explicit later in the book (3:8; 6:4), showing that Nebuchadnezzar is claiming prerogatives that belong exclusively to the God of Israel. See also introduction: *Themes and Characteristics*. **my hand:** An instance of irony. Nebuchadnezzar pounds weaker nations into submission by the power of his mighty hand, and yet he will be too weak to conquer Israel, for God will deliver his people by the "hand" of Judith (8:33; 9:10; 12:4; 16:6).

2:20 like a swarm of locusts: I.e., like an army of locusts overwhelming the countryside and causing massive damage to crops and orchards (Deut 28:38; Joel 1:4).

2:21–28 Holofernes' campaign against Asia Minor, Syria, Mesopotamia, northern Arabia, and the Mediterranean seacoast. The itinerary appears to be illogical and obscure at points, leading scholars to suspect either that the author was ignorant of the geography of these regions or that the text has been altered or rearranged in the course of being copied by hand. Particularly odd is 2:24, which describes Holofernes lunging eastward into the heart of Mesopotamia, despite Nebuchadnezzar's aim of punishing western nations that refused him assistance (2:6). Adding to the uncertainty, the Latin Vulgate differs from the Greek texts in identifying several of the locations in these verses.

2:21 three days: Perhaps a deliberate exaggeration to create the impression of a lightning campaign. The distance from Nineveh to Upper Cilicia is roughly 300 miles, and it is next to impossible that 120,000 soldiers could advance on foot at this rate with supply caravans in tow (2:15–17). **Cilicia:** In southeast Asia Minor (modern Turkey).

2:23 Put and Lud: Descendants of Noah's sons Ham and Shem, respectively (Gen 10:6, 22). Put is usually located in northern Africa (modern Libya), and Lud is thought to be Lydia in western Asia Minor. It is unclear what regions are in view here. **Rassis:** Not otherwise known but perhaps associated with the city of Tarsus in Cilicia. **Ishmaelites:** Descendants of Abraham's oldest son, Ishmael (Gen 25:12–18). **the Chelleans:** Possibly the inhabitants of ancient Cholle, near the upper Euphrates River.

2:24 the brook Abron: Remains unidentified.

2:25 borders of Japheth: By mentioning Noah's third son, Japheth, following the mention of Put and Lud, descendants of Noah's first and second son, the author highlights the extent of Nebuchadnezzar's conquests. According to Genesis, the whole earth was repopulated by the offspring of Noah's three sons after the flood (Gen 10:1–32). **Arabia:** Here a reference to the Syrian Desert east of Damascus (1 Mac 11:16).

2:26 the Midianites: A Semitic people of western Arabia. The Bible traces their ancestry to Abraham through his second wife, Keturah (Gen 25:1–2).

2:27 the wheat harvest: In early summer, around May-June.

ᵈ Gk *he.*
ᵉ Or *crossed.*

cities and ravaged their lands and put to death all their young men with the edge of the sword.

28 So fear and terror of him fell upon all the people who lived along the seacoast, at Si′don and Tyre, and those who lived in Sur and Oci′na and all who lived in Jam′nia. Those who lived in Azo′tus and Asca′lon feared him exceedingly.

Entreaties for Peace

3 So they sent messengers to sue for peace, and said, ²"Behold, we the servants of Nebuchadnez′zar, the Great King, lie prostrate before you. Do with us whatever you will. ³Behold, our buildings, and all our land, and all our wheat fields, and our flocks and herds, and all our sheepfolds with their tents, lie before you; do with them whatever you please. ⁴Our cities also and their inhabitants are your slaves; come and deal with them in any way that seems good to you."

5 The men came to Hol″ofer′nes and told him all this. ⁶Then he went down to the seacoast with his army and stationed garrisons in the hilltop cities and took picked men from them as his allies. ⁷And these people and all in the country round about welcomed him with garlands and dances and tambourines.

⁸And he demolished all their shrines ᶠ and cut down their sacred groves; for it had been given to him to destroy all the gods of the land, so that all nations should worship Nebuchadnez′zar only, and all their tongues and tribes should call upon him as god.

9 Then he came to the edge of Esdrae′lon, near Do′than, fronting the great ridge of Jude′a; ¹⁰here he camped between Ge′ba and Scythop′olis, and remained for a whole month in order to assemble all the supplies for his army.

Judea Prepares for Defense

4 By this time the people of Israel living in Judea heard of everything that Hol″ofer′nes, the general of Nebuchadnez′zar the king of the Assyrians, had done to the nations, and how he had plundered and destroyed all their temples; ²they were therefore very greatly terrified at his approach, and were alarmed both for Jerusalem and for the temple of the Lord their God. ³For they had only recently returned from the captivity, and all the people of Jude′a were newly gathered together, and the sacred vessels and the altar and the temple had been consecrated after their profanation. ⁴So they sent to every district of Samar′ia, and to Kona and Beth-ho′ron and Bel′main

---

2:28 fear and terror: This situation will be reversed in 15:2, when the Assyrian army flees in terror before the Israelites. **the seacoast:** The eastern Mediterranean seaboard. **Sidon and Tyre:** Phoenician port cities northwest of Galilee. **Sur and Ocina:** Otherwise unknown. **Jamnia:** A coastal city of Palestine south of Joppa. **Azotus and Ascalon:** Cities formerly controlled by the Philistines on the Mediterranean coast west of Jerusalem.

3:1–8 The cities mentioned in 2:28 announce their surrender before the oncoming hordes of Holofernes. The Ammonites, Moabites, and Idumeans must have done the same, since they are later found assisting the Assyrian army (5:2; 7:8). The point of this information is to show that Israel will be isolated and alone when the time comes to resist the Assyrian invasion in defense of Jerusalem and the Temple (4:2).

3:4 your slaves: Slavery is preferred to slaughter at the hands of Holofernes' warriors.

3:7 garlands: Wreathes woven of flowers and leaves and worn on the head like a crown. It is a Greek custom that spread to other lands in the Hellenistic period (Wis 2:8). **dances and tambourines:** Traditional forms of celebration after a victory over enemies (Ex 15:19–21; 1 Sam 18:6–7).

3:8 demolished all their shrines: Holofernes' military campaign is also a religious war on the native cults and sanctuaries of the western nations targeted for punishment. His aim is to eradicate their traditional religious practices and replace them with a mandatory "ruler cult" in which Nebuchadnezzar is worshiped exclusively. News of this development brings panic to Judea over the protection of the Jerusalem Temple (4:2). **sacred groves:** Trees or wooden poles that function as cult objects. They are typically associated with the Semitic fertility goddess, Asherah. The language used here recalls the Mosaic commandments that require the Israelites to destroy the cultic monuments of the Canaanite religion (Ex 34:13; Deut 7:5; 12:2–3). **given to him:** Suggests that Holofernes was acting, not on his own initiative, but on the orders of his superior, Nebuchadnezzar. For a similar instance in the Bible where Nebuchadnezzar II of Babylon forced his subjects to

worship according to his demands, see Dan 3:1–7. **call upon him as god:** For the divine pretentions of certain Near Eastern kings, see note on 2:12.

3:9 Esdraelon: The western extension of the Jezreel Valley. See note on 1:8. **Dothan:** About ten miles southwest of Mount Gilboa and known for its fertile pasturelands (Gen 37:17).

3:10 Geba: Exact location uncertain. **Scythopolis:** The Greek name for Beth-shean, located between Mount Gilboa and the Jordan River at the eastern end of the Jezreel Valley.

4:1–5 The prospect of Assyrian invasion moves the people of Israel to petition the Lord for help and to make preparations for a defense of the homeland. Once a state of emergency is declared, the covenant community prays as if everything depended on God and works as if everything depended on them.

4:1 Judea: Land of the former kingdom of Judah, which included most of southern Israel. In the early postexilic period, it was the Persian district of Yehud.

4:3 recently returned: The early postexilic period is meant, i.e., the late sixth or early fifth century B.C. **the captivity:** A reference to the Babylonian Exile, which began in earnest in 586 B.C. with the conquest of Jerusalem and the deportation of its population (2 Kings 25:8–12). The captivity officially ended in 538 B.C. with the emancipation of the Jewish exiles by a decree of Cyrus II of Persia (Ezra 1:1–4). A summary of this backstory is related by Achior in 5:18–19.

4:4 every district: Several places mentioned in this verse are otherwise unknown (e.g., Kona, Belmain, Choba, and Aesora). The Latin Vulgate mentions only Samaria and Jericho. **Samaria:** Refers either to the central highlands of Palestine or, more specifically, to the city of Samaria, which was formerly the capital of the Northern Kingdom of Israel over 40 miles north of Jerusalem (modern Sebaste). One of the main trade and travel routes connecting Galilee in the north with Judea in the south ran through the region of Samaria. **Beth-horon:** Twin settlements that guarded the approach to Jerusalem from the northwest. **Jericho:** In the western Jordan Valley north of the Dead Sea. Jericho at this time in history lay about one mile south of the ancient fortress of Jericho destroyed by Joshua (Josh 6:1–27). **valley of Salem:** Location uncertain but perhaps a reference to Salim in the western Jordan valley (Jn 3:23).

ᶠ Syr: Gk *borders.*

and Jericho and to Choba and Aeso'ra and the valley of Salem, ⁵and immediately seized all the high hilltops and fortified the villages on them and stored up food in preparation for war—since their fields had recently been harvested. ⁶And Jo'akim, the high priest, who was in Jerusalem at that time, wrote to the people of Beth"uli'a and Bet"omestha'im, which faces Esdrae'lon opposite the plain near Do'than, ⁷ordering them to seize the passes up into the hills, since by them Jude'a could be invaded, and it was easy to stop any who tried to enter, for the approach was narrow, only wide enough for two men at the most.

Israel's Prayer and Penance

8 So the Israelites did as Jo'akim the high priest and the senate of the whole people of Israel, in session at Jerusalem, had given order. ⁹And every man of Israel cried out to God with great fervor, and they humbled themselves with much fasting. ¹⁰They and their wives and their children and their cattle and every resident alien and hired laborer and purchased slave—they all clothed themselves with sackcloth. ¹¹And all the men and women of Israel, and their children, living at Jerusalem, prostrated themselves before the temple and put ashes on their heads and spread out their sackcloth before the Lord. ¹²They even surrounded the altar with sackcloth and cried out in unison, praying earnestly to the God of Israel not to give up their infants as prey and their wives as booty, and the cities they had inherited to be destroyed, and the sanctuary to be profaned and desecrated to the malicious joy of the Gentiles. ¹³So the Lord heard their prayers and looked upon their affliction; for the people fasted many days throughout Jude'a and in Jerusalem before the sanctuary of the Lord Almighty. ¹⁴And Jo'akim the high priest and all the priests who stood before the Lord and ministered to the Lord, with their loins clothed with sackcloth, offered the continual burnt offerings and the vows and freewill offerings of the people. ¹⁵With ashes upon their turbans, they cried out to the Lord with all their might to look with favor upon the whole house of Israel.

4:5 harvested: Suggests a time in mid-to-late summer.

4:6 Joakim: Son and successor of Jeshua, the first high priest to minister in Jerusalem after the Babylonian Exile (Ezra 3:2; 4:3; Neh 12:10). His name is given in the Latin Vulgate as Heliachim (= Eliakim). **high priest:** Confirms the postexilic setting of the story (4:3). At this time, Israel was no longer governed by kings, and so the high priest in Jerusalem assumed the role of national figurehead. **Bethulia:** The hometown of Judith and the focal point of the story in chaps. 8–16. The site remains unidentified to this day, although it is described as a hilltop town on the edge of Samaritan territory overlooking the Plain of Esdraelon from the south—a key defensive position guarding the mountain passes toward Jerusalem from the north. Ancient manuscripts of Judith preserve several different spellings of the city's name, making it difficult to determine its original Hebrew spelling. The ancient town of Beth-eked has been suggested for its location (2 Kings 10:12). Since Bethulia is home to members of the tribe of Simeon (6:15; 8:7), it is possible the name is a variation on the old Simeonite town of Bethul in southern Israel (Josh 19:4). **Betomesthaim:** Otherwise unknown. **Esdraelon:** See note on 1:8. **Dothan:** Known for its fertile pasturelands (Gen 37:17).

4:7 only wide enough for two: A rhetorical exaggeration to say that Holofernes' army did face one disadvantage on its march toward Jerusalem from the north.

4:9 fasting: Temporarily denying oneself food is a form of supplication for God's guidance and intervention in a desperate situation (Judg 20:26; Ezra 8:21–23; Jer 36:9; 1 Mac 3:44–48).

4:10 sackcloth: A coarse fabric spun of goat hair and worn in times of great distress. Sackcloth could be worn beneath regular clothing (9:1; 2 Kings 6:30) as a prayerful act of supplication (Dan 9:3) or repentance (1 Kings 21:27).
• Putting sackcloth on animals recalls the repentance of Nineveh at the preaching of the prophet Jonah, who warned that God would bring judgment on the city unless its inhabitants repented of their sins (Jon 3:8).

4:11 ashes on their heads: A sign of intense mourning (Esther 4:1).

4:12 the altar with sackcloth: A unique event otherwise unattested in Scripture. For its meaning, see note on 4:10.

4:13 the Lord heard their prayers: A pivotal detail in the Judith story, indicating that God is moved by the pleas of his people and is ready to take action on their behalf. The news is heartening for readers, although the Israelites in the story are not privy to this information. Hence they continue to pray for more than a month (7:19, 30) before the Lord turns away the enemy threat (13:14–15). **the Lord Almighty:** Probably a rendering of the Hebrew expression "the Lᴏʀᴅ of hosts". See note on 1 Sam 1:3.

4:14 the continual burnt offerings: The morning and evening lamb sacrifice offered each day in the Temple (Ex 29:38–42).

4:15 turbans: The Greek term *kidaris* is a Persian loanword for the linen headdress worn by Levitical priests (Ex 28:4; Ezek 44:18).

WORD STUDY

Senate (4:8)

gerousia (Gk.): an "assembly of elders". In the Greek translation of the Pentateuch, the term corresponds to the Hebrew *zĕqēnîm*, meaning "elders", and refers to a body of tribal leaders under the headship of Moses and Aaron (Ex 3:16; 24:9; Lev 9:1). The Book of Deuteronomy institutionalizes their role as local magistrates charged with adjudicating civil cases in the towns of Israel (Deut 21:19; 25:7). Occasionally, the elders administered civil punishments (Deut 22:18) and conducted ritual acts of purgation (Deut 21:1–9). In the postexilic period, a council of elders was established in Jerusalem (Jud 4:8; 11:14; 15:8) that exercised some political and religious authority alongside Israel's priestly leadership (1 Mac 12:6; 2 Mac 1:10; 4:44; 11:27). By NT times, the senate of elders formed part of the Jewish high council, called the Sanhedrin, whose membership also included chief priests and scribes (Acts 5:21; Josephus, *Antiquities* 12, 142).

Holofernes' Council against the Israelites

5 When Hol"ofer'nes, the general of the Assyrian army, heard that the people of Israel had prepared for war and had closed the passes in the hills and had fortified all the high hilltops and set up barricades in the plains, ²he was very angry. So he called together all the princes of Moab and the commanders of Ammon and all the governors of the coastland, ³and said to them, "Tell me, you Canaanites, what people is this that lives in the hill country? What cities do they inhabit? How large is their army, and in what does their power or strength consist? Who rules over them as king, leading their army? ⁴And why have they alone, of all who live in the west, refused to come out and meet me?"

Achior's Report

5 Then A'chior, the leader of all the Am'monites, said to him, "Let my lord now hear a word from the mouth of your servant, and I will tell you the truth about this people that dwells in the nearby mountain district. No falsehood shall come from your servant's mouth. ⁶This people is descended from the Chalde'ans. ⁷At one time they lived in Mesopota'mia, because they would not follow the gods of their fathers who were in Chaldea. ⁸For they had left the ways of their ancestors, and they worshiped the God of heaven, the God they had come to know; hence they drove them out from the presence of their gods; and they fled to Mesopota'mia, and lived there for a long time. ⁹Then their God commanded them to leave the place where they were living and go to the land of Canaan. There they settled, and prospered, with much gold and silver and very many cattle. ¹⁰When a famine spread over Canaan they went down to Egypt and lived there as long as they had food; and there they became a great multitude—so great that they could not be counted. ¹¹So the king of Egypt became hostile to them; he took advantage of them and set them to making bricks, and humbled them and made slaves of them. ¹²Then they cried out to their God, and he afflicted the whole land of Egypt with incurable plagues; and so the Egyptians drove them out of their sight. ¹³Then God dried up the Red Sea before them, ¹⁴and he led them by the way of Sinai and Ka'desh-bar'nea, and drove out all the people of the wilderness. ¹⁵So they lived in the land of the Am'orites, and by their might destroyed all the inhabitants of Heshbon; and crossing over the Jordan they took possession of all the hill country. ¹⁶And they drove out before them the Canaanites and the Per'izzites and the Jeb'usites and the She'chemites and all the Ger'gesites, and lived there a long time. ¹⁷As long as they did not sin against their God they prospered, for the God who hates iniquity is with them. ¹⁸But when they departed from the way which he had appointed for them, they were utterly defeated in many battles and were led away captive to a foreign country; the temple of their God was razed to the ground, and

---

5:1–4 Tension increases as Holofernes descends into rage after learning of Israel's plan to resist the Assyrians.
5:1 barricades: May include pitfalls and other traps.
5:2 Moab ... Ammon: Traditional enemies of Israel from east of the Dead Sea and the upper Jordan River. The Bible traces the ancestry of Moabites and Ammonites back to Abraham's nephew, Lot (Gen 19:37–38). **governors:** The term *satrapai* is Persian. Here it basically means "commanders" (7:8). **the coastland:** The cities and seaports mentioned in 2:28.
5:4 come out and meet me: I.e., with an announcement of surrender.
5:5–21 An overview of biblical history from Abraham to the Babylonian Exile. • The story is told from the theological perspective of Deuteronomy, in which Israel's historical fortunes are tied up with the nation's commitment to God and his covenant. The obedience or disobedience of Israel thus determines whether it experiences national prosperity or adversity (5:17–18). Judith articulates the same theology in 11:10. For the blessings and curses of the covenant, see Deut 28–29.
5:5 Achior: An Ammonite general. He cautions Holofernes against a hasty attack on Israel (5:20–21), only to find himself rejected and handed over to Bethulia, the first town targeted for conquest (6:5–14). Achior will later become a convert to Judaism (14:10). Beyond this, the name Achior means "my brother is light"—a subtle indication that he will be welcomed into the community of Israel. According to the Bible, the Israelites and the Ammonites are kinsmen, being descended from Abraham and his nephew Lot, respectively. See note on 5:2.
5:6 the Chaldeans: Another name for the Babylonians of Lower Mesopotamia.
5:7 Mesopotamia: Abraham and his family moved to Upper Mesopotamia when they left the city of Ur and resettled in Haran (Gen 11:31). No reason is given in the Book of Genesis for this change of residence. However, an ancient Jewish tradition holds that Abraham left his hometown of Ur because of disturbances incited by his criticisms of idolatry (Josephus, *Antiquities* 1, 154–57; cf. *Jubilees* 12:1–8). Achior follows this tradition in his account of Abraham's migration. **gods of their fathers:** The Semitic deities worshiped by Abraham's ancestors (Josh 24:2).
5:8 God of heaven: A divine appellation popular in the Persian period (Ezra 1:2; 5:11; 6:9; Dan 2:18–19).
5:9 God commanded: For the divine call that brought Abraham and his family to the land of Canaan, see Gen 12:1–5.
5:10 went down to Egypt: For the account of Abraham's descendants moving to Egypt, see Gen 46:1–34.
5:11–15 A summary of events recounted in Exodus and Numbers. A fuller account of the sea crossing, along with mention of two subsequent miracles, appears in the Latin Vulgate.
5:15 Amorites: Designates the various peoples who occupied Canaan before its seizure by the Israelites (Gen 15:16). **Heshbon:** A major city east of the Jordan that was conquered by the Israelites in the days of Moses (Num 21:25–26).
5:16 Canaanites: One of several peoples who dwelt in Canaan before the arrival of Joshua and the incoming Israelites (Gen 15:19–21; Deut 7:1). **Shechemites:** Inhabitants of the city of Shechem in central Israel, which was named after Shechem, son of Hamor. In patriarchal times, the Shechemites were slaughtered by the enraged sons of Jacob because Shechem had raped their sister Dinah (Gen 34:1–31). Judith alludes to this violent episode later in the book (9:2).
5:18 led away captive: I.e., exiled to Babylon. **the temple:** Destroyed by the Babylonians in 586 B.C. (2 Kings 25:8–9).

their cities were captured by their enemies. ¹⁹But now they have returned to their God, and have come back from the places to which they were scattered, and have occupied Jerusalem, where their sanctuary is, and have settled in the hill country, because it was uninhabited. ²⁰Now therefore, my master and lord, if there is any unwitting error in this people and they sin against their God and we find out their offense, then we will go up and defeat them. ²¹But if there is no transgression in their nation, then let my lord pass them by; for their Lord will defend them, and their God will protect them, and we shall be put to shame before the whole world."

22 When A'chior had finished saying this, all the men standing around the tent began to complain; Hol″ofer′nes' officers and all the men from the seacoast and from Moab insisted that he must be put to death. ²³"For," they said, "we will not be afraid of the Israelites; they are a people with no strength or power for making war. ²⁴Therefore let us go up, Lord Hol″ofer′nes, and they will be devoured by your vast army."

Achior Handed over to the Israelites

6 When the disturbance made by the men outside the council died down, Hol″ofer′nes, the commander of the Assyrian army, said to A'chior and all the Moabites in the presence of all the foreign contingents:

2 "And who are you, A'chior, and you hirelings of E'phraim, to prophesy among us as you have done today and tell us not to make war against the people of Israel because their God will defend them? Who is God except Nebuchadnez′zar? ³He will send his forces and will destroy them from the face of the earth, and their God will not deliver them—we the king's ^f servants will destroy them as one man. They cannot resist the might of our cavalry. ⁴We

will burn them up, ^g and their mountains will be drunk with their blood, and their fields will be full of their dead. They ^h cannot withstand us, but will utterly perish. So says King Nebuchadnez′zar, the lord of the whole earth. For he has spoken; none of his words shall be in vain.

5 "But you, A'chior, you Am′monite hireling, who have said these words on the day of your iniquity, you shall not see my face again from this day until I take revenge on this race that came out of Egypt. ⁶Then the sword of my army and the spear ⁱ of my servants shall pierce your sides, and you shall fall among their wounded, when I return. ⁷Now my slaves are going to take you back into the hill country and put you in one of the cities beside the passes, ⁸and you will not die until you perish along with them. ⁹If you really hope in your heart that they will not be taken, do not look downcast! I have spoken and none of my words shall fail."

10 Then Hol″ofer′nes ordered his slaves, who waited on him in his tent, to seize A'chior and take him to Beth″uli′a and hand him over to the men of Israel. ¹¹So the slaves took him and led him out of the camp into the plain, and from the plain they went up into the hill country and came to the springs below Beth″uli′a. ¹²When the men of the city saw them, ^j they caught up their weapons and ran out of the city to the top of the hill, and all the slingers kept them from coming up by casting stones at them. ¹³However, they got under the shelter of the hill and they bound A'chior and left him lying at the foot of the hill, and returned to their master.

14 Then the men of Israel came down from their city and found him; and they untied him and brought him into Beth″uli′a and placed him before the magistrates of their city, ¹⁵who in those days were Uzzi′ah the son of Micah, of the tribe of Simeon,

---

5:19 returned to their God: I.e., repented (as in Deut 30:1–2). **come back:** The return of Jewish exiles from Babylon began in 538 B.C. with the decree of Cyrus II (Ezra 1:1–4).

5:21 their Lord will defend them: Achior speaks the truth about God and his covenant with Israel. In doing so, he provokes the boastful but foolish assertion that Assyria will determine the outcome of battle by military might alone (5:23). Israel's enemy trusts only in the strength of arms and is blind to the laws of the covenant.

6:2 who are you ...?: The question is a rebuke. Judith will use the same words to the same effect in 8:12. **hirelings:** Mercenaries. **Ephraim:** Meaning obscure, since Ephraim is a tribal territory in central Israel, not a territory of the Ammonites. Perhaps Holofernes addresses defectors from Israel who joined his ranks. **to prophesy:** An instance of irony. Achior spoke the truth when he announced that "the Lord will defend" Israel while the Assyrians will be "put to shame before the whole world" (5:21). **Who is God except Nebuchadnezzar?:** The

theological claim at the heart of the Book of Judith. It is tested and disproved by the events of later chapters. See introduction: *Themes and Characteristics*.

6:3 their God will not deliver them: Not the first time this false promise was uttered by a bragging Assyrian (see 2 Kings 18:32–35).

6:5 not see my face again: An instance of irony. Holofernes has no idea that when Achior next sees his face, he will be looking at the severed head of the general's decapitated corpse (14:6).

6:7 in one of the cities: Achior will be placed in the warpath of Holofernes, thus dooming him to a violent death together with the Israelites. As later chapters will show, this attempt of the general to refute the laws of the covenant explained in 5:20–21 is futile.

6:10 Bethulia: See note on 4:6.

6:14 magistrates: The triumvirate of city rulers named in 6:15.

6:15 Uzziah: The name in Hebrew means "the LORD is my strength". Ironically, Judith will outshine Uzziah for her strength of faith in the midst of the present crisis (see 8:9–17). **the tribe of Simeon:** One of the southern tribes of Israel that inherited towns in the midst of Judah (Josh 19:1–9). For various reasons, settlement patterns changed over the centuries,

---

^f Gk *his.*
^g Other authorities add *with it.*
^h Gk *The track of their feet.*
ⁱ Lat Syr: Gk *people.*
^j Other authorities add *on the top of the hill.*

and Chabris the son of Gotho'niel, and Charmis the son of Melchi'el. [16]They called together all the elders of the city, and all their young men and their women ran to the assembly; and they set A'chior in the midst of all their people, and Uzzi'ah asked him what had happened. [17]He answered and told them what had taken place at the council of Hol"ofer'nes, and all that he had said in the presence of the Assyrian leaders, and all that Holofernes had said so boastfully against the house of Israel. [18]Then the people fell down and worshiped God, and cried out to him, and said,

[19] "O Lord God of heaven, behold their arrogance, and have pity on the humiliation of our people, and look this day upon the faces of those who are consecrated to you."

[20] Then they consoled A'chior, and praised him greatly. [21]And Uzzi'ah took him from the assembly to his own house and gave a banquet for the elders; and all that night they called on the God of Israel for help.

The Campaign against Bethulia

[7] The next day Hol"ofer'nes ordered his whole army, and all the allies who had joined him, to break camp and move against Beth"uli'a, and to seize the passes up into the hill country and make war on the Israelites. [2]So all their warriors moved their camp that day; their force of men of war was one hundred and seventy thousand infantry and twelve thousand cavalry, together with the baggage and the foot soldiers handling it, a very great multitude. [3]They encamped in the valley near Beth"uli'a, beside the spring, and they spread out in breadth over Do'than as far as Balba'im and in length from Bethulia to Cy'amon, which faces Esdrae'lon.

[4] When the Israelites saw their vast numbers they were greatly terrified, and every one said to his neighbor, "These men will now lick up the face of the whole land; neither the high mountains nor the valleys nor the hills will bear their weight." [5]Then each man took up his weapons, and when they had kindled fires on their towers they remained on guard all that night.

[6] On the second day Hol"ofer'nes led out all his cavalry in full view of the Israelites in Beth"uli'a, [7]and examined the approaches to the city, and visited the springs that supplied their water, and seized them and set guards of soldiers over them, and then returned to his army.

[8] Then all the chieftains of the people of Esau and all the leaders of the Moabites and the commanders of the coastland came to him and said, [9]"Let our lord hear a word, lest his army be defeated. [10]For these people, the Israelites, do not rely on their spears but on the height of the mountains where they live, for it is not easy to reach the tops of their mountains. [11]Therefore, my lord, do not fight against them in battle array, and not a man of your army will fall. [12]Remain in your camp, and keep all the men in your forces with you; only let your servants take possession of the spring of water that flows from the foot of the mountain—[13]for this is where all the people of Beth"uli'a get their water. So thirst will destroy them, and they will give up their city. We and our people will go up to the tops of the nearby mountains and camp there to keep watch that not a man gets out of the city. [14]They and their wives and children will waste away with famine, and before the sword reaches them they will be strewn about in the streets where they live. [15]So you will pay them back with evil, because they rebelled and did not receive you peaceably."

[16] These words pleased Hol"ofer'nes and all his servants, and he gave orders to do as they had said. [17]So the army of the Am'monites moved forward, together with five thousand Assyrians, and they encamped in the valley and seized the water supply

---

and the Bible speaks of Simeonites living among the survivors of the northern tribes just prior to the Babylonian conquest of Jerusalem and the exile of the people of Judah (2 Chron 34:6). A community of Simeonites in north central Israel thus fits the circumstances of this time period. See note on 8:1.

6:19 God of heaven: See note on 5:8. **have pity:** The prayerful humility of Bethulia stands in sharp contrast to the boastful arrogance of Assyria in 6:2-4 (CCC 2559). **consecrated to you:** A description of Israel, a people set apart to serve the Lord as a "holy nation" (Ex 19:6; Deut 7:6).

6:20 they consoled Achior: In sharp contrast to his humiliation and rejection at the hands of the Assyrians in 6:5-13.

7:1-32 The siege of Bethulia begins. Warriors surround the city, pinch off its water supply, and then watch as the townspeople slowly die of thirst. The situation becomes so dire after 34 days of entrapment that only a miracle of God could save them. The stage is now set for the appearance of Judith in the following chapter.

7:2 one hundred and seventy: The army of 120,000 that set out from Nineveh (2:15) has grown with the addition of auxiliary forces from regional "allies" (7:1).

7:3 Dothan: See note on 3:9. **Balbaim:** Reference obscure, owing to the various spellings of this name in ancient manuscripts. **Cyamon:** Otherwise unknown. **Esdraelon:** See note on 1:8.

7:4 lick up . . . the whole land: The words of the fearful townsfolk recall the words of the fearful Moabites, who described the Israelites in the wilderness as a multitude that will "lick up all that is round about us, as the ox licks up the grass of the field" (Num 22:4).

7:7 the springs: The Latin Vulgate also mentions an aqueduct on the south side of Bethulia.

7:8 people of Esau: The Edomites, who lived south of the Dead Sea (Gen 36:1). They are also called Idumeans in the postexilic period. **Moabites:** Lived east of the Dead Sea. Like the Ammonites, they are descendants of Lot (Gen 19:36-38). **the coastland:** Cities along the eastern Mediterranean seaboard are in view (2:28).

7:9 hear a word: Local military intelligence is offered by Israel's neighbors.

7:12 spring of water: Apparently this water source was overlooked at Holofernes' initial inspection in 7:7.

and the springs of the Israelites. ¹⁸And the sons of Esau and the sons of Ammon went up and encamped in the hill country opposite Do'than; and they sent some of their men toward the south and the east, toward Ac'raba, which is near Chu'si beside the brook Moch'mur. The rest of the Assyrian army encamped in the plain, and covered the whole face of the land, and their tents and supply trains spread out in great number, and they formed a vast multitude.

The Distress of the Israelites

19 The people of Israel cried out to the Lord their God, for their courage failed, because all their enemies had surrounded them and there was no way of escape from them. ²⁰The whole Assyrian army, their infantry, chariots, and cavalry, surrounded them for thirty-four days, until all the vessels of water belonging to every inhabitant of Beth"uli'a were empty; ²¹their cisterns were going dry, and they did not have enough water to drink their fill for a single day, because it was measured out to them to drink. ²²Their children lost heart, and the women and young men fainted from thirst and fell down in the streets of the city and in the passages through the gates; there was no strength left in them any longer.

23 Then all the people, the young men, the women, and the children, gathered about Uzzi'ah and the rulers of the city and cried out with a loud voice, and said before all the elders, ²⁴"God be judge between you and us! For you have done us a great injury in not making peace with the Assyrians. ²⁵For now we have no one to help us; God has sold us into their hands, to strew us on the ground before them with thirst and utter destruction. ²⁶Now call them in and surrender the whole city to the army of Hol"ofer'nes and to all his forces, to be plundered. ²⁷For it would be better for us to be captured by them;ᵏ for we will be slaves, but our lives will be spared, and we shall not witness the death of our infants before our eyes, or see our wives and children draw their last breath. ²⁸We call to witness against you heaven and earth and our God, the Lord of our fathers, who punishes us according to our sins and the sins of our fathers. Let him not do this day the things which we have described!"

29 Then great and general lamentation arose throughout the assembly, and they cried out to the Lord God with a loud voice. ³⁰And Uzzi'ah said to them, "Have courage, my brothers! Let us hold out for five more days; by that time the Lord our God will restore to us his mercy, for he will not forsake us utterly. ³¹But if these days pass by, and no help comes for us, I will do what you say."

32 Then he dismissed the people to their various posts, and they went up on the walls and towers of their city. The women and children he sent home. And they were greatly depressed in the city.

The Character of Judith

8 At that time Judith heard about these things: she was the daughter of Merar'i the son of Ox, son of Joseph, son of O'ziel, son of Elki'ah, son of Anani'as, son of Gideon, son of Raph'aim, son of Ahi'tub, son of Eli'jah, son of Hilki'ah, son of Eliab, son of Nathan'a-el, son of Sala'miel, son of Sara'sadai, son of Israel.* ²Her husband Manas'seh, who belonged

---

7:18 sons of Ammon: Living in the highlands east of the Jordan River. **Acraba:** The Greek spelling is Egrebel (or Ekrebel). It is often identified with the modern village of Akrabeh, roughly 25 miles north of Jerusalem. **Chusi:** Otherwise unknown. **Mochmur:** The seasonal stream in question is undetermined.

7:19 Israel cried out to the Lord: The people reach a point of extreme desperation, and yet they refuse to despair in the goodness and power of God to respond to their prayers.

7:20 thirty-four days: The siege grinds on for more than a month. This figure is matched in the second half of the book when Judith spends four days in the Assyrian camp (12:10) and the citizens of Bethulia plunder the abandoned camp for 30 days thereafter (15:11).

7:23 Uzziah: The chief magistrate of Bethulia (6:14–15). See note on 6:15.

7:25 no one to help us: The people's faith in God is failing since the earnest prayer of 6:21.

7:27 better ... to be captured: A life of slavery is preferred to slaughter (7:27). For a similar sentiment expressed at the time of the Exodus, see Ex 14:12.

7:28 punishes us according to our sins: The statement is true as a general rule of Israel's spiritual life but inapplicable in the present situation. Judith will correct this misperception of God's action in 8:25–27 by insisting that Bethulia's suffering is a divine test. **heaven and earth:** Possibly an allusion to Deut 31:28, where Moses invoked the witness of heaven and earth against the elders of Israel for their foreseen unfaithfulness.

7:30 hold out for five more days: In the hope that God will fill the town cisterns with rain (8:31).

8:1–16:25 The rest of the book features Judith and her daring triumph over Holofernes. Several reversals stand out in these chapters, teaching the lesson that God can use the weak to shame the strong, the female to outmaneuver the male, and the humble and prayerful to bring down the arrogant and boastful (9:11; 1 Cor 1:27–29).

8:1 Judith: The name in Hebrew means "Jewess". Judith is revered for her exceptional piety (8:5–6), beauty (8:7), wealth (8:7), and wisdom (8:29). Her genealogy, though abbreviated, traces back 16 generations and is the longest female ancestry in the Bible. For the author, Judith embodies the religious ideals of early Judaism. **Salamiel, son of Sarasadai:** A leader of the tribe of Simeon in the time of Moses. His name appears in the Book of Numbers as "Shelumiel the son of Zurishaddai" (Num 1:6; 2:12; 7:36). Judith is thus a Simeonite (9:2) like her husband (8:7). Several ancient manuscripts and versions of the book add the words "son of Simeon" after the name Sarasadai (as in 8:7). See note on 6:15. **Israel:** The patriarch Jacob, who was renamed Israel (Gen 32:28).

8:2 Manasseh: Probably named after the eldest son of the patriarch Joseph (Gen 48:1). **her tribe and family:** Endogamy, or marriage within one's own kinship group, was encouraged in Israel. See note on Tob 1:9. **barley harvest:** In late spring, April or May.

ᵏOther authorities add *than to die of thirst.*
*8:1: The names in this genealogy differ in the various texts and versions.

to her tribe and family, had died during the barley harvest. ³For as he stood overseeing the men who were binding sheaves in the field, he was overcome by the burning heat, and took to his bed and died in Beth″uli′a his city. So they buried him with his fathers in the field between Do′than and Bal′amon. ⁴Judith had lived at home as a widow for three years and four months. ⁵She set up a tent for herself on the roof of her house, and belted sackcloth about her loins and wore the garments of her widowhood. ⁶She fasted all the days of her widowhood, except the day before the sabbath and the sabbath itself, the day before the new moon and the day of the new moon, and the feasts and days of rejoicing of the house of Israel. ⁷She was beautiful in appearance, and had a very lovely face; she was prudent of heart, discerning in judgment, and quite virtuous. Her husband Manas′seh, the son of Joseph, the son of Ahi′tub, the son of Melchis, the son of E′liab, the son of Nathan′a-el, the son of Sara′sadai, the son of Simeon, had left her gold and silver, and men and women slaves, and cattle, and fields; and she maintained this estate. ⁸No one spoke ill of her, for she feared God with great devotion.

Judith Rebukes the Elders

9 When Judith heard the wicked words spoken by the people against the ruler, because they were faint for lack of water, and when she heard all that Uzziah said to them, and how he promised them under oath to surrender the city to the Assyrians after five days, ¹⁰she sent her maid, who was in charge of all she possessed, to summon¹ Chabris and Charmis, the elders of her city. ¹¹They came to her, and she said to them,

"Listen to me, rulers of the people of Beth″uli′a! What you have said to the people today is not right; you have even sworn and pronounced this oath between God and you, promising to surrender the city to our enemies unless the Lord turns and helps us within so many days. ¹²Who are you, that have put God to the test this day, and are setting yourselves up in the place ofᵐ God among the sons of men? ¹³You are putting the Lord Almighty to the test— but you will never know anything! ¹⁴You cannot plumb the depths of the human heart, nor find out what a man is thinking; how do you expect to search out God, who made all these things, and find out his mind or comprehend his thought? No, my brethren, do not provoke the Lord our God to anger. ¹⁵For if he does not choose to help us within these five days, he has power to protect us within any time he pleases, or even to destroy us in the presence of our enemies. ¹⁶Do not try to bind the purposes of the Lord our God; for God is not like man, to be threatened, nor like a human being, to be won over by pleading. ¹⁷Therefore, while we wait for his deliverance, let us call upon him to help us, and he will hear our voice, if it pleases him.

18 "For never in our generation, nor in these present days, has there been any tribe or family or people or city of ours which worshiped gods made with hands, as was done in days gone by—¹⁹and

---

8:3 burning heat: Judith's husband died of sunstroke. **Dothan:** See note on 3:9. **Balamon:** Identification uncertain.

8:4 a widow: By choice and not simply by circumstance (16:22). Throughout this season of life, she devotes herself to the Lord, the "protector of widows" (Ps 68:5; Sir 35:14). The prophetess Anna similarly adopted a life of consecrated widowhood after her husband's death (Lk 2:36–37).

8:5–6 Besides careful observance of the Law, Judith follows a regimen of ascetic practices, denying herself usual comforts associated with food, shelter, and clothing.

8:5 sackcloth: A penitential garment. See note on 4:10.

8:6 fasted: Fasting was required of an Israelite on the annual Day of Atonement, according to the Mosaic Law (Lev 16:29). It was practiced more frequently in postexilic Judaism (Zech 8:19) and would become a regular expression of piety among Jewish sectarian groups such as the Pharisees (Lk 18:11–12). Judith's commitment to fasting except on weekly (Sabbath), monthly (new moon), and yearly festivals (Passover, Pentecost, Tabernacles) is nothing short of heroic. Fasting on feast days was considered improper because these were days of celebrating the covenant between God and Israel (CCC 1434).

8:7 She was beautiful: Like several other matriarchs and heroines in the Bible (Gen 12:11; 29:17; Esther 2:7). **son of Simeon:** See note on 6:15. **maintained this estate:** Judith fits the description of the valiant wife in Prov 31:10–31.

8:8 she feared God: Explains why Judith remains fearless in the face of enemy threats.

8:9–36 Judith reprimands the rulers of Bethulia for their misguided leadership. By giving God a timetable for action

(7:30), they presume to limit the Lord's options for deliverance. This amounts to putting the Lord to the test (8:12). In reality, God is the One who is testing them (8:25). The setting of this private meeting is Judith's rooftop tent (8:5, 36).

8:9 under oath: The pledge to surrender the city in five days was a foolish attempt to force the hand of God (8:11–16). In OT times, an Israelite was forbidden to break an oath (8:30; Num 30:2), and failure to uphold an oath triggered a curse on the one who made the pledge (Num 5:19–22; 1 Sam 14:24; Dan 9:11).

8:10 Chabris and Charmis: Introduced in 6:14–15.

8:12 put God to the test: Strictly forbidden in Deut 6:16.

8:14 his mind: The hidden depths of God's mind are inaccessible to human probing, as also implied in Job 11:7. • The words of Judith may have inspired the words of Paul in 1 Cor 2:11. Both insist that no one can search the mind of another man, much less fathom the depths of God and discover the thoughts of his all-knowing intellect.

8:16 not like man: For similar statements in the Bible that contrast the perfections of God with the imperfections of man, see Num 23:19 and 1 Sam 15:29.

8:18 gods made with hands: Idol images. Bethulia is innocent of forsaking the Lord to worship other gods. Judith makes this point to show that the present crisis, with all its afflictions, must be viewed as a test from the Lord rather than a curse in punishment for breaking the covenant (explained in 8:25–27) (CCC 2113).

8:19 a great catastrophe: The conquest and the exile of Judah by the Babylonians in the early sixth century B.C. The prophets considered these events a divine chastisement for Judah's idolatry.

---

¹Some authorities add *Uzziah and* (see verses 28 and 35).
ᵐOr *above*.

that was why our fathers were handed over to the sword, and to be plundered, and so they suffered a great catastrophe before our enemies. [20]But we know no other god but him, and therefore we hope that he will not disdain us or any of our nation. [21]For if we are captured all Jude'a will be captured and our sanctuary will be plundered; and he will exact of us[n] the penalty for its desecration. [22]And the slaughter of our brethren and the captivity of the land and the desolation of our inheritance—all this he will bring upon our heads among the Gentiles, wherever we serve as slaves; and we shall be an offense and a reproach in the eyes of those who acquire us. [23]For our slavery will not bring us into favor, but the Lord our God will turn it to dishonor.

24 "Now therefore, brethren, let us set an example to our brethren, for their lives depend upon us, and the sanctuary and the temple and the altar rest upon us. [25]In spite of everything let us give thanks to the Lord our God, who is putting us to the test as he did our forefathers. [26]Remember what he did with Abraham, and how he tested Isaac, and what happened to Jacob in Mesopota'mia in Syria, while he was keeping the sheep of La'ban, his mother's brother. [27]For he has not tried us with fire, as he did them, to search their hearts, nor has he taken revenge upon us; but the Lord scourges those who draw near to him, in order to admonish them."

28 Then Uzzi'ah said to her, "All that you have said has been spoken out of a true heart, and there is no one who can deny your words. [29]Today is not the first time your wisdom has been shown, but from the beginning of your life all the people have recognized your understanding, for your heart's disposition is right. [30]But the people were very thirsty, and they compelled us to do for them what we have promised, and made us take an oath which we cannot break. [31]So pray for us, since you are a devout woman, and the Lord will send us rain to fill our cisterns and we will no longer be faint."

32 Judith said to them, "Listen to me. I am about to do a thing which will go down through all generations of our descendants. [33]Stand at the city gate tonight, and I will go out with my maid; and within the days after which you have promised to surrender the city to our enemies, the Lord will deliver Israel by my hand. [34]Only, do not try to find out what I plan; for I will not tell you until I have finished what I am about to do."

35 Uzzi'ah and the rulers said to her, "Go in peace, and may the Lord God go before you, to take revenge upon our enemies." [36]So they returned from the tent and went to their posts.

The Prayer of Judith

9 Then Judith fell upon her face, and put ashes on her head, and uncovered the sackcloth she was

---

8:21 if we are captured: Bethulia and its neighboring towns are viewed as the last line of defense against an Assyrian invasion of Judea from the north. **our sanctuary:** The Temple in Jerusalem (8:24).

8:22 bring upon our heads: I.e., "hold us responsible for" (cf. Josh 2:19).

8:26 Abraham: Faced several trials of faith in his relationship with God, from leaving his kindred and homeland (Gen 12:1-5) to waiting several years for a son (Gen 15:1-6), undergoing circumcision at age 99 (Gen 17:24), and offering his son as a sacrifice (Gen 22:1-14). **tested Isaac:** His trials included a time of childlessness (Gen 25:21), bitterness caused by Esau's foreign wives (Gen 26:34-35), and loss of eyesight in old age (Gen 27:1). Besides this, an ancient Jewish tradition held that Isaac was a grown man when Abraham bound him for sacrifice in Gen 22:9, implying that Isaac gave consent to forfeiting his life in obedience to God's command. For further details, see note on Gen 22:9. **Jacob in Mesopotamia:** The difficulties that Jacob overcame while working for Laban in Gen 29:15—31:42 are meant. **in Syria:** The region of Paddan-aram (Gen 28:2; 31:18).

8:27 the Lord scourges: A biblical interpretation of suffering that views the trials of life as fatherly discipline administered by God (Deut 8:5; Prov 3:11-12). From this perspective, divine chastisement is not simply an expression of God's anger that punishes violations of justice; it is an expression of God's love aimed at purifying his people and training them to grow in trust, obedience, and perseverance (Wis 3:4-6; Sir 2:1-5). It is because suffering makes possible a closer and stronger relationship between God and his people (Ps 94:12; Heb 12:7-11) that Judith urges the city leaders to "give thanks" in the midst of the present crisis (8:25).

8:30 they compelled us: A pathetic excuse for yielding to the demands of the people (cf. Ex 32:22-24).

8:31 pray for us: On the premise that the prayers of a righteous and humble person such as Judith are powerful with God (Sir 35:16-17; Jas 5:16-18), even to the point of bringing rain to end a drought (1 Kings 17:1; 18:41-45). Apparently, Uzziah has a limited view of God's ability to rescue his people, i.e., he trusts the Lord's sovereign control over nature but fails to consider his power to end the siege by breaking the stranglehold of the enemy.

8:33 my maid: Judith's silent and unnamed companion throughout the story (10:2, 10; 12:15; 13:3; etc.). **by my hand:** Introduces a prominent theme in the book, where eight times reference is made to the "hand" of Judith (9:10; 12:4; 13:14-15; 15:10; 16:6). Behind this expression is the Hebrew phrase *beyad*, literally "by the hand of". It signals that Judith is the instrument the Lord will use to save his people. The expression is doubly appropriate because it is Judith's hands that will grip the hair and sword of Holofernes to deliver the triumphant deathblow (13:6-8). • Multiple references to Judith's "hand" brings to mind the "hand" of Moses, which God used to show his power in saving Israel from bondage in Egypt (Ex 9:22; 10:12; 14:16, 21, 26-27). For additional allusions to the Exodus story, see notes on 15:13 and 16:1-17.

9:1-14 Judith prepares for her mission with prayer. Her impassioned pleas invoke biblical precedent (9:2-4), divine Providence (9:5-6), the pride of the enemy (9:7-10), and God's protection of the lowly (9:11-14). Judith's prayer for "strength" is a prayer for the help and grace of God to vanquish the present threat to her people (9:9) (CCC 2585).

9:1 ashes: A sign of humiliation and supplication (Esther 4:1). **sackcloth:** See note on 4:10. **incense:** Burned twice a day, in the morning and evening, in the Jerusalem Temple on a golden altar that stood before the veil that curtained off the most holy place (Ex 30:7-8; cf. Lk

---

[n] Gk *our blood.*

53

wearing; and at the very time when that evening's incense was being offered in the house of God in Jerusalem, Judith cried out to the Lord with a loud voice, and said,

2 "O Lord God of my father Simeon, to whom you gave a sword to take revenge on the strangers who had loosed the girdle° of a virgin to defile her, and uncovered her thigh to put her to shame, and polluted her womb to disgrace her; for you have said, 'It shall not be done'—yet they did it. ³So you gave up their rulers to be slain, and their bed, which was ashamed of the deceit they had practiced, to be stained with blood, and you struck down slaves along with princes, and princes on their thrones; ⁴and you gave their wives for a prey and their daughters to captivity, and all their booty to be divided among your beloved sons, who were zealous for you, and abhorred the pollution of their blood, and called on you for help—O God, my God, hear me also, a widow.

5 "For you have done these things and those that went before and those that followed; you have designed the things that are now, and those that are to come. Yes, the things you intended came to pass, ⁶and the things you willed presented themselves and said, 'Behold, we are here'; for all your ways are prepared in advance, and your judgment is with foreknowledge.

7 "Behold now, the Assyrians are increased in their might; they are exalted, with their horses and riders; they glory in the strength of their foot soldiers; they trust in shield and spear, in bow and sling, and know not that you are the Lord who crushes wars; the Lord is your name. ⁸Break their strength by your might, and bring down their power in your anger; for they intend to defile your sanctuary, and to pollute the tabernacle where your glorious name rests, and to cast down the horn of your altar with the sword. ⁹Behold their pride, and send your wrath upon their heads; give to me, a widow, the strength to do what I plan. ¹⁰By the deceit of my lips strike down the slave with the prince and the prince with his servant; crush their arrogance by the hand of a woman.

11 "For your power depends not upon numbers, nor your might upon men of strength; for you are God of the lowly, helper of the oppressed, upholder of the weak, protector of the forlorn, savior of those without hope. ¹²Hear, O hear me, God of my father, God of the inheritance of Israel, Lord of heaven and earth, Creator of the waters, King of all your creation, hear my prayer! ¹³Make my deceitful words to be their wound and stripe, for they have planned cruel things against your covenant, and against your consecrated house, and against the top of Zion, and against the house possessed by your children. ¹⁴And cause your whole nation and every tribe to know and understand that you are God, the God of all power and might, and that there is no other who protects the people of Israel but you alone!"

1:8–10). The evening offering took place in late afternoon, about 3 P.M. • Elsewhere in Scripture, petitions are offered at the hour of the evening sacrifice by Ezra (Ezra 9:4–5), Daniel (Dan 9:20–23), and Cornelius (Acts 10:1–4), hinting that the prayers of the covenant people are most effective when said at the time of the Temple liturgies.

9:2 Simeon: The second son of Jacob (Gen 29:33) and the tribal ancestor of Judith and her husband (8:1, 7). **take revenge:** Judith appeals to the actions of Simeon in Gen 34:1–31 as a precedent for her plan to take up the sword against the Assyrians. Simeon and Levi retaliated with deceit and bloodshed against the Gentile population of Shechem after their sister Dinah was raped by Hamor, the prince of the Shechemites. Judith, who admires her ancestor Simeon, prays for success in using the same weapons of deceit (9:10) and a sword (13:6–8) to take revenge on the Assyrians for their plan to defile the Lord's sanctuary (9:13). As the story unfolds, Judith will place herself in a perilous situation, much like the one that led to the rape of Dinah, but, instead of being victimized as Dinah was, she will play the part of the zealous Simeon, who shed the blood of wicked Gentiles for making a mockery of God's people. These actions, while tolerated as moral imperfections in OT times, fall short of the higher standards of NT morality, especially the gospel mandate to love even one's enemies (Mt 5:43–48). See note on 11:5–19.

9:4 their wives for a prey: Recalls how the rest of the sons of Jacob plundered Shechem, even taking their wives as captives of war (Gen 34:27–29).

9:5 before ... are now ... are to come: The God of Israel is the Lord of history. All events of the past, present, and future take place according to his Providence, i.e., either because he decreed them to happen or because he permitted them to happen. Other passages of Scripture that affirm God's foreknowledge and lordship over history include Is 42:9; 44:7; 46:9–11; Acts 2:23; Rom 8:29.

9:6 Behold, we are here: Events willed by God are poetically personified.

9:7 soldiers ... shield ... spear: Signs of earthly military strength that count for nothing in the eyes of the Lord (1 Sam 17:45–47). **the Lord who crushes wars:** An expression taken from the Greek LXX translation of the Song of the Sea in Ex 15:3 (as also in 16:3). The Hebrew reads: "The LORD is a man of war." The Latin Vulgate makes explicit mention of the Exodus and sea crossing in this verse, hinting that the Assyrians are the new Egyptians. See note on 16:1–17.

9:8 your glorious name: An idiom for the presence of the Lord dwelling in the sanctuary (Deut 12:11; 1 Chron 22:19). **the horn:** Four horns protruded from the top four corners of the altar of sacrifice (Ex 38:1–2).

9:10 the deceit of my lips: Judith plans to follow the example of Jacob's sons in Gen 34:13 in order to gain the advantage over her enemy (9:13). See notes on 9:2 and 11:5–19. **the hand of a woman:** Literally "the hand of a female". In biblical times, it was disgraceful for a man to be killed by a woman (Judg 9:53–54). See note on 8:33.

9:11 God of the lowly: In the OT, the lowly are the ʿanawim, the humble of heart who place their hopes and prayers in the hands of the Lord (Ps 10:17; 69:33). They are often despised by the wicked and suffer the injustice of oppression (Ps 9:12; Amos 2:7). The Lord is their Teacher (Ps 25:9) and Defender (Ps 147:6). **helper ... protector ... savior:** Another allusion to the Greek translation of the Song of the Sea, in addition to 9:7. Exodus 15:2a LXX says of the Lord: "He has become a helper and protector to me for salvation."

°Cn: Gk *womb*.

Judith Prepares to Go to Holofernes

10 When Judith[p] had ceased crying out to the God of Israel, and had ended all these words, ²she rose from where she lay prostrate and called her maid and went down into the house where she lived on sabbaths and on her feast days; ³and she removed the sackcloth which she had been wearing, and took off her widow's garments, and bathed her body with water, and anointed herself with precious ointment, and combed her hair and put on a tiara, and arrayed herself in her most festive apparel, which she used to wear while her husband Manas'seh was living. ⁴And she put sandals on her feet, and put on her anklets and bracelets and rings, and her earrings and all her ornaments,* and made herself very beautiful, to entice the eyes of all men who might see her. ⁵And she gave her maid a bottle of wine and a flask of oil, and filled a bag with parched grain and a cake of dried fruit and fine bread; and she wrapped up all her vessels and gave them to her to carry.

6 Then they went out to the city gate of Beth"u-li'a, and found Uzzi'ah standing there with the elders of the city, Chabris and Charmis. ⁷When they saw her, and noted how her face was altered and her clothing changed, they greatly admired her beauty, and said to her, ⁸"May the God of our fathers grant you favor and fulfil your plans, that the people of Israel may glory and Jerusalem may be exalted." And she worshiped God.

9 Then she said to them, "Order the gate of the city to be opened for me, and I will go out and accomplish the things about which you spoke with me." So they ordered the young men to open the gate for her, as she had said. ¹⁰When they had done this, Judith went out, she and her maid with her; and the men of the city watched her until she had gone down the mountain and passed through the valley and they could no longer see her.

Judith Is Captured

11 The women[q] went straight on through the valley; and an Assyrian patrol met her ¹²and took her into custody, and asked her, "To what people do you belong, and where are you coming from, and where are you going?" She replied, "I am a daughter of the Hebrews, but I am fleeing from them, for they are about to be handed over to you to be devoured. ¹³I am on my way to the presence of Hol"ofer'nes the commander of your army, to give him a true report; and I will show him a way by which he can go and capture all the hill country without losing one of his men, captured or slain."

14 When the men heard her words, and observed her face—she was in their eyes marvelously beautiful—they said to her, ¹⁵"You have saved your life by hurrying down to the presence of our lord. Go at once to his tent; some of us will escort you and hand you over to him. ¹⁶And when you stand before him, do not be afraid in your heart, but tell him just what you have said, and he will treat you well."

17 They chose from their number a hundred men to accompany her and her maid, and they brought them to the tent of Hol"ofer'nes. ¹⁸There was great excitement in the whole camp, for her arrival was

---

10:1–5 Having made spiritual preparations in 9:1–14, Judith makes practical preparations for the execution of her plan. She bathes herself in water, anoints herself with cosmetic oil, dresses herself in festive attire, and adorns herself with jewelry. Judith's aim is to disarm her male adversaries with her captivating beauty. Every man who encounters her in the following verses melts in admiration of her loveliness (10:7, 14, 18–19, 23).
10:2 went down: From her rooftop tent (8:5). **feast days:** The festivals of Israel's liturgical year when Judith refrained from fasting (8:6).
10:3 sackcloth: A penitential garment. See note on 4:10. **her husband Manasseh:** Died more than three years earlier of heatstroke (8:2–4).
10:4 very beautiful: Her physical appeal is further enhanced by the Lord according to the Latin Vulgate (see RSV note).
10:5 wine ... oil ... grain ... fruit ... bread: Foods permissible for Jewish consumption, i.e., not forbidden as unclean by Lev 11:1–47 and Deut 14:3–21. In addition to unclean foods, the faithful of Israel also avoided the foods and wines of the Gentiles, since these were often improperly prepared (meat not drained of blood) or connected with idolatry (consecrated by prayer to a deity other than Yahweh). Adherence to dietary laws was thus a vital part of Israel's devotion to God. Judith, having packed her own meals, can thus politely decline the non-Jewish delicacies of Holofernes' table (12:1–4, 19). • Judith is one of many figures of the OT who refused to defile themselves with Gentile foods. Others include Tobit, Esther, Daniel, and the martyrs of Maccabean times (Tob 1:10–12; Esther 14:17; Dan 1:8; 2 Mac 6:18—7:42).
10:6 Bethulia: See note on 4:6. **Uzziah ... Chabris ... Charmis:** Introduced in 6:14–15.
10:8 Israel may glory and Jerusalem may be exalted: Anticipates the celebratory words in 15:9.
10:10 Judith went out: The scene now shifts from Bethulia to the Assyrian camp.
10:11–13 Judith shows herself not only poised in dangerous circumstances but shrewd in handling questions.
10:12 Hebrews: A term sometimes applied to Israelites by foreigners. See note on 1 Sam 14:21. **I am fleeing:** Judith pretends to be a defector from Israel and a useful informant with military intelligence favorable to the Assyrians (10:13). Her plan of "deceit" is now underway (9:10). On the matter of Judith's deception, see note on 11:5–19.
10:13 without losing one: No field commander would ignore a plan that proposes victory without a single casualty. The siege of Bethulia began with this goal in mind (7:11–15).
10:16 he will treat you well: Reassuring words indicating that Judith has won the trust of the Assyrian soldiers.
10:17–19 Despite being an unarmed female captive, Judith has the soldiers of the Assyrian camp firmly—even comically—under her control.

---

[p] Gk *she.*
[q] Gk *They.*
*10:4: The remainder of this verse reads in the Vulgate (verse 4): "⁴And the Lord also gave her more beauty: because all this dressing–up did not proceed from sensuality, but from virtue: and therefore the Lord increased this her beauty, so that she appeared to all men's eyes incomparably lovely."

reported from tent to tent, and they came and stood around her as she waited outside the tent of Hol″ofer′nes while they told him about her. ¹⁹And they marveled at her beauty, and admired the Israelites, judging them by her, and every one said to his neighbor, "Who can despise these people, who have women like this among them? Surely not a man of them had better be left alive, for if we let them go they will be able to ensnare the whole world!"

Judith Is Brought before Holofernes

20 Then Hol″ofer′nes' companions and all his servants came out and led her into the tent. ²¹Hol″ofer′nes was resting on his bed, under a canopy which was woven with purple and gold and emeralds and precious stones. ²²When they told him of her he came forward to the front of the tent, with silver lamps carried before him. ²³And when Judith came into the presence of Hol″ofer′nes ˣ and his servants, they all marveled at the beauty of her face; and she prostrated herself and made obeisance to him, and his slaves raised her up.

11 Then Hol″ofer′nes said to her, "Take courage, woman, and do not be afraid in your heart, for I have never hurt any one who chose to serve Nebuchadnez′zar, the king of all the earth. ²And even now, if your people who live in the hill country had not slighted me, I would never have lifted my spear against them; but they have brought all this on themselves. ³And now tell me why you have fled from them and have come over to us—since you have come to safety. ⁴Have courage; you will live, tonight and from now on. No one will hurt you, but all will treat you well, as they do the servants of my lord King Nebuchadnez′zar."

Judith Deceives Holofernes

5 Judith replied to him, "Accept the words of your servant, and let your maidservant speak in your presence, and I will tell nothing false to my lord this night. ⁶And if you follow out the words of your maidservant, God will accomplish something through you, and my lord will not fail to achieve his purposes. ⁷Nebuchadnez′zar the king of the whole earth lives, and as his power endures, who had sent you to direct every living soul, not only do men serve him because of you, but also the beasts of the field and the cattle and the birds of the air will live by your power under Nebuchadnezzar and all his house. ⁸For we have heard of your wisdom and skill, and it is reported throughout the whole world that you are the one good man in the whole kingdom, thoroughly informed and marvelous in military strategy.

9 "Now as for the things A′chior said in your council, we have heard his words, for the men of Beth″uli′a spared him and he told them all he had said to you. ¹⁰Therefore, my lord and master, do not

---

10:21 canopy: An ornamented netting stretched over poles as a protective barrier against insects. It will become a trophy of war (13:9) that Judith dedicates to the Temple (16:19). Note the glaring contrast between Holofernes' luxury tent, where the general takes his rest from the concerns of the war, and Judith's ascetical tent, where she readies herself for battle with prayer and fasting (8:5).

10:22 silver lamps: Not only necessary to see in the dark but an indicator that Holofernes is a stately figure surrounded by pomp and ceremony.

11:1 Take courage, woman: Offering words of comfort, the general is unaware of the scam unfolding before him. The irony is that Judith, far from being fearful and fragile, acts with extraordinary courage and composure in a perilous situation. • Bravery is not often lacking in a good widow. Judith was able to rouse and defend men who were broken by a siege, overcome with fear and hunger. For when Holofernes had driven countless men behind walls, she ventured outside the walls, showing herself braver than the army she delivered and the army she caused to flee (St. Ambrose, *On Widows* 37). **Nebuchadnezzar:** See note on 1:1.

11:2 slighted me: By refusing to surrender to the Assyrians (5:1–4).

11:3 you have come to safety: An instance of irony, since Holofernes is the one placing himself in mortal danger.

11:5–19 Judith misleads Holofernes with a masterful use of ambiguous language that allows for more than one interpretation. The deliberate use of equivocation makes Judith's speech something of a moral problem. Several considerations are relevant to an evaluation of her words. **(1)** Deception was widely accepted as a stratagem of war in the world of the OT. Several war heroes of the Bible used it as a weapon to bring defeat to Israel's enemies (e.g., Simeon in Gen 34:13–25; Ehud in Judg 3:15–25; Jael in Judg 4:17–22).

In spite of these examples, Scripture never teaches that God approves of deception as a morally acceptable means of pursuing an honorable goal. **(2)** The Bible praises Judith for many extraordinary virtues, but it never says that God instructed her on the practical steps to be taken against the Assyrians, nor does it recommend duplicity as a norm for Jewish conduct. **(3)** Even the greatest OT figures cannot be held to NT standards of morality, many of which were simply unknown before the coming of the Messiah. God instructed his people only gradually over many centuries regarding his perfect will for human behavior. Consequently, he patiently tolerated—rather than endorsed—the imperfections and ignorance of those who lived before the revelation of the gospel (CCC 2480–86). • Some are commended in Scripture for a praiseworthy disposition that moved them to commit unjust deeds. In the case of Judith, it was not because she lied to Holofernes that she is praised, but because she desired to save her people and for this reason placed herself in danger (St. Thomas Aquinas, *Summa Theologiae* II-II, 110, 3).

11:5 my lord: Strategically ambiguous. Holofernes assumes this is a reference to himself, whereas Judith is speaking about her divine Lord, to whom she would never lie.

11:6 God will accomplish ... his purposes: Strategically ambiguous. Holofernes hears this as a promise about Israel's downfall, whereas Judith has in mind Israel's deliverance.

11:7-8 Judith appeals to Holofernes' vanity with shameless flattery, just as she appeals to his sensuality with her ravishing beauty (12:16).

11:7 beasts ... cattle ... birds: For a similar description of Nebuchanezzar's lordship over all creation, see Dan 4:12.

11:8 the one good man: A compliment so exaggerated as to be comical.

11:9 Achior: The Ammonite who cautioned Holofernes against attacking Israel in 5:5–21.

11:10 unless they sin: I.e., unless Israel transgresses the Lord's covenant and draws down its curses upon the nation.

ˣ Gk *him.*

disregard what he said, but keep it in your mind, for it is true: our nation cannot be punished, nor can the sword prevail against them, unless they sin against their God.

11 "And now, in order that my lord may not be defeated and his purpose frustrated, death will fall upon them, for a sin has overtaken them by which they are about to provoke their God to anger when they do what is wrong. ¹²Since their food supply is exhausted and their water has almost given out, they have planned to kill their cattle and have determined to use all that God by his laws has forbidden them to eat. ¹³They have decided to consume the first fruits of the grain and the tithes of the wine and oil, which they had consecrated and set aside for the priests who minister in the presence of our God at Jerusalem—although it is not lawful for any of the people so much as to touch these things with their hands. ¹⁴They have sent men to Jerusalem, because even the people living there have been doing this, to bring back to them permission from the senate. ¹⁵When the word reaches them and they proceed to do this, on that day they will be handed over to you to be destroyed.

16 "Therefore, when I, your servant, learned all this, I fled from them; and God has sent me to accomplish with you things that will astonish the whole world, as many as shall hear about them. ¹⁷For your servant is religious, and serves the God of heaven day and night; therefore, my lord, I will remain with you, and every night your servant will go out into the valley, and I will pray to God and he will tell me when they have committed their sins. ¹⁸And I will come and tell you, and then you shall go out with your whole army, and not one of them will withstand you. ¹⁹Then I will lead you through the middle of Jude′a, till you come to Jerusalem; and I will set your throne ˢ in the midst of it; and you will lead them like sheep that have no shepherd, and not a dog will so much as open its mouth to growl at you. For this has been told me, by my foreknowledge; it was announced to me, and I was sent to tell you."

20 Her words pleased Hol″ofer′nes and all his servants, and they marveled at her wisdom and said, ²¹"There is not such a woman from one end of the earth to the other, either for beauty of face or wisdom of speech!" ²²And Hol″ofer′nes said to her, "God has done well to send you before the people, to lend strength to our hands and to bring destruction upon those who have slighted my lord. ²³You are not only beautiful in appearance, but wise in speech; and if you do as you have said, your God shall be my God, and you shall live in the house of King Nebuchadnez′zar and be renowned throughout the whole world."

Judith as a Guest of Holofernes

12 Then he commanded them to bring her in where his silver dishes were kept, and ordered them to set a table for her with some of his own food and to serve her with his own wine. ²But Judith said, "I cannot eat it, lest it be an offense; but I will be provided from the things I have brought with me." ³Hol″ofer′nes said to her, "If your supply runs out, where can we get more like it for you? For none of your people is here with us." ⁴Judith replied, "As your soul lives, my lord, your servant will not use up the things I have with me before the Lord carries out by my hand what he has determined to do."

5 Then the servants of Hol″ofer′nes brought her into the tent, and she slept until midnight. Along toward the morning watch she arose ⁶and sent to Hol″ofer′nes and said, "Let my lord now command

---

For the theology of retribution that lies behind this statement, see note on 5:5–21.

11:11 my lord: Strategically ambiguous. See note on 11:5.

11:12 planned to kill their cattle: The slaughter of livestock for meat is lawful (Deut 12:15), but any consumption of blood is strictly forbidden (Lev 17:10–12; Deut 12:16). Out of desperation, the Israelites are on the verge of drinking blood in order to escape death by dehydration, a point made explicit in the Latin Vulgate.

11:13 the first fruits ... the tithes: Sacred food portions reserved for the ministers of the sanctuary in Jerusalem (Num 18:12–13, 21–32). **not lawful ... to touch:** The laypeople of Israel were not permitted to eat any consecrated foods in their towns (Deut 12:17), much less the tithe offerings intended for priests and Levites.

11:14 permission: A special dispensation from the strict demands of the Torah is sought. **the senate:** A ruling body of elders in Jerusalem. See word study: *Senate* at 4:8.

11:16 things that will astonish: Strategically ambiguous. Holofernes thinks of a smashing victory for Assyria, whereas Judith means a stunning triumph for Israel.

11:17 God of heaven: See note on 5:8. **every night:** Judith establishes a nightly routine of exiting the camp for prayer in order to win the trust of the Assyrian guards (12:7) and thereby ensure the success of her getaway plan once Holofernes is assassinated (see 13:9–10).

11:19 like sheep that have no shepherd: Judith promises the general a divided and leaderless Israel, but in fact the Assyrians will flee in panic when their leader is discovered slain (15:1–2). **not a dog will ... growl:** An idiom meaning that Holofernes will encounter no opposition (Ex 11:7).

11:23 your God shall be my God: A promise to adopt Judith's religion (Ruth 1:16). The general's words are probably insincere, since he believes that Nebuchadnezzar alone is God (6:2).

12:2 I cannot eat it: Holofernes is not offended by this refusal to eat at his table because it reinforces the credibility of Judith's claim to defect from Israel on the premise that Bethulia is about to consume prohibited food (11:11–16). For the reasons behind Jewish avoidance of Gentile food and drink, see note on 10:5.

12:4 As your soul lives: An oath formula. **my lord:** Strategically ambiguous. See note on 11:5. **my hand:** The Lord's instrument of deliverance. See note on 8:33.

12:5 the morning watch: The darkness before dawn. • The author seems to allude to Ex 14:24, which tells how the Lord saved Israel by destroying the Egyptian army in the sea at the morning watch. For other allusions to the Exodus story, see notes on 8:33, 9:7, 15:13, and 16:1–17.

ˢ Or *chariot*.

that your servant be permitted to go out and pray." ⁷So Hol″ofer′nes commanded his guards not to hinder her. And she remained in the camp for three days, and went out each night to the valley of Beth″uli′a, and bathed at the spring in the camp.ᵗ ⁸When she came up from the spring she prayed the Lord God of Israel to direct her way for the raising up of her people. ⁹So she returned clean and stayed in the tent until she ate her food toward evening.

Judith Attends Holofernes' Banquet

10 On the fourth day Hol″ofer′nes held a banquet for his slaves only, and did not invite any of his officers. ¹¹And he said to Bago′as, the eunuch who had charge of all his personal affairs, "Go now and persuade the Hebrew woman who is in your care to join us and eat and drink with us. ¹²For it will be a disgrace if we let such a woman go without enjoying her company, for if we do not embrace her she will laugh at us." ¹³So Bago′as went out from the presence of Hol″ofer′nes, and approached her and said, "This beautiful maidservant will please come to my lord and be honored in his presence, and drink wine and be merry with us, and become today like one of the daughters of the Assyrians who serve in the house of Nebuchadnez′zar." ¹⁴And Judith said, "Who am I, to refuse my lord? Surely whatever pleases him I will do at once, and it will be a joy to me until the day of my death!" ¹⁵So she got up and

arrayed herself in all her woman's finery, and her maid went and spread on the ground for her before Hol″ofer′nes the soft fleeces which she had received from Bago′as for her daily use, so that she might recline on them when she ate.

16 Then Judith came in and lay down, and Hol″ofer′nes' heart was ravished with her and he was moved with great desire to possess her; for he had been waiting for an opportunity to deceive her, ever since the day he first saw her. ¹⁷So Hol″ofer′nes said to her, "Drink now, and be merry with us!" ¹⁸Judith said, "I will drink now, my lord, because my life means more to me today than in all the days since I was born." ¹⁹Then she took and ate and drank before him what her maid had prepared. ²⁰And Hol″ofer′nes was greatly pleased with her, and drank a great quantity of wine, much more than he had ever drunk in any one day since he was born.

Judith Beheads Holofernes

13 When evening came, his slaves quickly withdrew, and Bago′as closed the tent from outside and shut out the attendants from his master's presence; and they went to bed, for they all were weary because the banquet had lasted long. ²So Judith was left alone in the tent, with Hol″ofer′nes stretched out on his bed, for he was overcome with wine.

12:7 bathed: Immersion in the spring below Bethulia is part of Judith's nightly routine of prayer. Perhaps she is purifying herself of uncleanness from the Assyrian camp. From a Jewish perspective, Gentiles were ritually unclean because they did not observe the Mosaic purity laws (Acts 10:28), and soldiers were unclean because of their regular contact with death (Num 19:1–11).

12:10 the fourth day: The day before Bethulia plans to surrender (7:30). **his officers:** The absence of military personnel indicates that Holofernes, who intends to seduce Judith, is leaving himself unprotected and thus vulnerable to Judith's designs.

12:11 Bagoas: A Persian name of uncertain meaning. An advisor of this name served the Persian king Artaxerxes III Ochus in the fourth century B.C. See introduction: *Literary Genre.* **eunuch:** A male servant, often castrated, who was entrusted with the care of a royal harem.

12:12 enjoying her company: A euphemism for sexual intimacy.

12:13 like one of the daughters of the Assyrians: Presumably female attendants in the royal court who are willing to do whatever pleases the king.

12:14 my lord: Strategically ambiguous. See note on 11:5.

12:15 her woman's finery: The articles of jewelry mentioned in 10:3–4.

12:16 lay down: Festive meals were eaten while reclining on one side.

12:19 what her maid had prepared: Instead of the food and drink offered by Holofernes (12:1).

13:1–20 The beheading of Holofernes is the climax of the Judith story. The heroine is left alone with the lustful and drunken general and exposed to sexual abuse, but the tables are quickly turned when she hacks off his head and slips out with the ghastly trophy tucked in her food sack. Judith's action is brutal, yet the author stresses that she

accomplished her mission in a spirit of prayer and patriotic zeal for the defense of Jerusalem (13:4–5, 7, 11). • Many women, made strong by the grace of God, have performed manly deeds. The blessed Judith, her city besieged, asked the elders to enter the camp of the enemy. So she placed herself in danger out of love for her homeland and people, and the Lord gave Holofernes into the hand of a woman (St. Clement of Rome, *1 Clement* 55, 3–5).

WORD STUDY

Deceive (12:16)

apataō (Gk.): A verb meaning "deceive" or "entice". Speech is often a means of deception in Scripture, as when the serpent beguiles Eve with his empty promises (Gen 3:13) and when Delilah uses feminine wiles to trick Samson into giving up the secret of his strength (Judg 16:5). The term can also mean "seduce", as when a man lures a woman into sexual relations (Ex 22:16). In the Book of Judith, the verb and its related noun (*apatē*) add to the drama of Judith and Holofernes facing off in a game of wits. Holofernes burns with lust for the heroine, and, over the course of several days, he devises a scheme to seduce her into his bed (Jud 12:16). The general has no idea, however, that Judith is working out her own plan of deception at the same time. By a clever use of vague and misleading speech, coupled with the disarming power of her beauty, she succeeds in tricking, distracting, and assassinating the wicked commander (Jud 9:10, 13; 13:16; 16:8).

ᵗOther authorities omit *in the camp.*

3 Now Judith had told her maid to stand outside the bedchamber and to wait for her to come out, as she did every day; for she said she would be going out for her prayers. And she had said the same thing to Bago'as. ⁴So every one went out, and no one, either small or great, was left in the bedchamber. Then Judith, standing beside his bed, said in her heart, "O Lord God of all might, look in this hour upon the work of my hands for the exaltation of Jerusalem. ⁵For now is the time to help your inheritance, and to carry out my undertaking for the destruction of the enemies who have risen up against us."

6 She went up to the post at the end of the bed, above Hol"ofer'nes' head, and took down his sword that hung there. ⁷She came close to his bed and took hold of the hair of his head, and said, "Give me strength this day, O Lord God of Israel!" ⁸And she struck his neck twice with all her might, and severed his head from his body. ⁹Then she tumbled his body off the bed and pulled down the canopy from the posts; after a moment she went out, and gave Hol"ofer'nes' head to her maid, ¹⁰who placed it in her food bag.

Then the two of them went out together, as they were accustomed to go for prayer; and they passed through the camp and circled around the valley and went up the mountain to Beth"uli'a and came to its gates. ¹¹Judith called out from afar to the watchmen at the gates, "Open, open the gate! God, our God, is still with us, to show his power in Israel, and his strength against our enemies, even as he has done this day!"

Judith Returns to Her People

12 When the men of her city heard her voice, they hurried down to the city gate and called together the elders of the city. ¹³They all ran together, both small and great, for it was unbelievable that she had returned; they opened the gate and admitted them, and they kindled a fire for light, and gathered around them. ¹⁴Then she said to them with a loud voice, "Praise God, O praise him! Praise God, who has not withdrawn his mercy from the house of Israel, but has destroyed our enemies by my hand this very night!"

15 Then she took the head out of the bag and showed it to them, and said, "See, here is the head of Hol"ofer'nes, the commander of the Assyrian army, and here is the canopy beneath which he lay in his drunken stupor. The Lord has struck him down by the hand of a woman. ¹⁶As the Lord lives, who has protected me in the way I went, it was my face that tricked him to his destruction, and yet he committed no act of sin with me, to defile and shame me."

17 All the people were greatly astonished, and bowed down and worshiped God, and said with one accord, "Blessed are you, our God, who have brought into contempt this day the enemies of your people."

18 And Uzzi'ah said to her, "O daughter, you are blessed by the Most High God above all women on earth; and blessed be the Lord God, who created the heavens and the earth, who has guided you to strike the head of the leader of our enemies. ¹⁹Your hope will never depart from the hearts of men, as

---

13:3 Bagoas: Introduced in 12:11.

13:4 the work of my hands: For the significance of this expression, see note on 8:33.

13:5 your inheritance: The people of Israel, who are descended from Jacob (Deut 32:9).

13:6 his sword: The Greek term *akinakēs* is a Persian loanword, referring to a short battle sword (Herodotus, *Histories* 7, 54). • Judith's triumph over Holofernes recalls similar acts of heroism in the OT, especially the killing of Sisera by Jael, the woman who struck a mortal blow to the general's head (Judg 4:17–22), and the slaying of Goliath by David, who severed the head of the Philistine warrior with his own sword (1 Sam 17:50–51) in order to deliver Israel from reproach (1 Sam 17:26).

13:7 Give me strength: Judith prays for divine help to save her people. Once victory is achieved, she humbly acknowledges that God is the true Deliverer whose power brought about these events (13:11, 14–15; 16:6).

13:9 the canopy: See note on 10:21.

13:10 went out together: Passing the unsuspecting guards, who had been accustomed to the women leaving the camp each night. See note on 11:17.

13:11 God ... is still with us: Thrilling news for the people of Bethulia, who wondered if God had abandoned them (7:25).

13:14 Praise God: Credit for Judith's success belongs to the Lord and his providential care for Israel. **my hand:** The Lord's instrument of deliverance. See note on 8:33.

13:16 As the Lord lives: An oath formula. **my face:** A reference to Judith's beauty (10:7, 14, 23). **no act of sin:** Judith's sexual purity was kept safe from the general's lustful intentions (12:12, 16). In the Latin Vulgate, she attributes her protection to an angel from God. • When Holofernes laid siege to Bethulia and the power of Israel grew weak, chastity marched forth to assault the desires of lust, and humility brought about the destruction of pride. What the entire people of Israel was unable to do, the widow Judith accomplished by the virtue of chastity (St. Fulgentius, *Letters* 2, 29).

13:18 Uzziah: Chief magistrate of Bethulia (6:14–15). **blessed by the Most High God above all women:** The first of several times that Judith is "blessed" by others (also 14:7; 15:9–10, 12). • Uzziah's benediction resembles Melchizedek's blessing upon Abraham (Gen 14:19) as well as Deborah's blessing of Jael (Judg 5:24). The benedictions of Deborah and Uzziah together inspired Elizabeth's words to Mary in the Gospel narrative: "Blessed are you among women" (Lk 1:42; CCC 2676). These words indicate that Mary plays a role in salvation history analogous to that of Jael and Judith—she is a woman who is blessed by God and raised up to crush the head of the enemy leader (Gen 3:15). But whereas Jael and Judith wielded lethal weapons, Mary gave birth to the Son of God, who came "to destroy the works of the devil" (1 Jn 3:8). Judith 13:18–19 is read in the Lectionary as a responsorial on several Marian feast days (CCC 64, 489). • It is equally possible for man and woman to share in perfection. Judith became perfect among women when she despised danger for the sake of her country and, putting faith in God, gave herself into the hand of the enemy (St. Clement of Alexandria, *Stromata* 4, 19).

they remember the power of God. [20]May God grant this to be a perpetual honor to you, and may he visit you with blessings, because you did not spare your own life when our nation was brought low, but have avenged our ruin, walking in the straight path before our God." And all the people said, "So be it, so be it!"*

Judith's Counsel

14 Then Judith said to them, "Listen to me, my brethren, and take this head and hang it upon the parapet of your wall. [2]And as soon as morning comes and the sun rises, let every valiant man take his weapons and go out of the city, and set a captain over them, as if you were going down to the plain against the Assyrian outpost; only do not go down. [3]Then they will seize their arms and go into the camp and rouse the officers of the Assyrian army; and they will rush into the tent of Hol"ofer'nes, and will not find him. Then fear will come over them, and they will flee before you, [4]and you and all who live within the borders of Israel shall pursue them and cut them down as they flee. [5]But before you do all this, bring A'chior the Am'-monite to me, and let him see and recognize the man who despised the house of Israel and sent him to us as if to his death."

[6] So they summoned A'chior from the house of Uzzi'ah. And when he came and saw the head of Hol"ofer'nes in the hand of one of the men at the gathering of the people, he fell down on his face and his spirit failed him. [7]And when they raised him up he fell at Judith's feet, and knelt before her, and said, "Blessed are you in every tent of Judah! In every nation those who hear your name will be alarmed. [8]Now tell me what you have done during these days."

Then Judith described to him in the presence of the people all that she had done, from the day she left until the moment of her speaking to them. [9]And when she had finished, the people raised a great shout and made a joyful noise in their city. [10]And when A'chior saw all that the God of Israel had done, he believed firmly in God, and was circumcised, and joined the house of Israel, remaining so to this day.

Holofernes' Death Is Discovered

[11] As soon as it was dawn they hung the head of Hol"ofer'nes on the wall, and every man took his weapons, and they went out in companies to the passes in the mountains. [12]And when the Assyrians saw them they sent word to their commanders, and they went to the generals and the captains and to all their officers. [13]So they came to Hol"ofer'nes' tent and said to the steward in charge of all his personal affairs, "Wake up our lord, for the slaves have been so bold as to come down against us to give battle in order to be destroyed completely."

[14] So Bago'as went in and knocked at the door of the tent, for he supposed that he was sleeping with Judith. [15]But when no one answered, he opened it and went into the bedchamber and found him thrown down on the platform dead, with his head cut off and missing. [16]And he cried out with a loud

---

13:20 **perpetual honor:** Foreshadows the perpetual honor bestowed on Mary, the Mother of Jesus, who foresaw that "all generations" would call her "blessed" (Lk 1:48; CCC 971). **So be it:** The Greek is a literal translation of the Hebrew acclamation 'āmēn.

14:1 **hang it:** Displaying the head of a slain enemy is a feature of Near Eastern warfare (see 1 Sam 17:54; 2 Kings 10:8; 2 Mac 15:35). Like the judge Deborah, Judith boldly takes charge of directing Israel's military strategy (Judg 4:4–7).

14:3 **they will flee:** Mobilizing Israel's warriors will lead to the discovery of Holofernes' body and cause the leaderless Assyrians to panic (14:19) and run for their lives (15:1–3).

14:6 **Achior:** The Ammonite commander handed over to Bethulia (6:1–17). He is called to verify that the severed head belonged to Holofernes, for he is the only person in the town who has seen the general face-to-face (5:1–21). The epi-sode is highly ironic in view of Holofernes' threatening words to Achior in 6:5. **his spirit failed him:** Suggests that Achior fainted at the gruesome spectacle.

14:10 **believed:** Achior comes to faith in the God of Israel after witnessing the divine protection of Israel. The wording of the passage recalls Abraham's act of faith in Gen 15:6. **circumcised:** Achior's conversion is sealed by accepting circumcision, the rite of initiation into the covenant community (Gen 17:10). Tension is oftentimes felt between this verse and Deut 23:3, where Moses bans Ammonites and Moabites from joining the assembly of Israel for ten generations. The story of Judith, set in the postexilic period, takes place well after this restriction was in force (although it was still applied to mixed marriages at this time in Neh 13:1–2). Besides this, there were exceptions to the general rule even in earlier times, e.g., with the conversion of Ruth the Moabite (Ruth 1:16–17). See note on Gen 17:11. **to this day:** May mean, as specified in the Latin Vulgate, that Achior's descendants were still known in Israel in the author's day (cf. Josh 6:25).

14:13 **the steward:** The eunuch Bagoas (12:11). **the slaves:** The Latin Vulgate reads: "the mice".

14:14 **knocked at the door:** Suggests the general's bed-chamber was a walled enclosure set within his war tent.

14:15 **found him ... dead:** Recalls how the servants of Eglon the Moabite discovered his lifeless body after he had been deceived and assassinated by Ehud (Judg 3:24–25).

14:16 **tore his garments:** A sign of extreme distress (Gen 37:29).

---

*13:20: Vulgate adds (verses 27–31): "[27]And Achior being called for came, and Judith said to him: The God of Israel, to whom you gave testimony, that he revenge himself of his enemies, he has cut off the head of all the unbelievers this night by my hand. [28]And that you may find that it is so, behold the head of Holofernes, who in the contempt of his pride despised the God of Israel, and threatened you with death, saying: When the people of Israel shall be taken, I will command your sides to be pierced with a sword. [29]Then Achior, seeing the head of Holofernes, being seized with a great fear he fell on his face upon the earth, and his soul swooned away. [30]But after he had recovered his spirits, he fell down at her feet, and reverenced her, and said: [31]Blessed are you by your God in every tabernacle of Jacob, for in every nation which shall hear your name, the God of Israel shall be magnified on occasion of you."

voice and wept and groaned and shouted, and tore his garments. ¹⁷Then he went to the tent where Judith had stayed, and when he did not find her he rushed out to the people and shouted, ¹⁸"The slaves have tricked us! One Hebrew woman has brought disgrace upon the house of King Nebuchadnez′zar! For look, here is Hol″ofer′nes lying on the ground, and his head is not on him!"

19 When the leaders of the Assyrian army heard this, they tore their tunics and were greatly dismayed, and their loud cries and shouts arose in the midst of the camp.

The Assyrian Army Flees

15 When the men in the tents heard it, they were amazed at what had happened. ²Fear and trembling came over them, so that they did not wait for one another, but with one impulse all rushed out and fled by every path across the plain and through the hill country. ³Those who had camped in the hills around Beth″uli′a also took to flight. Then the men of Israel, every one that was a soldier, rushed out upon them. ⁴And Uzz′iah sent men to Bet″omastha′im and Bebai and Choba and Ko′la, and to all the frontiers of Israel, to tell what had taken place and to urge all to rush out upon their enemies to destroy them. ⁵And when the Israelites heard it, with one accord they fell upon the enemy,ᵘ and cut them down as far as Cho′ba. Those in Jerusalem and all the hill country also came, for they were told what had happened in the camp of the enemy; and those in Gilead and in Galilee outflanked them with great slaughter, even beyond Damascus and its borders. ⁶The rest of the people of Beth″uli′a fell upon the Assyrian camp and plundered it, and were greatly enriched.

⁷And the Israelites, when they returned from the slaughter, took possession of what remained, and the villages and towns in the hill country and in the plain got a great amount of booty, for there was a vast quantity of it.

The Israelites Celebrate

8 Then Jo′akim the high priest, and the senate of the people of Israel who lived at Jerusalem, came to witness the good things which the Lord had done for Israel, and to see Judith and to greet her. ⁹And when they met her they all blessed her with one accord and said to her, "You are the exaltation of Jerusalem,* you are the great glory of Israel, you are the great pride of our nation! ¹⁰You have done all this singlehanded; you have done great good to Israel, and God is well pleased with it. May the Almighty Lord bless you for ever!" And all the people said, "So be it!"

11 So all the people plundered the camp for thirty days. They gave Judith the tent of Hol″ofer′nes and all his silver dishes and his beds and his bowls and all his furniture; and she took them and loaded her mule and hitched up her carts and piled the things on them.

12 Then all the women of Israel gathered to see her, and blessed her, and some of them performed a dance for her; and she took branches in her hands and gave them to the women who were with her; ¹³and they crowned themselves with olive wreaths, she and those who were with her; and she went before all the people in the dance, leading all the women, while all the men of Israel followed, bearing their arms and wearing garlands and with songs on their lips.

14:18 disgrace: It was shameful in biblical times for a man to be killed by a woman (Judg 9:53–54).

15:1–15 The warriors of Israel cut off the retreating Assyrians, while the rest of the people plunder the abandoned camp for an entire month (15:11). From the spoils of victory, Judith is given all that belonged to Holofernes.

15:3 camped in the hills: The sons of Ammon and Edom, neighbors of Israel who played a supportive role in the Assyrian siege (7:18).

15:4 Betomasthaim ... Bebai ... Choba ... Kola: Unidentified locations in Israel. Kola may be a reference to the Judahite town of Holon (Josh 15:51).

15:5 with one accord: Israelites from all over rally together to rout the enemy in an act of national solidarity. **the hill country:** The highlands of Judah around Jerusalem. **Gilead:** The highlands east of the Jordan River. **Galilee:** The northern region of Israel west of the Sea of Galilee. **Damascus:** In Syria north of Israelite territory.

15:8 Joakim: See note on 4:6. **the senate:** See word study: *Senate* at 4:8.

15:9 exaltation of Jerusalem: Judith executed her daring plan to save Jerusalem and the Temple from foreign conquest and desecration (9:8, 13; 13:4). • The benediction here pronounced on Judith is applied to the Blessed Virgin Mary in Catholic liturgy. The application is based on the Church's typological reading of Scripture, which considers Judith to be one of the outstanding women of the OT who prepares the way for the Messiah's Mother (CCC 489).

15:10 singlehanded: Not a denial of the Lord's primary role in Israel's deliverance but an acknowledgment of Judith's contribution of bravery and faith.

15:11 thirty days: Parallels the 34 days of the Assyrian siege (7:20) if one adds the four days that Judith spent in the enemy camp (12:10).

15:12 the women of Israel: Traditionally led a victory dance following a military triumph (Ex 15:20; 1 Sam 18:6). **branches:** Like the festal bundles of palms, willows, and other greens waved during occasions of national celebration (2 Mac 10:7) such as the feast of Booths/Tabernacles (Lev 23:40).

15:13 olive wreaths: A Greek cultural custom. The detail suggests the Book of Judith was either written or last edited in the Hellenistic period between 332 and 63 B.C. **leading all the women:** The parade of celebrants is traveling to Jerusalem (16:18). • The event recalls how Miriam, the sister of Moses, led the women of Israel in song and dance after the drowning of the Egyptian army made the Exodus from Egypt complete (Ex 15:20–21).

ᵘGk *them.*
*15:9, *You are the exaltation of Jerusalem:* This passage is included in the office for feasts of the Blessed Virgin Mary, e.g., the little chapter for None on the Assumption, 15 August.

The Song of Praise of Judith

16 Then Judith began this thanksgiving before all Israel, and all the people loudly sang this song of praise. ²And Judith said,

Begin a song to my God with tambourines,
> sing to my Lord with cymbals.
Raise to him a new psalm;ᵛ
> exalt him, and call upon his name.
³For God is the Lord who crushes wars;
> for he has delivered me out of the hands of my
> > pursuers,
> and brought me to his camp, in the midst of
> > the people.

⁴The Assyrian came down from the mountains of
> the north;
> he came with myriads of his warriors;
> their multitude blocked up the valleys,
> > their cavalry covered the hills.
⁵He boasted that he would burn up my territory,
> and kill my young men with the sword,
and dash my infants to the ground
> and seize my children as prey,
> > and take my virgins as booty.

⁶But the Lord Almighty has foiled them
> by the hand of a woman.
⁷For their mighty one did not fall by the hands of
> the young men,
> nor did the sons of the Titans strike him,
> nor did tall giants set upon him;
but Judith the daughter of Merar'i undid him
> with the beauty of her countenance.

⁸For she took off her widow's mourning
> to exalt the oppressed in Israel.

She anointed her face with ointment
> and fastened her hair with a tiara
> and put on a linen gown to deceive him.
⁹Her sandal ravished his eyes,
> her beauty captivated his mind,
> and the sword severed his neck.
¹⁰The Persians trembled at her boldness,
> the Medes were daunted at her daring.

¹¹Then my oppressed people shouted for joy;
> my weak people shoutedʷ and the enemyˣ
> > trembled;
> they lifted up their voices, and the enemyˣ
> > were turned back.
¹²The sons of maidservants have pierced them
> > through;
> they were wounded like the children of
> > fugitives,
> they perished before the army of my Lord.

¹³I will sing to my God a new song:
O Lord, you are great and glorious,
> wonderful in strength, invincible.
¹⁴Let all your creatures serve you,
> for you spoke, and they were made.
You sent forth your Spirit,ʸ and it formed them;
> there is none that can resist your voice.
¹⁵For the mountains shall be shaken to their
> foundations with the waters;
> at your presence the rocks shall melt like wax,
but to those who fear you
> you will continue to show mercy.
¹⁶For every sacrifice as a fragrant offering is a
> small thing,
> and all fat for burnt offerings to you is a very
> > little thing,
but he who fears the Lord shall be great for ever.

16:1–17 The Song of Judith. It is a thanksgiving hymn that exalts the God of Israel as a divine Warrior (16:3–6), Creator (16:13–15), and Judge (16:17). Verses 4–12 summarize the Judith story in poetic form; vv. 13–17 praise Yahweh in terms that recall several of the psalms. Its main lesson is that mercy and greatness belong to those who "fear" the Lord (16:15–16). • The primary inspiration behind the Song of Judith is the Song of the Sea in Ex 15:1–18. In both, Yahweh is described as the Lord who "crushes wars" (compare 16:3 with Ex 15:3 LXX), confronts a boastful enemy (compare 16:5 with Ex 15:9), and causes other nations to tremble with fear at the news of God's triumph (compare 16:10 with Ex 15:14–15). Likewise, the mention of God using "the hand" of a woman to save Israel from the Assyrians (16:6) recalls how he used the hand of Moses to save Israel from the Egyptians. For details, see note on 8:33.

16:1 Then Judith began: In the NABRE, this sentence is printed as the final verse of chap. 15 rather than the first verse of chap. 16, with the result that 16:1–8 is divided differently in the two translations.

16:3 the Lord who crushes wars: See note on 9:7.

16:4 with myriads: Holofernes invaded Israel with 182,000 troops at his command (7:2).

16:7 their mighty one: Or "their champion". The same term is used for Goliath of Gath in the Greek LXX translation of 1 Sam 17:4. **the Titans:** Divine giants who battled the gods of Olympus in Greek mythology. **giants:** Men of imposing stature and strength from ancient times (e.g., the Nephilim, Gen 6:4; the Anakim/Rephaim, Num 13:32–33; Deut 2:11).

16:8 ointment ... tiara: A summary of 10:1–4.

16:10 Persians ... Medes: The story of Judith is set in the postexilic period when the Medo-Persian empire was the mightiest in the Near East.

16:13 a new song: Compare with Ps 144:9; 149:1.

16:14 all your creatures: Compare with Ps 148:1–12. **you spoke, and they were made:** Compare with Ps 33:6–9. **You sent forth your Spirit:** Compare with Ps 104:30.

16:15 the rocks shall melt: Compare with Ps 97:5 and Mic 1:4. **those who fear you:** Judith is the foremost example in the book (8:8).

16:16 sacrifice ... a small thing: Fear of the Lord is the heart of Israel's faith (Prov 1:7; Sir 1:11–20). The liturgical rites of worship, while not unimportant, are a means to express the fear of the Lord in an outward, tangible way (cf. 1 Sam 15:22; Ps 51:16–17).

ᵛOther authorities read *a psalm and praise.*
ʷOther authorities read *feared.*
ˣGk *they.*
ʸOr *breath.*

[17]Woe to the nations that rise up against my people!
The Lord Almighty will take vengeance on
them in the day of judgment;
fire and worms he will give to their flesh;
they shall weep in pain for ever.

18 When they arrived at Jerusalem they worshiped God. As soon as the people were purified, they offered their burnt offerings, their freewill offerings, and their gifts. [19]Judith also dedicated to God all the vessels of Hol"ofer'nes, which the people had given her; and the canopy which she took for herself from his bedchamber she gave as a votive offering to the Lord. [20]So the people continued feasting in Jerusalem before the sanctuary for three months, and Judith remained with them.

The Renown and Death of Judith

21 After this every one returned home to his own inheritance, and Judith went to Beth"uli'a, and remained on her estate, and was honored in her time throughout the whole country. [22]Many desired to marry her, but she remained a widow all the days of her life after Manas'seh her husband died and was gathered to his people. [23]She became more and more famous, and grew old in her husband's house, until she was one hundred and five years old. She set her maid free. She died in Beth"uli'a, and they buried her in the cave of her husband Manas'seh, [24]and the house of Israel mourned for her seven days. Before she died she distributed her property to all those who were next of kin to her husband Manas'seh, and to her own nearest kindred. [25]And no one ever again spread terror among the people of Israel in the days of Judith, or for a long time after her death.*

16:17 fire and worms: The terrible fate in store for those who rebel against the Lord according to Is 66:24 and Sir 7:17. • Jesus uses the imagery of fire and worms to depict the woes of eternal damnation in Mk 9:47-48 (CCC 1034-35).

16:18 purified: I.e., cleansed of ritual defilement incurred by contact with slain soldiers in the Assyrian camp (see Num 19:11-13, 16; 31:19). Purification from corpse impurity was necessary before worship in the Temple was allowed (cf. Jn 11:55).

16:19 the vessels of Holofernes: Listed in 15:11. **the canopy:** See note on 10:21. **a votive offering:** An item devoted to the Lord. Once given to the priests at the sanctuary, it could not be bought back (Lev 27:28).

16:21 her estate: Described in 8:7.

16:22 she remained a widow: Literally "no man knew her". Judith chose to remain unmarried and celibate after the Assyrian crisis had passed. Just as God guarded her sexual purity from the lustful Holofernes (13:16), so she guarded her sexual purity from all other men for the rest of her life. Remarriage would not have compromised her sexual purity, but Judith's celibacy allowed her to dedicate the remainder of her life to God without the added responsibilities of married life. Consecrated widowhood was unusual in biblical Israel and was not widely esteemed as a religious ideal until early Christian times (1 Cor 7:39-40; 1 Tim 5:9-10). • Judith was a widow, renowned of family, rich in goods, attractive in appearance; and yet she despised wealth and luxury and trampled down the delights of the flesh. By the witness of her brilliant feat, it is clear that God loves a widow's continence (St. Fulgentius, *Letters* 2, 29).

16:23 one hundred and five: A long life is sometimes a reward for righteousness (Prov 16:31). Scholars who read the Judith story as an allegory of the Maccabean period often point out that it lasted 105 years (168-63 B.C.). An intended allusion to this period seems unlikely, however, since Judith was almost certainly written before the latter half of the first century B.C. **in the cave of her husband:** The Genesis matriarchs were likewise buried in the same cave as the Patriarchs (Gen 49:29-32).

16:24 seven days: A traditional period for mourning the deceased (Sir 22:12).

16:25 for a long time: Years of peace following war was also a legacy of the biblical Judges (see Judg 3:11, 30; 5:31). The Latin Vulgate concludes the book with an additional verse stating that the anniversary of Judith's victory was celebrated as a Jewish feast day. No such feast is known from ancient sources. Perhaps the story was retold in connection with the festival of Hanukkah.

---

*16:25: Vulgate adds (verse 31): "[31]But the day of the festivity of this victory is received by the Hebrews in the number of holy days, and is religiously observed by the Jews from that time until this day."

Study Questions
Judith

Chapter 1

For understanding

1. **1:1.** Who is the Nebuchadnezzar mentioned in the story usually thought to be, and when did he reign? What problem does this identification pose? What three explanations for this historical discrepancy have been proposed? What is the city of Nineveh, and when was it destroyed? Given the setting of the Book of Judith after 515 B.C., what is it possible that the author is doing? Who is Arphaxad? Where is Ecbatana?
2. **1:2.** What does history know of the fortifications at Ecbatana? What is the purpose of the detailed description in 1:2–4? If the mighty fortress of Ecbatana could not withstand the king's forces, what could the small town of Bethulia expect? How long is a cubit?
3. **1:8.** Where are Carmel, Gilead, and Galilee? What does the fertile Esdraelon valley form? Of what Hebrew name is Esdraelon a Greek spelling?
4. **1:12.** Where are Moab and Ammon? To what might "two seas" possibly refer?

For application

1. **1:1–4.** The three traditional enemies of the human spirit are the world, the flesh, and the devil. In your experience, which do you think is the most powerful? Which seems most unstoppable? Which causes the most destruction? What defenses can you build against such an enemy?
2. **1:5.** Why do you think Nebuchadnezzar is making war against King Arphaxad? According to CCC 2317, what are some of the reasons why nations wage war, and how can the threat of violence be vanquished? What is the *root cause* of war implied in this explanation?

Chapter 2

For understanding

1. **2:1.** What is the "eighteenth year" referred to in the text? Why might the timing be mentioned? In the Latin Vulgate, when does the king reveal his plans? What is the "first month", and to what does it correspond? What day is Nisan 22?
2. **2:4.** What kind of name is Holofernes? As commander of the Assyrian forces, what will his role be?
3. **2:12.** What kind of formula is "as I live"? How did ancient Jewish readers probably hear Nebuchadnezzar's words? What does the proclamation of Nebuchadnezzar as a god, made explicit later in the book, show about him? What irony lies behind Nebuchadnezzar's reference to his mighty hand?
4. **2:21–28.** With what do these verses deal? Since the itinerary appears to be illogical and obscure at points, what do scholars suspect? How does the Latin Vulgate add to the uncertainty?

For application

1. **2:1–3.** Have you ever felt the urge to retaliate against someone who has interfered with your plans, harshly criticized you, or pointedly ignored you? If so, how long did you spend ruminating on how you would execute your revenge before acting on it?
2. **2:7–11.** In connection with the previous question, how publicly did you speak about your plans to others? What is the purpose of making your threats known in advance of action? How many of these threats did you actually end up carrying out?

Chapter 3

For understanding

1. **3:1–8.** What do the cities mentioned in 2:28 do before the oncoming hordes of Holofernes? How do we know the Ammonites, Moabites, and Idumeans must have done the same? What is the point of this information?
2. **3:7.** What are garlands? Where did the custom of weaving them originate? What do the dances and tambourines signify?
3. **3:8.** What kind of war is Holofernes' military campaign? What is his aim? What are "sacred groves", and with what are they typically associated? What does the language used here recall? On whose initiative is Holofernes acting?
4. **3:9.** Where is Esdraelon? Where is Dothan, and for what is it known?

For application

1. **3:1–4.** Under what circumstances would you surrender, as these cities did, without a fight? Why would you do it? Under what circumstances or according to what values might you fight, even knowing that defeat is all but certain?
2. **3:6–8.** If you were to lead an invading army, how would you attack the base culture of the country you were invading? If you were among the populace being invaded, how far would you allow an attack on your culture to go? How would you resist?

Chapter 4

For understanding

1. **4:4.** Which are some of the sites mentioned in this verse that are otherwise unknown? To what does the mention of Samaria refer? What route runs through the region of Samaria? What is Beth-horon? Where is Jericho? To what is the "valley of Salem" perhaps a reference?

2. **4:6.** Who is Joakim? What does the mention of him as high priest confirm, and what role does he assume? What is Bethulia? Where is the site, and how is it described? Why is it difficult to determine the original Hebrew spelling of the city's name? What ancient town has been suggested for its location?

3. **Word Study: Senate (4:8).** In the Greek translation of the Pentateuch, to what Hebrew term does the Greek word *gerousia* correspond, and to what does that term refer? In the Book of Deuteronomy, with what was this group of magistrates charged? In the postexilic period, what did the council of elders in Jerusalem do, and what had it become by NT times?

4. **4:10.** What is sackcloth, and when would it be worn? What does putting sackcloth on animals recall?

For application

1. **4:1–5.** Read the note for these verses. What is the worst emergency you personally or your family or community has faced? How did you prepare to meet it? What part did prayer play in your preparation?

2. **4:6.** For various reasons or according to need, the Church proclaims days or seasons of prayer and fasting. How do you respond to those proclamations? What is your rationale for deciding to participate or not?

3. **4:9.** What is your practice of fasting? In other words, how often do you fast, and what in your mind constitutes a true fast? What are some of your reasons for fasting (or for avoiding it)?

4. **4:12.** In penitential seasons such as Lent, how does your parish church approach decorating the sanctuary (including the altar, the crucifix, and the ambo)? What changes are made to the colors of cloth, banners, hangings, or other decorations? How do these changes affect your own spirituality?

Chapter 5

For understanding

1. **5:5–21.** What are these verses about? From what perspective is the story told? What determines whether Israel experiences national prosperity or adversity?

2. **5:5.** Who is Achior? What happens to him when he cautions Holofernes against a hasty attack on Israel? What will he later become? Beyond this, what does the name Achior mean, and what does it subtly indicate? According to the Bible, how are the Israelites and Ammonites kinsmen?

3. **5:7.** Where did Abraham and his family move when they left the city of Ur? Though no reason is given in the Book of Genesis for the change of residence, what does an ancient Jewish tradition hold? How does that tradition apply to Achior? Who are "the gods of their fathers"?

4. **5:16.** Who are the Canaanites? Who are the Shechemites? In patriarchal times, what happened to the Shechemites? What does Judith do with this violent episode later in the book?

For application

1. **5:5–21.** According to the note for these verses, Israel's historical fortunes are tied up with its commitment to God and his covenant. With what commitments are *our* national fortunes connected? In what do you think our obedience or disobedience would result?

2. **5:5.** Have you ever had to deliver bad news to a superior or offer advice that you were sure would not please the superior? If so, how did you feel about offering that kind of input? How was it received?

3. **5:21.** Psalm 91 promises that those who abide under the shelter of the Most High will enjoy the Lord's protection. What does the word *abide* mean to you? How sincerely do you trust this promise of divine protection? How willing are you to trust in it?

4. **5:22–24.** If you have opposed the plans of a superior, what support have you had from colleagues? If all of them were against you even though you felt that evidence was on your side, how firmly would you hold to your position despite the potential fallout?

Chapter 6

For understanding

1. **6:2.** Who are the "hirelings" to whom Holofernes refers? What does he mean by "hirelings of Ephraim", and who is he perhaps addressing? How is Holofernes' reference to prophecy an instance of irony? What is the theological claim at the heart of the Book of Judith, and how is it tested?

2. **6:5.** What is the instance of irony in this verse?

3. **6:7.** Where will Holofernes have Achior placed, and why? What will later chapters show of this attempt to refute the laws of the covenant explained in the previous chapter?

4. **6:15.** What does the name Uzziah mean in Hebrew, and how will Judith outshine him? Where did the southern tribe of Simeon inherit towns? Since settlement patterns shifted over the centuries, where else does the Bible speak of Simeonites living, and when?

For application

1. **6:2.** Christians are often criticized, mocked, and even threatened for defending Christian moral teachings. How do you respond to such opposition? How well do you understand Christian moral teachings, and how equipped do you feel to defend them? If someone were to challenge your credentials ("Who are you …?"), how would you reply?

2. **6:5.** Name-calling is a technique (called *ad hominem*) for attacking or dismissing an opponent without having to deal with his position. Have you ever used this technique in an argument, and, if so, why did you resort to it? Has it ever been used on you, and to what effect?

3. **6:19.** How would you apply the prayer in this verse to present-day circumstances? What sorts of arrogance and humiliation do Christians face today? What does it mean to ask God to "look upon the faces" of those who are praying?

Chapter 7

For understanding

1. **7:1–32.** What happens in these verses? What do the warriors do? For what is the stage now set?
2. **7:4.** What do the words of the fearful townsfolk recall about the Israelites in the wilderness?
3. **7:20.** How long does the siege last? How is this figure matched in the second half of the book?
4. **7:28.** What is the truth of the statement that God punishes us according to our sins? How will Judith correct this misperception? To what is the expression "heaven and earth" possibly an allusion in this instance?

For application

1. **7:1–32.** Read the note for these verses. What examples of siege warfare in recent times can you think of? How are they similar to and different from the type of siege being waged in the Book of Judith? What do you think of the morality of this type of warfare?
2. **7:4–5.** Which is more frightening: watching the movement of a powerful enemy into position against you or beginning the actual combat? What is so terrifying about the anticipation of a looming battle?
3. **7:19.** Read the note for this verse. Have you ever reached a "point of extreme desperation" over a problem you have faced? If so, how did your desperation affect your trust that the Lord would hear your prayer?
4. **7:30–31.** Have you ever tried to make an if-then deal with God, as Uzziah is doing in these verses? What was the issue? How spiritually prudent is such deal-making?

Chapter 8

For understanding

1. **8:1.** What does the name Judith mean in Hebrew? For what is she revered? How long is her genealogy? For the author, what does Judith embody? Who was Salamiel, son of Sarasadai? What does that make Judith, like her husband?
2. **8:6.** When was fasting required of an Israelite? When was it practiced more frequently? What makes Judith's commitment to fasting nothing short of heroic? Why was fasting on feast days considered improper?
3. **8:26.** What trials of faith did Abraham face? How did God test Isaac? What did an ancient Jewish tradition about Isaac as a grown man when Abraham bound him for sacrifice imply that Isaac did? Which of Jacob's difficulties in Syrian Mesopotamia are meant?
4. **8:27.** What biblical interpretation of suffering is described here? From this perspective, of what is divine chastisement an expression? How, then, is Judith able to urge city leaders to give thanks in the midst of the present crisis?
5. **8:33.** How many times is reference made to the "hand" of Judith? What does the Hebrew phrase *beyad* ("by the hand of") signal? How is the expression doubly appropriate in her case? What do multiple references to Judith's "hand" bring to mind?

For application

1. **8:1.** What is the narrator's point in listing Judith's ancestry? How much do you know about your own? What benefit would you derive from knowing more about your lineage?
2. **8:4.** Although remarriage is permitted and sometimes encouraged following the death of a spouse (cf. 1 Tim 5:14), some surviving spouses choose to remain single. What are some reasons for this choice? Why is consecrated widowhood better than simply choosing to remain single?
3. **8:12.** What does it mean to "put God to the test"? What is the difference between "putting the Lord to the test" and asking him for a sign suggesting the direction he wants one to go? Why is the first forbidden but the second allowed?
4. **8:25.** Judith encourages the elders to give thanks to God for putting *them* to the test. Why should we be grateful when God tests our faith and perseverance? According to Heb 12:5–7, what are the benefits of divine discipline?

Chapter 9

For understanding

1. **9:1.** Of what are ashes a sign? When and on what is incense burned in the Jerusalem Temple? At what time of day does the evening sacrifice take place? Where else in Scripture are petitions offered at the evening sacrifice, and at what does the practice hint?
2. **9:2.** Why does Judith appeal to the actions of her ancestor Simeon in Gen 34:1–31? What did Simeon and Levi do to the Gentile population of Shechem? What does Judith, who admires her ancestor Simeon, pray for success in doing? As the story unfolds, how will Judith place herself in a position much like that of Dinah, first, and, then, of Simeon?
3. **9:5.** How does the God of Israel show himself the Lord of history?
4. **9:11.** In the OT, who are the lowly? How are they often treated by the wicked? What does the Lord become for them?

For application

1. **9:1.** Why do Catholics (and some other Christians) put ashes on their foreheads on Ash Wednesday? In the formulas used for imposition of the ashes, what does the minister advise us to remember or to do?
2. **9:5.** Read the note for this verse. What is the relation between God's foreknowledge of future events and human free will? Does his knowledge of what I will do determine my will, including my eternal fate?
3. **9:7.** Psalm 46:10 encourages the reader to "be still, and know that I am God"; the context is that God puts a stop to wars. How do you apply this psalm verse to your own struggles? What does the verb "know" in this verse mean for you?
4. **9:11.** The note for this verse defines who "the lowly" are as Scripture uses the term. Who are the lowly of your acquaintance? Would you place yourself among them? How does the picture of "the lowly" presented here accord with "the blessed" in Mt 5:3–12?

Chapter 10

For understanding
1. **10:1–5.** Having made spiritual preparations, what does Judith do? What is her aim? How does every man who encounters her in the following verses react?
2. **10:5.** What kinds of foods did Judith give her maid to take with her? In addition to unclean foods, why did the Israelites avoid other kinds of Gentile foods and wines? Having packed her own meals, what is Judith able politely to do? Who else of the many figures in the OT refused to defile themselves with Gentile foods?
3. **10:12.** What was the term sometimes applied to Israelites by foreigners? What is Judith pretending to be?
4. **10:21.** What is the canopy under which Holofernes is resting? What will it become? What glaring contrast is the reader asked to note?

For application
1. **10:3–4.** The clothes people wear convey messages to others. If you wished to attract others' attention to yourself, what sort of clothing would you select? How would you dress if you did *not* want people to notice you? When you see someone dressed for attendance at Mass in faded or torn clothing, what do you think that person is communicating to others?
2. **10:5.** What limitations do you place on the kinds of food you eat? On the kinds of food you serve? Are there foods that you consider immoral to eat, or at least questionable? How might your diet provide either encouragement or scandal to someone else (cf. 1 Cor 8:9–13)?
3. **10:17–19.** Read the note for this verse. How do industries such as the advertising, entertainment, or fashion industries use female beauty to captivate an audience? For what purposes? What do sexually alluring women have to do with buying goods like automobiles or furniture?

Chapter 11

For understanding
1. **11:1.** Offering words of comfort, of what is the general unaware? What is the irony about Judith? According to St. Ambrose, how does Judith, a good widow, demonstrate bravery?
2. **11:5–19.** How does Judith mislead Holofernes? Since the deliberate use of equivocation makes Judith's speech something of a moral problem, what considerations are relevant to an evaluation of her words? According to St. Thomas Aquinas, what is the real reason Judith is praised by Scripture?
3. **11:12.** While the slaughter of livestock for meat is lawful, what is strictly forbidden about it? Out of desperation, what are the Israelites on the verge of doing?
4. **11:17.** By establishing a nightly routine of exiting the camp for prayer, what is Judith accomplishing?

For application
1. **11:1.** The note for this verse refers to Holofernes' ignorance of how Judith is "playing" him. What kinds of skill does it take to become a good con artist? How would such a person introduce himself to you? How does the devil tend to operate when he tempts?
2. **11:5–19.** The note for these verses presents some important considerations for evaluating the moral use of language. How do you evaluate these considerations? For example, if "Scripture never teaches that God approves of deception as a morally acceptable means of pursuing an honorable goal", does that mean that he explicitly disapproves it? Is it *ever* licit to lie to an enemy in order to save another's life (cf. CCC 2488–89)?
3. **11:13.** What is sacrilege (CCC 2120)? By describing sacrilege as a "grave sin", what is the *Catechism* saying about its seriousness? How sacrilegious is the Israelites' consumption of food that Judith is describing to Holofernes, given their dire circumstances?

Chapter 12

For understanding
1. **12:10.** What is the significance of the fourth day? What does the absence of military personnel indicate that Holofernes is doing relative to Judith's designs?
2. **12:11.** What kind of name is Bagoas? Whom did an advisor of this name serve? What is a eunuch?
3. **Word Study: Deceive (12:16).** What does the Greek verb *apataō* mean? When is speech used as a means of deception in Scripture? When can the term mean "seduce"? In the Book of Judith, how do the verb and its related noun (*apatē*) add to the drama of Judith and Holofernes facing off in a game of wits? How does Judith succeed?

For application
1. **12:2.** If you had medical limitations such as allergies on the kinds of food you could eat and were invited to a banquet, how would you politely decline to eat what was served? What if your reasons were religious rather than medical or hygienic?
2. **12:7.** Why does the priest at Mass wash his hands before consecrating the bread and wine? What prayer does he say? How might ritual actions such as washing highlight the prayers being recited?
3. **12:13.** Notice the delicacy of Bagoas' invitation to Judith to join Holofernes at his banquet. If you were Judith, how would you interpret his meaning, especially as it concerns becoming "like one of the daughters of the Assyrians"? As a serious Christian, how would you take an invitation to join others' revelry so as to be like everyone else?
4. **12:16.** Read the "Word Study" for this verse. In terms of the virtue of chastity, what is the danger of flirting with someone of either sex? Why is it best to avoid even the appearance of flirting?

Chapter 13

For understanding

1. **13:1–20.** What is the climax of the Judith story? Although Judith's action is brutal, what does the author stress about it? According to St. Clement of Rome, how did Judith, made strong by the grace of God, perform her manly deed?
2. **13:6.** To what does the Greek term *akinakēs* refer? What other acts of heroism in the OT does Judith's triumph over Holofernes recall?
3. **13:16.** What kind of formula is "as the Lord lives"? What happens regarding Judith's sexual purity? In the Latin Vulgate, to what does she attribute her protection? According to St. Fulgentius, what powers marched forth to assault the desires of lust and bring about the destruction of pride?
4. **13:18.** What position does Uzziah hold? What other blessings does Uzziah's benediction resemble? What inspired Elizabeth's words to Mary in the Gospel narrative? To whom do these words indicate that Mary's role in salvation history is analogous? What is the difference between Mary's weapon and theirs? According to St. Clement of Alexandria, when did Judith become perfect among women?

For application

1. **13:4–5.** Think of a time when you faced a necessary but unpleasant duty. How did you stir up the willingness to go through with it? What part, if any, did prayer play in your preparation? What would you change about the way you readied yourself?
2. **13:14.** Reflecting on the duty you faced in the previous question, how well did you succeed? How did you feel about it afterward? What part do you think God may have played in your success, and what thanks did you give him for it?
3. **13:16.** From your adolescence until now, how have your own attitudes toward sexual integrity or chastity changed? How important would you say this virtue is to you now? If you had the chance, how would you work to promote chastity in adolescents?
4. **13:18.** Many representations of the Virgin Mary show her with her foot on the head of a serpent. To what does that depiction allude? In terms of importance, how would you rate the roles of Judith and Mary in the salvation of their people, and why?

Chapter 14

For understanding

1. **14:1.** What action described in this verse is a grisly feature of Near Eastern warfare? Like the judge Deborah, of what does Judith take charge?
2. **14:6.** What is Achior, the Ammonite commander handed over to Bethulia, called to do, and why? How is the episode highly ironic?
3. **14:10.** When does Achior come to faith in the God of Israel? How is Achior's conversion sealed? What tension is oftentimes felt between this verse and Deut 23:3? How does that affect the story of Judith, set in the postexilic period? Besides this, what is an example of an exception to the general rule cited in the note?

For application

1. **14:1.** Beheadings, whether accidental or deliberate, still occur and are reported in the news. What is there about a beheading that arouses both horror and fascination in us? Why display the head of a victim?
2. **14:10.** Can you pinpoint a time in your life when you came to believe firmly in God? If so, what happened to seal your conversion? If not, how would you describe your growth toward a personal, living relationship with God?
3. **14:14–18.** Imagine yourself in the place of Bagoas. What would have been your responsibilities to Holofernes? What sort of shock or panic would you feel when you discovered what Judith had done? Since you were responsible for Holofernes' security, how would you regard your failure to protect him? Does his situation compare with any experience in your own life?

Chapter 15

For understanding

1. **15:1–15.** What do the warriors of Israel do to the retreating Assyrians? What is Judith given from the spoils of victory?
2. **15:9.** What was the result of Judith's daring plan? To whom does the benediction here pronounced on Judith apply in the Catholic liturgy?
3. **15:12.** What did the women of Israel traditionally do following a military triumph? What kinds of branches would they wave and when?
4. **15:13.** What does the Greek custom of crowning people with olive wreaths suggest about when the Book of Judith was written or last edited? Where is the parade of celebrants going? What does the event recall?

For application

1. **15:4–5.** The events in these verses imply some sort of swift communication. How quickly would news of the Assyrian rout have traveled throughout what would be the equivalent of modern Palestine? How quickly might news of such a rout travel with our current means of communication?
2. **15:9.** Read the note for this verse. What are some of the reasons this blessing upon Judith is applied to the Blessed Virgin Mary in the Catholic liturgy?
3. **15:12–13.** When might modern peoples engage in dancing and victory parades like those described in these verses? In addition to dancing, what are some other ways for groups to express joy?

Study Questions: Judith

Chapter 16

For understanding
1. **16:1–17.** By what titles does the Song of Judith exalt the God of Israel? What is the main lesson of the Song? What is the primary inspiration behind the Song of Judith, and how is Yahweh described in both? Likewise, what does the mention of God using "the hand" of a woman to save Israel from the Assyrians recall?
2. **16:16.** What is the heart of Israel's faith? In what way do the liturgical rites express fear of the Lord?
3. **16:22.** After the Assyrian crisis passes, what does Judith choose to do? How does she handle her sexual purity for the rest of her life? How usual was consecrated widowhood in biblical Israel? According to St. Fulgentius, what makes it clear that God loves a widow's continence?
4. **16:23.** For what is a long life sometimes a reward? What do scholars who read the Judith story as an allegory of the Maccabean period often point out? Why does an intended allusion to this period seem unlikely?

For application
1. **16:1–2.** Judith praises God using rhythm instruments (tambourines and cymbals). What instruments would you choose if you wanted to "loudly sing" a song of praise? How can musical instruments enhance prayer?
2. **16:14.** How does Judith describe in this verse God's manner of creating? According to the *Catechism* (687–88), how do we come to know the Holy Spirit?
3. **16:16.** Read the note for this verse. If fear of the Lord is the heart of Israel's faith, what place should it hold in Christian faith? How does fear of the Lord contribute to love of the Lord?
4. **16:19.** The note for this verse defines what a "votive offering" is. What kinds of votive offerings do Christians make (e.g., at Lourdes and similar shrines)? What do these offerings express?

INTRODUCTION TO ESTHER

Author and Date The origin of the Book of Esther is somewhat obscure, not least because the book exists in two distinct forms: a shorter version in Hebrew (as found in Jewish and Protestant Bibles) and a longer version in Greek (as found in Catholic and Orthodox Bibles). Both ancient versions are anonymous, although the Greek version cites two royal decrees issued in the name of King Artaxerxes of Persia, one dictated by Haman the Agagite (*13:1–13*), and another by Mordecai the Jew (*16:1–24*). Judging from internal evidence, the author of the (Hebrew) Book of Esther was a Jew from the eastern Diaspora who was familiar with Persian vocabulary, Persian court customs, and the royal palace in the Persian capital of Susa. If the story has its basis in history, it may have come from one of the characters featured in the book, most likely Mordecai. Not only did Mordecai hold an official position in the Persian government, presumably giving him access to royal archives, but he is said to have recorded some of the things that took place in the story (*12:4; 9:20*). Nonetheless, the evidence is too meager to warrant a definitive judgment on who produced the biblical book in its present form.

The date of the Book of Esther is likewise uncertain, although a few parameters can be established. The book cannot have been written before the time of the story itself, which takes place in the first half of the reign of Ahasuerus/Xerxes, king of Persia (485–465 B.C.). On the other hand, the story is known in its Greek form to writers in the first century A.D., such as the Jewish historian Josephus and St. Clement of Rome. It is hard to say when the book was written between these two endpoints, but virtually all scholars agree that the Hebrew version is older than the Greek version. Evidence suggests the Hebrew version originated in the Persian period (fifth or fourth century B.C.), whereas the Greek version appears to come from the Hellenistic period (second or first century B.C.). The librarian's note at *11:1* indicates that the Greek edition of Esther was in circulation by at least 48 B.C. and possibly as early as 114 B.C. For the different versions of Esther, see *Literary Background*.

Title The book is named after its Jewish heroine, Esther. A few scholars have correlated her name with an Old Iranian word meaning "star", but most think it derives from the name of the Babylonian goddess Ishtar. Esther's birth name, Hadassah, means "myrtle" (*2:7*). The title of the book appears as *'Ester* in the Hebrew Bible, as *Esthēr* in the Greek Septuagint, and as *Liber Hesther* in the Latin Vulgate.

Place in the Canon The Book of Esther had a rather mixed reception among ancient Jews and Christians. Esther's inclusion in the Greek OT suggests that it may have been canonical for Greek-speaking Jews outside the land of Israel. At the same time, no copies of the book have been found among the Dead Sea Scrolls, nor did the Qumran community in Judea that produced these scrolls include the Feast of Purim, which is instituted in the Book of Esther, as part of its liturgical calendar. Scholars hypothesize that some Jews may have rejected the book as canonical since the Hebrew version never mentions God and since the Jewish heroine of the story shares a table and a bed with a Gentile king. Nevertheless, Esther was eventually accepted into the Jewish canon of the Bible, where it stands among the *Ketuvim*, or Writings. One likely reason for its acceptance is liturgical usage: from ancient times, Esther was read in synagogues at the yearly Feast of Purim (Mishnah *Megillah* 1, 1).

In early Christian times, Esther was considered non-canonical by a handful of Church Fathers such as St. Athanasius of Alexandria and St. Gregory Nazianzen. Most, however, including St. Cyril of Jerusalem, St. Augustine of Hippo, and St. John of Damascus, accepted it as an inspired book of Scripture. Likewise, Esther is included in the canon of biblical books drawn up at the early synods of Laodicea (A.D. 360), Rome (A.D. 382), and Hippo (A.D. 393). In the Christian OT, Esther is counted as one of the Historical Books.

Structure The Book of Esther is a classic example of artful Jewish storytelling. Emphasis is placed squarely on the plot, with the reader constantly drawn forward by the use of irony and suspense. Fuller development of the characters of Esther and Mordecai is noticeable in the Greek version of the story. The canonical structure of Greek Esther (whose additions are printed in italics) exhibits a concentric design in which key episodes in the first half of the book are mirrored in reverse order in the second half. The story's outer frame consists of *11:2–12* and *10:4–13*, which recount Mordecai's dream and its interpretation. Within this frame, the lavish feast hosted by Ahasuerus in 1:1–20 is matched by the celebratory feast of Purim in 9:16–32. A third point of correspondence is the reversal that takes place between *13:1–7*, the king's edict against the Jews, and *16:1–24*, the king's edict in favor of the Jews. The central segment of the book, which pivots the storyline toward its resolution, consists of the prayers of Mordecai and Esther in

13:8—14:19 and the account of Esther's appeal to the king in *15:1–16*. The book ends with a short postscript about the translation of the book and its arrival in Egypt (*11:1*).

Literary Background Looking at the chapter numbers in the RSV2CE, the Book of Esther appears to be in serious disarray. The reason is because Esther survives in two primary editions, one written in Hebrew, which is ten chapters long, and another in Greek, which is sixteen chapters long. The Greek version is a translation and expansion of the Hebrew version that includes an additional 107 verses not found in the Hebrew text. In the Greek OT, this additional material is placed in its proper chronological place in the story; but when St. Jerome translated the Book of Esther into Latin, he first rendered the Hebrew version in its entirety, and then he grouped the Greek additions together in an appendix at the end of the book, making them chapters 10:4—16:24 in the Vulgate. This is why the RSV2CE appears shuffled out of order: the chapter numbers of the Vulgate are retained, but the additions are restored to their logical place in the story (printed in italics), as in the Greek OT. Other modern translations deal with this differently. The Douay-Rheims follows the order of the Latin Vulgate on which it is based, with the additions lumped together at the very end. The NABRE only uses numbers for the chapters that appear in the Hebrew version, whereas the expansions found in the Greek version are inserted into their proper place in the story and labeled Additions A–F. Regardless of editorial arrangement, Catholic and Eastern Orthodox traditions concur in canonizing the expanded edition of Esther, since this was the form of the book embraced by the early Church.

Literary Genre Since ancient times, both Jews and Christians have read the Book of Esther as a book of history. Modern scholarship, however, is divided over its proper classification. Some continue to read Esther as a historical account that tells us about persons and events of the past, while others classify the book as a form of historical fiction in which an edifying story is given a realistic historical setting (i.e., as a "novella" or "court tale"). The primary reasons given for these respective interpretations may be outlined as follows.

Scholars who read the Book of Esther as *history* make several points to support their position. **(1)** The author of Esther presents his story in the same manner as other historical books of the OT, situating the plot during the reign of a known historical king (Ahasuerus/Xerxes, son of Darius I), in a known historical location (Susa, capital of Persia), and against a known historical backdrop (the eastern Jewish Diaspora). **(2)** The story includes several details that accurately represent ancient Persian practices, e.g., the seven advisor princes in 1:14; the crown placed on the king's horse in 6:8;

the execution of criminals by hanging in 7:10, etc. **(3)** The story abounds with authentic Persian names and includes at least a dozen Persian loanwords, e.g., "nobles" (1:3), "palace" (1:5), "decree" (1:20), "satraps" (3:12), etc. **(4)** The writer claims that the actions of Ahasuerus/Xerxes and Mordecai could be verified by consulting a government logbook called "the Book of the Chronicles of the kings of Media and Persia" (10:2). **(5)** The Greek edition of Esther inserts citations that allegedly come from Persian government edicts (see *13:1–7*; *16:1–24*).

Scholars who read the Book of Esther as *historical fiction* also support their position with critical observations. **(1)** The Esther story has not been independently corroborated by historical sources outside the Bible. Literary and archaeological evidence related to the Persian period appear to know nothing about either Vashti or Esther, the queens featured in the biblical story. Nor has evidence come to light that confirms the crisis at the heart of the book, namely, the government-sponsored decree to wipe out the Jewish population of Persia in the fifth century B.C. **(2)** The biblical account appears to stand in conflict with the testimony of other ancient sources. For instance, the Book of Esther identifies the wife of the Persian king Ahasuerus/Xerxes as Vashti (1:9); but, according to Herodotus, the ancient historian who documented Persia's invasion of Greece in 480 B.C., Xerxes' wife was named "Amestris" (*Histories* 7, 114). **(3)** The author of Esther appears to exaggerate select features of the story as a way of signaling his intention to write fiction. One example appears in 1:1, which asserts that Ahasuerus/Xerxes ruled a vast empire of 127 provinces. The statement is problematic because the Persian Empire, even at its height, ruled over no more than 31 administrative districts called "satrapies".

Given the number of arguments on both sides of the issue, scholars are not likely to reach a consensus on the genre of the Book of Esther anytime soon. Both positions have their strengths and weaknesses, and so both are worthy of serious consideration. Reading Esther as history offers a plausible interpretation of the book, especially in view of its many genuine details relating to Persian court life. Moreover, unless one assumes that ancient readers were ill-equipped to read ancient literature, the longstanding tradition among Jews and Christians of reading Esther as a historical book can be said to favor this position. Reading Esther as historical fiction is likewise a plausible approach to the book, which tells a story that sometimes seems exaggerated and sometimes seems to disagree with ancient sources outside the Bible. In the end, one should keep in mind that the Catholic Church has never officially defined the genre of the book, and so the issue remains open for discussion.

Content and Themes The story of the Book of Esther takes place in the Persian capital of Susa during the reign of King Xerxes I, usually known in English translations as Ahasuerus. At this time, the Jewish people living in the capital and throughout the Persian Empire are a vulnerable minority in the midst of a sometimes hostile majority. Anti-Semitism, common among the Gentiles of the ancient world, is taken to a new extreme when a Persian official named Haman is offended by a Jewish exile named Mordecai (3:1–5) and tricks the king into sanctioning a daylong holocaust to exterminate the Jewish population of Persia (3:6–13; *13:1–7*). The massacre is narrowly averted by the wisdom of Mordecai and the courage of his niece Esther, who recently became the queen (7:9–10; 8:1–8). Not only do the Jews of Persia escape the terrible fate decreed against them, they secure their right to live in peace by acting on a second government decree that allows them to preempt the schemes of their enemies (8:9–12; *16:1–24*). Successful escape from the threat leads to the establishment of a new Jewish holiday, the Feast of Purim, which celebrates the deliverance of the Jewish people from total destruction at the hands of the Persians (9:1–32). The Book of Esther was written to explain the origin of this yearly festival.

Theologically, the story has everything to do with God's Providence. At first glance, this is a curious claim, since the Hebrew text of Esther makes no explicit reference to God or religious matters at all (apart from fasting, 4:16). Still, God is present in a hidden way in the form of happy "coincidences" that ensure the plan to execute Mordecai and his people is not only thwarted but turned against Haman and those who would harm the Jewish people. These are implicitly portrayed as moments of divine intervention. Thus, it is not by chance that Esther becomes queen at this particular time and place in history (4:14); it is not blind fate that positioned Mordecai to learn of assassination plots against the king (*12:1–6*; 2:19–23); nor is it sheer luck that the king has insomnia and is reminded of Mordecai's loyalty on the very night that Haman comes seeking authorization for Mordecai's execution (6:1–11). In these and other passages, the hand of God is the unseen factor that guides the story to its remarkable outcome. The Greek version of Esther makes this implicit theology of divine Providence fully explicit, describing God as the sovereign Lord of history (*13:9, 11*) who steers the course of earthly events toward the fulfillment of his plan (*11:12*).

God's Providence is likewise behind a number of "ironic reversals" that add drama and depth to the story. These are pivotal moments when the tables are turned suddenly in favor of the Jews, while their opponents are confounded and cast down. So, for instance, Vashti, the reigning queen of Persia, is stripped of her crown because she defies an order of the king to appear before him and his guests (1:10–12), while Esther, an orphaned Jewish girl of no account, becomes queen (2:1–17) and is exempted from punishment despite her uninvited appearance in the royal throne room (4:11; *15:1–16*; 5:3–8). The fortunes of Haman and Mordecai are likewise reversed in sudden, unexpected ways. Haman is furious that Mordecai the Jew refuses to honor him with a bow (3:1–5), and so he plans to hang him on the gallows (5:14) and to plunder the property of his fellow Jews (3:13). But just before his plans can take effect, Haman is forced to honor Mordecai, instead (6:7–11); he is hanged on the very gallows prepared for Mordecai (7:9–10); his property is seized by the Persian crown (8:1); and Mordecai is promoted to his place as the king's prime minister (8:2, 15). Most significant of all, the Jewish people, condemned to annihilation, become victors over their enemies (9:1–15) rather than victims of an ethnic slaughter (3:7–13). This reversal appears in two royal edicts, the first dictated by Haman, which calls for the elimination of the Jews (*13:1–7*), and the second dictated by Mordecai, which counteracts the first decree point for point (*16:1–24*).

Divine Providence favoring the Jewish community in exile presupposes the election of Israel in the larger plan of God. This, too, is more implicit than explicit in the book, and yet it underlies the significance of everything that takes place. It is because the Lord has chosen Israel to be his covenant people that he intervenes on their behalf when danger threatens, just as a father rushes to the aid of his children or a husband defends his bride. As the Book of Esther illustrates, God will not allow the nations of the world to wipe out the family of Abraham, for this family is the special instrument God has chosen to restore his blessings to the nations in the age of messianic fulfillment (Gen 22:16–18).

Christian Perspective The New Testament never cites or makes direct reference to the Book of Esther. The clearest allusion is a remark made by Herod Antipas, who echoes the promise of Ahasuerus (5:3, 6; 7:2) by offering a young woman "even half" of his kingdom (Mk 6:23). Theologically, however, one can identify common themes shared by Esther and the books of the NT. For example, God's deliverance of the Jews in Esther anticipates the deliverance of Israel announced in Romans, where Paul insists that, despite the exile of the covenant people among the nations, God has not rejected his people (Rom 11:1) but loves them (Rom 11:28) and desires to save them (Rom 11:26). In later Christian centuries, the Book of Esther was read as a foreshadowing of persecutions against the Church, with Mordecai representing Christ the Savior, Haman signifying the enemies of the gospel, and Esther assuming the role of the Church, or sometimes of the Virgin Mary, the queen who intercedes for the endangered People of God (CCC 489).

OUTLINE OF ESTHER

1. Prologue (*11:2—12:6*)

2. Esther Becomes Queen (1:1—2:23)
    A. The Deposition of Queen Vashti (1:1–22)
    B. The Coronation of Queen Esther (2:1–18)
    C. Mordecai Discovers a Plot (2:19–23)

3. Destruction of the Jews Planned (3:1—5:14 including chaps. *13, 14, 15*)
    A. Destruction of the Jews Is Plotted and Decreed (3:1–13; *13:1–7*; 3:14–15)
    B. Mordecai Convinces Esther to Intercede (4:1–17)
    C. The Prayers of Mordecai and Esther (*13:8—14:19*)
    D. Esther Appears before the King (*15:1–16*; 5:3–8)
    E. Haman Plans to Hang Mordecai (5:9–14)

4. Deliverance of the Jews Accomplished (6:1—9:32 including chap. *16*)
    A. The Rise of Mordecai and the Fall of Haman (6:1—8:2)
    B. Esther Pleads for Her People (8:3–12)
    C. Protection of the Jews Is Decreed (*16:1–24*; 8:13–17)
    D. The Enemies of the Jews Are Destroyed (9:1–15)
    E. The Feast of Purim (9:16–32)

5. Epilogue (10:1–3; *10:4–11:1*)

THE BOOK OF
ESTHER

Mordecai's Dream

11 *²In the second year of the reign of Arta-xerxes the Great, on the first day of Nisan, Mordecai the son of Jair, son of Shimei, son of Kish, of the tribe of Benjamin, had a dream. ³He was a Jew, dwelling in the city of Susa, a great man, serving in the court of the king. ⁴He was one of the captives whom Nebuchadnezzar king of Babylon had brought from Jerusalem with Jeconiah king of Judea. And this was his dream:*

5 Behold, noise[a] and confusion, thunders and earthquake, tumult upon the earth! ⁶And behold, two great dragons came forward, both ready to fight, and they roared terribly. ⁷And at their roaring every nation prepared for war, to fight against the nation of the righteous. ⁸And behold, a day of darkness and gloom, tribulation and distress, affliction and great tumult upon the earth! ⁹And the whole righteous nation was troubled; they feared the evils that threatened them, and were ready to perish. ¹⁰Then

---

11:2—12:6 Also known as Addition A:1–17. For the non-sequential chapter numbers in Esther, see introduction: *Literary Background.*

11:2 the second year: ca. 483 B.C. **Artaxerxes:** The same person as "Ahasuerus" (1:1). See word study: *Ahasuerus* at 1:1. **Nisan:** The first month of ancient Israel's liturgical calendar, originally called Abib (Ex 12:2; Deut 16:1). It corresponds to March–April. **Mordecai:** A Jew from the tribe of Benjamin and a servant in the Persian government. He is the kinsman and adoptive guardian of Esther (2:5–7). His name is derived from Marduk, the chief deity in the Babylonian pantheon. The name *Marduka* appears in several Near Eastern records from Persian antiquity, but it remains unknown whether any of the figures bearing the name can be identified with the biblical Mordecai. Perhaps he was given this non-Jewish name when he entered government service, as in the case of Daniel and his friends in Dan 1:7.

Set in the Persian capital Susa, this story relates how God saved his people from the hands of an enemy, this time in a foreign country. As in the book of Judith, the deliverance is brought about through the instrumentality of a woman. The book gives details for the keeping of the feast of Purim in memory of this deliverance.

[a] Or *voices.*

*11:2: The disarrangement of the chapter and verse order is due to the insertion of the deuterocanonical portions in their logical place in the story of Esther, as narrated in the Greek version from which they are taken. They are printed in italics to enable the reader to recognize them at once.

In the old Vulgate these portions were placed by Jerome immediately after the Hebrew text of Esther, regardless of their logical position, because he himself did not regard them as canonical. Hence they came to be numbered 10:4—16:24. It has been thought best to leave the chapter and verse numbering unchanged in the present edition.

11:3 Susa: The winter capital of the Persian Empire at this time. The city, known in Hebrew as *Shushan*, was built on a fertile plain about 150 miles north of the Persian Gulf (the site of modern Shush in southwest Iran). Nehemiah, who organized the effort to rebuild the walls of Jerusalem after the Babylonian Exile, also served at the court in Susa (Neh 1:1).

11:4 one of the captives: If this refers to Mordecai himself, then he was exiled from Israel during the Babylonian deportation of 597 B.C. (2 Kings 24:10–14). This creates a difficulty, however, since he would be over 100 years old at the time of the story. On the other hand, if the expression refers to Mordecai's great-grandfather Kish, then there is no problem with the chronology. In support of the latter possibility, see note on 2:6. **Jeconiah:** Another name for Jehoiachim, king of Judah (1 Chron 3:16–17; Jer 24:1). **his dream:** A symbolic vision of the drama at the heart of the book. The story will unfold as an apocalyptic struggle between two men, Mordecai and Haman, representing two peoples, Jews and Gentiles. The dream and its interpretation follow the order of prophecy and fulfillment, standing at both ends of the book as prologue (11:5–12) and epilogue (10:4–13). Dreams are often vehicles of divine revelation in the Bible (Gen 37:5–11; 41:15–32; Dan 2:25–45; Mt 1:20–21).

11:6 two great dragons: Later identified as Haman and Mordecai (10:7).

11:7 the nation of the righteous: Israel, the nation chosen by God (10:9) to follow the way of righteousness marked out by the Torah (Deut 6:25).

11:10 God: The Hebrew text of Esther never mentions God or religious matters at all. The Greek text of Esther, however, supplies these references in abundance. **a great river:** Later identified as Esther (10:6).

The Additional Chapters in Greek Esther

Additional Chapters	RSV2CE, Vulgate, etc.		NABRE
Mordecai's Dream	Esther *11:2–12*	=	Esther A:1–11
Mordecai Discovers a Plot	Esther *12:1–6*	=	Esther A:12–17
First Letter of Artaxerxes	Esther *13:1–7*	=	Esther B:1–7
Prayer of Mordecai	Esther *13:8–18*	=	Esther C:1–11
Prayer of Esther	Esther *14:1–19*	=	Esther C:12–30
Esther before the King	Esther *15:1–16*	=	Esther D:1–16
Second Letter of Artaxerxes	Esther *16:1–24*	=	Esther E:1–24
Mordecai's Dream	Esther *10:4–13*	=	Esther F:1–10
Postscript	Esther *11:1*	=	Esther F:11

they cried to God; and from their cry, as though from a tiny spring, there came a great river, with abundant water; ¹¹light came, and the sun rose, and the lowly were exalted and consumed those held in honor.

12 Mordecai saw in this dream what God had determined to do, and after he awoke he had it on his mind and sought all day to understand it in every detail.

Mordecai Discovers a Plot against the King

12 *Now Mordecai took his rest in the courtyard with Gabatha and Tharra, the two eunuchs of the king who kept watch in the courtyard. ²He overheard their conversation and inquired into their purposes, and learned that they were preparing to lay hands upon Artaxerxes the king; and he informed the king concerning them. ³Then the king examined the two eunuchs, and when they confessed they were led to execution. ⁴The king made a permanent record of these things, and Mordecai wrote an account of them. ⁵And the king ordered Mordecai to serve in the court and rewarded him for these things. ⁶But Haman, the son of Hammedatha, a Bougaean, was in great honor with the king, and he sought to injure Mordecai and his people because of the two eunuchs of the king.*

King Ahasuerus Deposes Queen Vashti

1 In the days of Ahas′u-e′rus, the Ahasu-erus who reigned from India to Ethiopia over one hundred and twenty-seven provinces, ²in those days when King Ahas′u-e′rus sat on his royal throne in Susa the capital, ³in the third year of his reign he gave a banquet for all his princes and servants, the army chiefs ᵃ of Persia and Med′ia and the nobles and governors of the provinces being before him, ⁴while he showed the riches of his royal glory and the splendor and pomp of his majesty for many days, a hundred and eighty days. ⁵And when these days were completed, the king gave for all the people present in Susa the capital, both great and small, a banquet lasting for seven days, in the court of the garden of the king's palace. ⁶There were white cotton curtains and blue hangings caught up with cords of fine linen and purple to silver rings ᵇ and marble pillars, and also couches of gold and silver on a mosaic pavement of porphyry, marble, mother-of-pearl and precious stones. ⁷Drinks were served in golden goblets, goblets of different kinds, and the royal wine was lavished according to the bounty of the king. ⁸And drinking was according to the law, no one was compelled; for the king had given orders to all the officials of his palace to do as every man desired. ⁹Queen Vashti also gave a banquet for

---

11:11 light came: Anticipates the miraculous reversal noted in 8:16.

12:1 eunuchs: Royal servants in the Persian government (1:10) having charge of the king's harem of women (2:3, 14).

12:2 overheard: Mordecai discovers a plot against King Ahasuerus/Xerxes. It is uncertain whether *12:1–6* recounts the same event that occurs in the seventh year of the king's reign in the Hebrew text (2:19–23). Many scholars regard the two accounts as two versions of the same episode, the names of the conspirators being similar in both. Others treat them as two different episodes. Eventually, Ahasuerus/Xerxes will be assassinated in the twentieth year of his reign (465 B.C.) in a palace conspiracy headed by his chief bodyguard.

12:6 Haman: The archvillain of the book. *Bougaean:* Meaning uncertain. The Hebrew text calls Haman an "Agagite". See note on 3:1. *sought to injure:* Over time, Haman's desire for revenge will boil over into a murderous hatred for Mordecai and his fellow Jews (3:5).

1:1 India to Ethiopia: The vast dimensions of the Persian Empire achieved by Darius I, the father of Ahasuerus/Xerxes. **provinces:** Persian lands were divided into at least 20 major administrative districts called satrapies. The number 127 is not necessarily in conflict with this fact. Either the author is using hyperbole to enhance the king's claims to greatness, or perhaps the figure includes the many subdistricts within each satrapy. For the use of hyperbole in some of the Bible's historical texts, see note on 1 Kings 3:4.

1:3 the third year: Ca. 482 B.C. **banquet:** The first of several banquet scenes in Esther (1:5, 9; 2:18; 3:15; etc.). Persian kings were known for hosting lavish feasts and drinking parties (Herodotus, *Histories* 1, 126; Xenophon, *Cyropaedia* 8, 8, 10). **Media:** Formerly a neighbor of Persia in ancient Iran but incorporated into the Persian Empire ca. 550 B.C.

1:9 Vashti: Not mentioned outside the Bible. The Greek historian Herodotus names Xerxes' wife "Amestris", although he never calls her a queen (*Histories* 7, 61). Too little information about Ahasuerus/Xerxes survives to insist that the discrepancy between Herodotus and the Bible is irreconcilable, especially since Persian monarchs kept a harem of multiple wives.

WORD STUDY

Ahasuerus (1:1)

'Ahashwerosh (Heb.): The name of the Persian king in the Hebrew text of Esther. It renders an Old Persian term, *Khshayarshan*, meaning "ruler over men". Greek writers reproduce the Hebrew name as *Asouēros* (Ezra 4:6 LXX) and the Persian name as *Xerxēs* (Herodotus, *Histories* 7, 2). The king in question is Xerxes I, ruler of the Persian Empire from 485 to 465 B.C. In the Greek version of Esther, however, his name is given the longer form *Artaxerxēs* (Esther 11:2; 12:2). Despite this expansion of the usual Greek spelling, the reference is still to Ahasuerus/Xerxes, in which case he must not be confused with later Persian kings who bore the name "Artaxerxes" (cf. Ezra 4:7–8; Neh 2:1). Outside the Bible, Ahasuerus/Xerxes is described as a devotee of the Persian deity Ahuramazda and is best remembered for his massive invasion of Greece in 480 B.C., which was extensively documented by the Greek historian Herodotus.

ᵃ Heb *the army.*
ᵇ Or *rods.*

the women in the palace which belonged to King Ahas′u-e′rus.

10 On the seventh day, when the heart of the king was merry with wine, he commanded Mehu′man, Biztha, Harbo′na, Bigtha and Abagtha, Ze′thar and Car′kas, the seven eunuchs who served King Ahas′-u-e′rus as chamberlains, [11]to bring Queen Vashti before the king with her royal crown, in order to show the peoples and the princes her beauty; for she was fair to behold. [12]But Queen Vashti refused to come at the king's command conveyed by the eunuchs. At this the king was enraged, and his anger burned within him.

13 Then the king said to the wise men who knew the times—for this was the king's procedure toward all who were versed in law and judgment, [14]the men next to him being Carshe′na, She′thar, Adma′tha, Tar′shish, Me′res, Marse′na, and Memu′-can, the seven princes of Persia and Med′ia, who saw the king's face, and sat first in the kingdom—: [15]"According to the law, what is to be done to Queen Vashti, because she has not performed the command of King Ahas′u-e′rus conveyed by the eunuchs?" [16]Then Memu′can said in presence of the king and the princes, "Not only to the king has Queen Vashti done wrong, but also to all the princes and all the peoples who are in all the provinces of King Ahas′u-e′rus. [17]For this deed of the queen will be made known to all women, causing them to look with contempt upon their husbands, since they will say, 'King Ahas′u-e′rus commanded Queen Vashti to be brought before him, and she did not come.' [18]This very day the ladies of Persia and Med′ia who have heard of the queen's behavior will be telling it to all the king's princes, and there will be contempt and wrath in plenty. [19]If it please the king, let a royal order go forth from him, and let it be written among the laws of the Persians and the Medes so that it may not be altered, that Vashti is to come no more before King Ahas′u-e′rus; and let the king give her royal position to another who is better

than she. [20]So when the decree made by the king is proclaimed throughout all his kingdom, vast as it is, all women will give honor to their husbands, high and low." [21]This advice pleased the king and the princes, and the king did as Memu′can proposed; [22]he sent letters to all the royal provinces, to every province in its own script and to every people in its own language, that every man be lord in his own house and speak according to the language of his people.

Esther Is Chosen as Queen

2 After these things, when the anger of King Ahas′u-e′rus had abated, he remembered Vashti and what she had done and what had been decreed against her. [2]Then the king's servants who attended him said, "Let beautiful young virgins be sought out for the king. [3]And let the king appoint officers in all the provinces of his kingdom to gather all the beautiful young virgins to the harem in Susa the capital, under custody of Hegai the king's eunuch who is in charge of the women; let their ointments be given them. [4]And let the maiden who pleases the king be queen instead of Vashti." This pleased the king, and he did so.

5 Now there was a Jew in Susa the capital whose name was Mor′decai, the son of Ja′ir, son of Shim′e-i, son of Kish, a Benjaminite, [6]who had been carried away from Jerusalem among the captives carried away with Jeconi′ah king of Judah, whom Nebu-chadnez′zar king of Babylon had carried away. [7]He had brought up Hadas′sah, that is Esther, the daughter of his uncle, for she had neither father nor mother; the maiden was beautiful and lovely, and when her father and her mother died, Mor′-decai adopted her as his own daughter. [8]So when the king's order and his edict were proclaimed, and when many maidens were gathered in Susa the capital in custody of Hegai, Esther also was taken into the king's palace and put in custody of Hegai who had charge of the women. [9]And the maiden pleased him and won his favor; and he quickly

---

1:12 refused to come: The queen rejects the summons to display herself before the men of Susa. Court etiquette normally dictated that the royal women be concealed from the public (Josephus, *Antiquities* 11, 191). Beyond that, Vashti may have refused out of self-respect, perhaps supposing the king was drunk. One Jewish tradition speculates that Vashti was asked to come wearing nothing but her crown (*Targum and Midrash on Esther*).

1:17 known to all women: The sages fear a wave of domestic chaos throughout Persia.

1:19 the laws of the Persians and the Medes: Also mentioned in Dan 6:8, 12, 15. **another who is better:** Vashti's demotion sets the stage for Esther's promotion (2:17). The king's deposition of the queen is not a formal divorce; it simply means that she is bumped down to a lower position in the royal harem.

1:22 its own language: The Persian Empire encompassed an array of peoples who spoke Persian, Akkadian, Elamite, Aramaic, Phoenician, Egyptian, and Greek.

2:1–18 Persia searches for a new queen to replace Vashti. She is found in the young and beautiful Esther, whose Jewish identity is concealed from the king until 7:3–4.

2:5 Mordecai: His second introduction in the Greek version of the book. See note on *11:2*.

2:6 who: The pronoun could refer to Mordecai, indicating that he was taken captive from Jerusalem in 597 B.C., but this would make him over 100 years old at the time of the story. It is also possible on grammatical grounds that the pronoun refers back to Kish, the great-grandfather of Mordecai (2:5). See note on *11:4*. **Jeconiah:** King Jehoiachim.

2:7 Hadassah: Esther's birth name, which in Hebrew means "myrtle" (as in Is 55:13). The name Esther is likely derived from that of Ishtar, the Babylonian goddess of love, and may have been given to her at her coronation as queen of Persia. Esther is a Jewess of the tribe of Benjamin. **his uncle:** Abihail, the father of Esther (2:15).

2:8 was taken: Esther has no choice but to comply with the royal decree.

provided her with her ointments and her portion of food, and with seven chosen maids from the king's palace, and advanced her and her maids to the best place in the harem. [10]Esther had not made known her people or kindred, for Mor'decai had charged her not to make it known. [11]And every day Mor'decai walked in front of the court of the harem, to learn how Esther was and how she fared.

12 Now when the turn came for each maiden to go in to King Ahas'u-e'rus, after being twelve months under the regulations for the women, since this was the regular period of their beautifying, six months with oil of myrrh and six months with spices and ointments for women—[13]when the maiden went in to the king in this way she was given whatever she desired to take with her from the harem to the king's palace. [14]In the evening she went, and in the morning she came back to the second harem in custody of Shaash'gaz the king's eunuch who was in charge of the concubines; she did not go in to the king again, unless the king delighted in her and she was summoned by name.

15 When the turn came for Esther the daughter of Ab'ihail the uncle of Mor'decai, who had adopted her as his own daughter, to go in to the king, she asked for nothing except what Hegai the king's eunuch, who had charge of the women, advised. Now Esther found favor in the eyes of all who saw her. [16]And when Esther was taken to King Ahas'u-e'rus into his royal palace in the tenth month, which is the month of Te'beth, in the seventh year of his reign, [17]the king loved Esther more than all the women, and she found grace and favor in his sight more than all the virgins, so that he set the royal crown on her head and made her queen instead of Vashti. [18]Then the king gave a great banquet to all his princes and servants; it was Esther's banquet. He also granted a remission of taxes[c] to the provinces, and gave gifts with royal liberality.

Mordecai Discovers a Plot

19 When the virgins were gathered together the second time, Mor'decai was sitting at the king's gate. [20]Now Esther had not made known her kindred or her people, as Mor'decai had charged her; for Esther obeyed Mordecai just as when she was brought up by him. [21]And in those days, as Mor'decai was sitting at the king's gate, Bigthan and Te'resh, two of the king's eunuchs, who guarded the threshold, became angry and sought to lay hands on King Ahas'u-e'rus. [22]And this came to the knowledge of Mor'decai, and he told it to Queen Esther, and Esther told the king in the name of Mordecai. [23]When the affair was investigated and found to be so, the men were both hanged on the gallows. And it was recorded in the Book of the Chronicles in the presence of the king.

Haman Seeks to Destroy the Jews

3 After these things King Ahas'u-e'rus promoted Ha'man the Ag'agite, the son of Hammeda'tha,

---

2:10 her people: Concealment of Esther's Jewish identity is central to the drama of later chapters.

2:12 to go in: Suggests that Ahasuerus/Xerxes will select his new queen on the basis of sexual preference. beautifying: The young virgins underwent an entire year of cosmetic preparation before their night with the king.

2:14 the second harem: The women who had already had sexual relations with the king. The first harem consisted of virgins who had not yet been summoned to the royal bedroom (2:3).

2:16 Tebeth: Corresponds to December–January. the seventh year: Ca. 478 B.C., four years after the king deposed Vashti. The prolonged delay is unexplained for the reader of Esther, but Herodotus tells us that Xerxes spent the intervening years abroad in his military campaign against the Greek states.

2:17 the royal crown: Esther becomes the queen and principal wife of Ahasuerus/Xerxes from the seventh (2:16) to the twelfth year of his reign (3:7). Herodotus makes no mention of Esther; however, his account of Xerxes' reign breaks off soon after his return from the Greek campaign in his seventh year.

2:18 a great banquet: Esther's banquet signifies the bliss of Christ's spiritual union with the Church. Those worthy to participate consume, not carnal foods, but a spiritual meal of wisdom and virtue. At this feast, the faithful partake of the sacred mysteries of [the] Lord's Body and Blood as a remedy for salvation (Rabanus Maurus, *Explanation of Esther* 3).

2:19-23 Mordecai foils a plot against the king. It is unclear whether this is the same event as *12:1-6* or whether they are two separate events. See note on *12:2*.

2:19 at the king's gate: May imply that Mordecai was a member of the palace guard (cf. 11:3; 12:1). Archaeology has determined that the royal palace in Susa was encircled by a defensive wall with a massive gate on the east side.

2:23 hanged: Not hung by the neck with a rope and but impaled on a wooden gibbet. In some cases, this was an early form of execution by crucifixion; in others, it was a means of displaying the corpses of victims who had died in some other way. For ancient testimony to this Persian practice, see Herodotus, *Histories* 3, 125, and 3, 159. Book of the Chronicles: A logbook of noteworthy deeds and events in the Persian Empire. Mordecai's role as a loyal informant is recorded in the book but forgotten until 6:1-2.

3:1-13 Haman uses false accusations to procure an edict of genocide against the Jews. His pride offended, he wants to wipe out the entire Jewish population of Persia down to the last woman and child (3:13).

3:1 Haman: Branded "the enemy of the Jews" (3:10). He was introduced in the Greek version already in *12:6*. Agagite: A descendant of the Amalekite king Agag (1 Sam 15:8). • This detail is highly significant from the standpoint of biblical history. Saul of Benjamin, the first king of Israel, was commanded to administer the Lord's judgment on the Amalekites by destroying all the people and their property, including their king, Agag (1 Sam 15:1-23). This was to be an act of just punishment on a people whom God swore to eradicate because they fought against the Israelites at the time of the Exodus (Ex 17:8-16; Deut 25:17-19). Saul, however, disobeyed God's command by sparing Agag's life and by laying hands on the plunder of the Amalekites. For this reason, he was stripped of the kingship. Now, centuries later, Mordecai and Esther will restore honor to their native tribe of Benjamin (2:5-7) by bringing down Haman, a wicked Agagite. And, unlike Saul and his army,

---

[c] Or *a holiday*.

and advanced him and set his seat above all the princes who were with him. [2]And all the king's servants who were at the king's gate bowed down and did obeisance to Ha'man; for the king had so commanded concerning him. But Mor'decai did not bow down or do obeisance. [3]Then the king's servants who were at the king's gate said to Mor'decai, "Why do you transgress the king's command?" [4]And when they spoke to him day after day and he would not listen to them, they told Ha'man, in order to see whether Mor'decai's words would avail; for he had told them that he was a Jew. [5]And when Ha'man saw that Mor'decai did not bow down or do obeisance to him, Ha'man was filled with fury. [6]But he disdained to lay hands on Mor'decai alone. So, as they had made known to him the people of Mordecai, Ha'man sought to destroy all the Jews, the people of Mordecai, throughout the whole kingdom of Ahas'u-e'rus.

[7] In the first month, which is the month of Ni'san, in the twelfth year of King Ahas'u-e'rus, they cast Pur, that is the lot, before Ha'man day after day; and they cast it month after month till the twelfth month, which is the month of Adar'. [8]Then Ha'man said to King Ahas'u-e'rus, "There is a certain people scattered abroad and dispersed among the peoples in all the provinces of your kingdom; their laws are different from those of every other people, and they do not keep the king's laws, so that it is not for the king's profit to tolerate them. [9]If it please the king, let it be decreed that they be destroyed, and I will pay ten thousand talents of silver into the hands of those who have charge of the king's business, that they may put it into the king's treasuries." [10]So the king took his signet ring from his hand and gave it to Ha'man the Ag'agite, the son of Hammeda'tha, the enemy of the Jews. [11]And the king said to Ha'man, "The money is given to you, the people also, to do with them as it seems good to you."

[12]Then the king's secretaries were summoned on the thirteenth day of the first month, and an edict, according to all that Ha'man commanded, was written to the king's satraps and to the governors over all the provinces and to the princes of all the peoples, to every province in its own script and every people in its own language; it was written in the name of King Ahas'u-e'rus and sealed with the king's ring. [13]Letters were sent by couriers to all the king's provinces, to destroy, to slay, and to annihilate all Jews, young and old, women and children, in one day, the thirteenth day of the twelfth month, which is the month of Adar', and to plunder their goods.

The King's Letter

13 *This is a copy of the letter: "The Great King, Artaxerxes, to the rulers of the hundred and twenty-seven provinces from India to Ethiopia and to the governors under them, writes thus:*

2 "Having become ruler of many nations and master of the whole world, not elated with presumption of authority but always acting reasonably and with kindness, I have determined to settle the lives of my subjects in lasting tranquillity and, in order to make my kingdom peaceable and open to travel throughout all its extent, to re-establish the peace which all men desire.

3 "When I asked my counselors how this might be accomplished, Haman, who excels among us in

---

who confiscated the plunder of the Amalekites, the Jews of Persia refuse to lay hands on the spoils of the enemy (9:10, 15, 16), despite being authorized to do so (8:11). **above all the princes:** Haman is made the vizier or prime minister of Persia, second only to the king as the most powerful man in the empire (*13:3; 16:11*).

3:2 did not bow: The Torah does not forbid acts of homage such as bowing. Indeed, it was an attested practice in ancient Israel (Gen 23:7; 1 Sam 24:8; 1 Kings 1:16). The explanation in *13:12–14* is that Mordecai bows to God alone, lest the glory of men be esteemed as equal to the glory of God. Another possible reason for Mordecai's action is that Haman, being an Amalekite descendant of Agag (3:1), is an accursed enemy of Israel (Ex 17:16; Deut 25:17–19). According to one Jewish tradition, Mordecai refused to bow because Haman displayed an idol on his chest (*Targum on Esther*).

3:6 destroy all the Jews: Haman turns a personal insult into an ethnic war. His thirst for vengeance is far out of proportion to the perceived crime—an indication that anti-Semitism was rampant throughout the Gentile world and needed only the smallest excuse to flare up in violent ways.

3:7 Nisan: Corresponds to March–April. See note on *11:2*. **the twelfth year:** Ca. 473 B.C., five years after Esther became queen (2:16–17). **Pur:** Means "lot". See word study: *Pur* at 9:24. **Adar:** Corresponds to February–March.

3:8 the king's laws: Haman misrepresents the Jews and recommends their elimination. It is true that the Jewish people honor their ancestral customs and laws, but the accusation is false that they disregard the civil laws of Persia. The king shows himself irresponsible and naïve in accepting this lie without inquiry into the allegation.

3:9 ten thousand talents: About 375 pounds of silver.

3:10 signet ring: Used to authorize official state documents and edicts in the name of the king (8:8).

3:12 thirteenth day: Two days before the Jewish feast of Passover (Lev 23:5–6).

3:13 by couriers: The Persian postal system fanned out across the Near East as a network of roads, riders, and relay points. **to destroy, to slay, and to annihilate:** Underscores the severity of the catastrophe that is being plotted against the Jews (7:4).

13:1–7 Also known as Addition B:1–7. It purports to be a copy of the government edict that sentences the Jewish population of Persia to death. Haman, the architect behind the letter, paints the Jews as a threat to the unity and stability of the Persian Empire. The edict calls for an ethnic cleansing in the name of peace and voices common Gentile criticisms of Jews that are also known from other ancient sources.

13:1 provinces: The Persian satrapies with their subdistricts. See note on 1:1.

13:3 asked my counselors: The king makes himself appear concerned for his subjects and their welfare. In reality, Haman took the initiative in exposing the Jewish "problem" to the king (3:8–9). ***second place:*** As the vizier or prime minister, Haman outranks every official in the Persian government except the king (3:1–2).

sound judgment, and is distinguished for his un-changing good will and steadfast fidelity, and has attained the second place in the kingdom, ⁴pointed out to us that among all the nations in the world there is scattered a certain hostile people, who have laws contrary to those of every nation and continually disregard the ordinances of the kings, so that the unifying of the kingdom which we honorably intend cannot be brought about. ⁵We understand that this people, and it alone, stands constantly in opposition to all men, perversely following a strange manner of life and laws, and is ill-disposed to our government, doing all the harm they can so that our kingdom may not attain stability.

6 "Therefore we have decreed that those indicated to you in the letters of Haman, who is in charge of affairs and is our second father, shall all, with their wives and children, be utterly destroyed by the sword of their enemies, without pity or mercy, on the fourteenth day of the twelfth month, Adar, of this present year, ⁷so that those who have long been and are now hostile may in one day go down in violence to Hades, and leave our government completely secure and untroubled hereafter."

¹⁴A copy of the document was to be issued as a decree in every province by proclamation to all the peoples to be ready for that day. ¹⁵The couriers went in haste by order of the king, and the decree was issued in Susa the capital. And the king and Ha'man sat down to drink; but the city of Susa was perplexed.

Esther Agrees to Help the Jews

4 When Mor'decai learned all that had been done, Mordecai tore his clothes and put on sackcloth and ashes, and went out into the midst of the city, wailing with a loud and bitter cry; ²he went up to the entrance of the king's gate, for no one might enter the king's gate clothed with sackcloth. ³And in every province, wherever the king's command and

his decree came, there was great mourning among the Jews, with fasting and weeping and lamenting, and most of them lay in sackcloth and ashes.

4 When Esther's maids and her eunuchs came and told her, the queen was deeply distressed; she sent garments to clothe Mor'decai, so that he might take off his sackcloth, but he would not accept them. ⁵Then Esther called for Ha'thach, one of the king's eunuchs, who had been appointed to attend her, and ordered him to go to Mor'decai to learn what this was and why it was. ⁶Ha'thach went out to Mor'decai in the open square of the city in front of the king's gate, ⁷and Mor'decai told him all that had happened to him, and the exact sum of money that Ha'man had promised to pay into the king's treasuries for the destruction of the Jews. ⁸Mor'decai also gave him a copy of the written decree issued in Susa for their destruction, that he might show it to Esther and explain it to her and charge her to go to the king to make supplication to him and entreat him for her people, *"Remembering the days of your lowliness, when you were cared for by me, because Haman, who is next to the king, spoke against us for our destruction. Beseech the Lord and speak to the king concerning us and deliver us from death."* ⁹And Ha'thach went and told Esther what Mor'decai had said. ¹⁰Then Esther spoke to Ha'thach and gave him a message for Mor'decai, saying, ¹¹"All the king's servants and the people of the king's provinces know that if any man or woman goes to the king inside the inner court without being called, there is but one law; all alike are to be put to death, except the one to whom the king holds out the golden scepter that he may live. And I have not been called to come in to the king these thirty days." ¹²And they told Mor'decai what Esther had said. ¹³Then Mor'decai told them to return answer to Esther, "Think not that in the king's palace you will escape any more than all the other Jews. ¹⁴For if you keep silence at

---

13:4 hostile: A baseless accusation.

13:6 those indicated: The Jews are not named in the decree. It is assumed that Gentiles throughout the empire can identify the culprits without difficulty. **the fourteenth day:** It is uncertain why the Greek version of Esther puts the extermination date one day after the Hebrew version of 3:13. Perhaps it is a scribal mistake that was introduced in the course of copying the book by hand. In any case, both the 13th and 14th of Adar were remembered as days of deliverance among the Jews (9:1–15).

13:7 Hades: Greek name for the realm of the dead, known in Hebrew as *She'ol*.

4:1–17 Mordecai pleads with Esther to intervene for the Jewish people by exerting her influence in the Persian court. Pressure is applied with the reminder that Esther owes her life to Mordecai (4:8) as well as a warning that her position as queen will be no protection against an edict of death (4:13–14).

4:1 tore his clothes: A sign of grief and distress (Gen 37:34). **sackcloth and ashes:** Signs of mourning and supplication for God's mercy. Sackcloth was a coarse, hair-spun fabric worn next to the skin (1 Kings 21:27), and ashes were sprinkled on the head (2 Sam 13:19).

4:5 Hathach: A royal servant who carries communications between Mordecai and Esther.

4:7 the exact sum: The ten thousand silver talents mentioned in 3:9.

4:8 Remembering ... death: Italicized in the RSV2CE because these two sentences are found in the Greek version of Esther but not the Hebrew version.

4:11 put to death: No one dared to make an uninvited appearance before the king, since it was a capital crime to violate this security precaution. At his discretion, however, the king could use his royal authority to grant an exemption from the death penalty. Josephus says that men armed with axes stood around the royal throne (*Antiquities* 11, 205). **thirty days:** Esther had not been summoned by Ahasuerus/Xerxes for an entire month, suggesting her favor with the king was at a low point. This small detail adds dramatic tension to the scene.

4:14 from another quarter: God is not explicitly mentioned, but his will to protect Israel is implicit as theological background. **such a time as this:** Mordecai invites Esther to see the hand of God in her unique situation. Has not divine Providence placed her next to the king in view of the crisis that

such a time as this, relief and deliverance will rise for the Jews from another quarter, but you and your father's house will perish. And who knows whether you have not come to the kingdom for such a time as this?" ¹⁵Then Esther told them to reply to Mor′decai, ¹⁶"Go, gather all the Jews to be found in Susa, and hold a fast on my behalf, and neither eat nor drink for three days, night or day. I and my maids will also fast as you do. Then I will go to the king, though it is against the law; and if I perish, I perish." ¹⁷Mor′decai then went away and did everything as Esther had ordered him.

Mordecai's Prayer

[13] 8 Then Mordecai[b] prayed to the Lord, and said: "O God of Abraham, God of Isaac, God of Jacob, blessed are you:

9 "O Lord, Lord, King who rule over all things, for the universe is in your power and there is no one who can oppose you if it is your will to save Israel. ¹⁰For you have made heaven and earth and every wonderful thing under heaven, ¹¹and you are Lord of all, and there is no one who can resist you. ¹²You know all things; ¹³you know, O Lord, that I would have been willing to kiss the soles of Haman's feet to save Israel! ¹⁴But I did not do this, lest I set the glory of man above the glory of God; I will not bow down to any one but you, O Lord, my God. ¹⁵And now, O Lord God and King, God of Abraham, God of Isaac, and God of Jacob, spare your people; for the eyes

of our foes are upon us[c] to annihilate us, and they desire to destroy your inheritance. ¹⁶Do not neglect your portion, which you redeemed for yourself out of the land of Egypt. ¹⁷Hear my prayer, and have mercy upon your inheritance; turn our mourning into feasting, that we may live and sing praise to your name, O Lord; do not destroy the mouth of those who praise you."

18 And all Israel cried out mightily, for their death was before their eyes.

Esther's Prayer

14 And Esther the queen, seized with deathly anxiety, fled to the Lord; ²she took off her splendid apparel and put on the garments of distress and mourning, and instead of costly perfumes she covered her head with ashes and dung, and she utterly humbled her body, and every part that she loved to adorn she covered with her tangled hair. ³And she lay on the earth together with all her maidservants, from morning until evening, and said: "God of Abraham, God of Isaac, and God of Jacob, blessed are you; help me, who am alone and have no helper but you, ⁴for my danger is in my hand. ⁵Ever since I was born I have heard in the tribe of my family that you, O Lord, took Israel out of all the nations, and our fathers from among all their ancestors, for an everlasting inheritance, and that you did for them all that you promised. ⁶And now we have sinned before you, and you have given us

---

now faces her people? If so, his grace will prove sufficient for the task that is set before her (CCC 306–8).

4:16 hold a fast: Fasting is a form of prayerful intercession, a way of beseeching God to intervene favorably in a desperate situation (Ezra 8:21; Dan 9:3; Joel 2:12; Acts 13:2–3). **if I perish:** The heroic moment when Esther summons the courage to risk her own life in order to save her people. Bravery and a spirit of self-sacrifice combine to make her "the reluctant heroine" of the story and not simply its lead actress. • Esther, a woman perfect in faith, put herself in danger in order to rescue the twelve tribes of Israel from perishing. For by fasting and humiliation, she petitioned the all-seeing God, who saw the humility of her soul and delivered the people for whom she confronted danger (St. Clement of Rome, *1 Clement* 55, 6).

13:8–14:19 Also known as Addition C:1–30, which consists of the prayers of Mordecai (*13:8–17*) and Esther (*14:3–19*). Their supplications make explicit in the Greek version what is only implicit in the Hebrew version, namely, that God is the one who will rescue the Jews from the mortal threat that approaches.

13:8–17 The prayer of Mordecai, who appeals to God as the King of the universe and the Redeemer of Israel. His hope for salvation rests on the Lord's all-powerful will (*13:9*), his all-knowing intellect (*13:12*), and his deliverance of Israel in the past (*13:16*) (CCC 268). • Mordecai was persecuted by wicked Haman just as Jesus was persecuted by the rebellious people. By his prayer, Mordecai rescued his people from the power of Haman; by his prayer, Jesus rescued his people from the power of Satan. Mordecai clothed himself with sackcloth and saved Esther and his people from the sword, while Jesus clothed himself with a body and saved

the Church and her children from death (St. Aphrahat, *Demonstrations* 21, 20).

13:14–15 I will not bow: The Greek version of Esther, unlike the Hebrew, makes known the reason behind Mordecai's refusal to show homage to Haman (3:2). **God of Abraham ... Isaac ... Jacob:** Mordecai appeals to God's relationship with the Patriarchs, which includes the promise to make a great nation of their descendants (Gen 12:2; 15:5; 22:17, etc.). Moses did the same at Mount Sinai when it looked as if Israel might be destroyed (Ex 32:9–14).

13:16 you redeemed: A reference to the Exodus from Egypt (Ex 15:13).

14:1–19 The prayer of Esther. Mirroring the prayer of Mordecai, her hope for divine deliverance is based on the knowledge (*14:15*) and power of God (*14:19*) as well as his saving actions in the past (*14:5*). For herself, she asks for the grace of persuasive speech (*14:13*) and the courage to overcome fear (*14:12, 19*). Esther's prayer shows many similarities to that of Daniel (Dan 9:3–19) and Judith (Jud 9:1–14). See note on *13:8–17*. • Esther delivered Israel from the power of the king and the cruelty of his vizier. She alone, afflicted with fasting, held back ten thousand hands, her faith canceling the tyrant's decree. The king she appeased, Haman she restrained, and Israel she preserved by her perfect prayer to God (St. Clement of Alexandria, *Stromata* 4, 19).

14:2 ashes and dung: Take the place of the queen's crown (2:17). Esther is both humbling herself before the Lord and, by removing the royal headpiece, symbolically renouncing human pride (*14:16*).

14:5 tribe of my family: The tribe of Benjamin (2:5–7).

14:6 we have sinned: The reason Esther and her fellow Jews find themselves scattered throughout the Gentile world. Exile as a curse and a punishment for the sins of the nation is a feature of the Deuteronomic covenant (Deut 28:63–68; cf. Dan 9:4–19).

---

[b]Gk *he.*
[c]Gk *for they are looking upon us.*

into the hands of our enemies, [7]because we glorified their gods. You are righteous, O Lord! [8]And now they are not satisfied that we are in bitter slavery, but they have covenanted with their idols [9]to abolish what your mouth has ordained and to destroy your inheritance, to stop the mouths of those who praise you and to quench your altar and the glory of your house, [10]to open the mouths of the nations for the praise of vain idols, and to magnify for ever a mortal king. [11]O Lord, do not surrender your scepter to what has no being; and do not let them mock at our downfall; but turn their plan against themselves, and make an example of the man who began this against us. I have heard from the books of my ancestors that you liberate all those who are pleasing to you, O Lord, until the very end. And now, assist me, who am all alone, and have no one but you, O Lord, my God. Come to my aid, for I am an orphan. [12]Remember, O Lord; make yourself known in this time of our affliction, and give me courage, O King of the gods and Master of all dominion! [13]Put eloquent speech in my mouth before the lion, and turn his heart to hate the man who is fighting against us, so that there may be an end of him and those who agree with him. [14]But save us from the hand of our enemies; turn our mourning into gladness and our affliction into well-being. [15]You have knowledge of all things; and you know that I hate the splendor of the wicked and abhor the bed of the uncircumcised and of any alien. [16]You know my necessity—that I abhor the sign of my proud position, which is upon my head on the days when I appear in public. I abhor it like a menstruous rag, and I do not wear it on the days

when I am at leisure. [17]And your servant has not eaten at Haman's table, and I have not honored the king's feast or drunk the wine of the libations. [18]Your servant has had no joy since the day that I was brought here until now, except in you, O Lord God of Abraham. [19]O God, whose might is over all, hear the voice of the despairing, and save us from the hands of evildoers. And save me from my fear!"

Esther's Invitation to the King and Haman

15 [*]On the third day, when she ended her prayer, she took off the garments in which she had worshiped, and clothed herself in splendid attire. [2]Then, majestically adorned, after invoking the aid of the all-seeing God and Savior, she took her two maids with her, [3]leaning daintily on one, [4]while the other followed carrying her train. [5]She was radiant with perfect beauty, and she looked happy, as if beloved, but her heart was frozen with fear. [6]When she had gone through all the doors, she stood before the king. He was seated on his royal throne, clothed in the full array of his majesty, all covered with gold and precious stones. And he was most terrifying.

7 Lifting his face, flushed with splendor, he looked at her in fierce anger. And the queen faltered, and turned pale and faint, and collapsed upon the head of the maid who went before her. [8]Then God changed the spirit of the king to gentleness, and in alarm he sprang from his throne and took her in his arms until she came to herself. And he comforted her with soothing words, and said to her, [9]"What is it, Esther? I am your brother. Take courage; [10]you shall not die, for our law applies only to the people. [d] Come near."

14:9 abolish what your mouth has ordained: Esther appeals to God's reputation as an additional motive to intervene, as Moses and David did (see Ex 32:12; 1 Sam 17:45). **quench your altar**: Destruction of the covenant people will result in a permanent cessation of worship in the Jerusalem Temple, which resumed after the Babylonian Exile ca. 520 B.C. This is the only mention of Israel's land and sanctuary in the book.

14:13 the lion: Symbol of the king of Persia. **turn his heart to hate the man**: Exactly what happens when the king learns of Haman's treachery in 7:5-10.

14:15 the uncircumcised: A derogatory reference to Gentiles, who are not incorporated by circumcision into the Lord's covenant with Abraham (Gen 17:9-14). Despite the prestige of her position, Esther takes no delight in her marriage to an uncircumcised Persian.

14:16 like a menstruous rag: Menstruation was a cause of ritual impurity for women in Israel (Lev 15:19).

14:17 wine of the libations: I.e., wine offered to a pagan deity in the setting of a meal or religious rite. Esther is careful

to avoid foods connected with idolatry, as were other pious Israelites living in Palestine (Jud 12:1-2) and abroad in the Diaspora (Tob 1:10-11; Dan 1:8; 10:3).

15:1-16 Also known as Addition D:1-16. It is a Greek expansion of the Hebrew version of 5:1-2 and is here printed in its place. The Greek and Hebrew texts coincide from 5:3 to the end of the chapter. The Greek account is the more dramatic, accentuating both the outward splendor and the inward emotions of the characters.

15:1 the third day: I.e., since Esther resolved to plead for the life of her people (4:15-16).

15:2 her two maids: Not mentioned in the Hebrew version.

15:6 she stood before the king: A crime punishable by death (4:11). Beyond this, Esther's bold action points to an antithetical parallel in the book: whereas Vashti incurred the king's wrath by refusing to appear before him when summoned (1:12), Esther risks a far worse fate by approaching the throne unsummoned.

15:7 fierce anger: Recalls the king's reaction in 1:12, hinting that Esther has made a fatal mistake unless the Lord intervenes to save her. **collapsed**: The queen faints, not as a ploy to win sympathy from the king, but because she is overcome with fear and fatigue. Recall that Esther is not only jeopardizing her life (4:11) but has been fasting for three days (4:16).

15:8 God changed the spirit: God is in control of the situation, guiding the course of events to fulfill his purposes. A theology of divine Providence is implicit in the Hebrew version of Esther but is made explicit in the Greek version (CCC 269). See introduction: *Content and Themes*.

---

[d]The meaning of the Greek text of this clause is obscure.

[*]15:1-16: This deuterocanonical passage is a later expansion of the Hebrew text 5:1-2, which is as follows: "On the third day Esther put on her royal robes and stood in the inner court of the king's palace, opposite the king's hall. The king was sitting on his royal throne inside the palace opposite the entrance to the palace; [2]and when the king saw Queen Esther standing in the court, she found favor in his sight and he held out to Esther the golden scepter that was in his hand. Then Esther approached and touched the top of the scepter." Greek and Hebrew rejoin at verse 3.

11 Then he raised the golden scepter and touched it to her neck; ¹²*and he embraced her, and said, "Speak to me."* ¹³*And she said to him, "I saw you, my lord, like an angel of God, and my heart was shaken with fear at your glory.* ¹⁴*For you are wonderful, my lord, and your countenance is full of grace."* ¹⁵*But as she was speaking, she fell fainting.* ¹⁶*And the king was agitated, and all his servants sought to comfort her.*

[5] ³And the king said to her, "What is it, Queen Esther? What is your request? It shall be given you, even to the half of my kingdom." ⁴And Esther said, "If it please the king, let the king and Ha′man come this day to a dinner that I have prepared for the king." ⁵Then said the king, "Bring Ha′man quickly, that we may do as Esther desires." So the king and Ha′man came to the dinner that Esther had prepared. ⁶And as they were drinking wine, the king said to Esther, "What is your petition? It shall be granted you. And what is your request? Even to the half of my kingdom, it shall be fulfilled." ⁷But Esther said, "My petition and my request is: ⁸If I have found favor in the sight of the king, and if it please the king to grant my petition and fulfil my request, let the king and Ha′man come tomorrow^d to the dinner which I will prepare for them, and tomorrow I will do as the king has said."

Haman Plans to Have Mordecai Hanged

9 And Ha′man went out that day joyful and glad of heart. But when Haman saw Mor′decai in the king's gate, that he neither rose nor trembled before him, he was filled with wrath against Mordecai. ¹⁰Nevertheless Ha′man restrained himself, and went home; and he sent and fetched his friends and his wife Ze′resh. ¹¹And Ha′man recounted to them the splendor of his riches, the number of his sons, all the promotions with which the king had honored him, and how he had advanced him above the princes and the servants of the king. ¹²And Ha′man added, "Even Queen Esther let no one come with the king to the banquet she prepared but myself. And tomorrow also I am invited by her together with the king. ¹³Yet all this does me no good, so long as I see Mor′decai the Jew sitting at the king's gate." ¹⁴Then his wife Ze′resh and all his friends said to him, "Let a gallows fifty cubits high be made, and in the morning tell the king to have Mor′decai hanged upon it; then go merrily with the king to the dinner." This counsel pleased Ha′man, and he had the gallows made.

The King Honors Mordecai

6 On that night the king could not sleep; and he gave orders to bring the book of memorable deeds, the chronicles, and they were read before the king. ²And it was found written how Mor′decai had told about Big′thana and Te′resh, two of the king's eunuchs, who guarded the threshold, and who had sought to lay hands upon King Ahas′u-e′rus. ³And the king said, "What honor or dignity has been bestowed on Mor′decai for this?" The king's servants who attended him said, "Nothing has been done for him." ⁴And the king said, "Who is in the court?" Now Ha′man had just entered the outer court of the king's palace to speak to the king about having Mor′decai hanged on the gallows that he had prepared for him. ⁵So the king's servants told him, "Ha′man is there, standing in the court." And the king said, "Let him come in." ⁶So Ha′man came in, and the king said to him, "What shall be done to the man whom the king delights to honor?" And Haman said to himself, "Whom would the king delight to honor more than me?" ⁷And Ha′man said

---

5:3, 6: Mk 6:23.

---

^d Gk: Heb lacks *tomorrow.*

15:11 the golden scepter: Used to exempt a lawbreaker from the death penalty (4:11).

15:13 like an angel of God: A reference to the king's dazzling and dreadful appearance. In other contexts, the simile can suggest innocence (1 Sam 29:9) or wisdom (2 Sam 14:20).

15:16 agitated: In the sense of being "troubled" rather than "annoyed".

5:3 half of my kingdom: A rhetorical expression of generosity not intended literally. The offer is made twice more in the context of a dinner party (5:6; 7:2). • Herod Antipas echoes these words when he solicits a request from the daughter of Herodias in the setting of a banquet (Mk 6:23). Ironically, Esther intervenes to save the Jewish people from death (7:3), whereas Herodias and her daughter request the death of John the Baptist (Mk 6:25).

5:4 to a dinner: An unexpected response, suggesting that Esther's courage is faltering. The invitation intensifies the suspense of the story.

5:8 come tomorrow: A second dinner is planned for the following day. This pair of feasts mirrors the two banquets hosted by Ahasuerus/Xerxes at the beginning of the book (1:2–8) and anticipates the two-day Feast of Purim instituted at the end of the book (9:17–19).

5:10 Zeresh: Haman's wife, whose name means "gold". Haman will not value her as such when he is hanged on the very gallows (7:10) that were built at her prompting (5:14).

5:11 splendor ... promotions: Haman's gloating over his personal wealth and honor, along with his seething hatred for Mordecai, is the prelude to his downfall (Prov 16:18; 29:23).

5:14 fifty cubits high: About 75 feet high. Either the height of the gibbet is exaggerated for dramatic effect, or else it will rise from the top of a solid structure or hilltop. The Persians used gallows for impalement. See note on 2:23.

6:1 could not sleep: The king's insomnia is no mere coincidence but is orchestrated by divine Providence. The Greek version of Esther says explicitly, "the Lord took sleep from the king." **book of memorable deeds:** A logbook of noteworthy deeds and events in the Persian Empire. Mordecai's discovery of a plot to assassinate the king was recorded in this volume (2:19–23).

6:6 more than me?: Haman's ego proves to be his undoing. Presumption that more royal honors are in store for him leads directly to his public humiliation (6:11–12).

to the king, "For the man whom the king delights to honor, [8]let royal robes be brought, which the king has worn, and the horse which the king has ridden, and on whose head a royal crown is set; [9]and let the robes and the horse be handed over to one of the king's most noble princes; let him[e] clothe the man whom the king delights to honor, and let him[e] conduct the man on horseback through the open square of the city, proclaiming before him: 'Thus shall it be done to the man whom the king delights to honor.'" [10]Then the king said to Ha'man, "Make haste, take the robes and the horse, as you have said, and do so to Mor'decai the Jew who sits at the king's gate. Leave out nothing that you have mentioned." [11]So Ha'man took the robes and the horse, and he clothed Mor'decai and made him ride through the open square of the city, proclaiming, "Thus shall it be done to the man whom the king delights to honor."

12 Then Mor'decai returned to the king's gate. But Ha'man hurried to his house, mourning and with his head covered. [13]And Ha'man told his wife Ze'resh and all his friends everything that had befallen him. Then his wise men and his wife Zeresh said to him, "If Mor'decai, before whom you have begun to fall, is of the Jewish people, you will not prevail against him but will surely fall before him."

Haman's Downfall and Mordecai's Advancement

14 While they were yet talking with him, the king's eunuchs arrived and brought Ha'man in haste to the banquet that Esther had prepared.

7 So the king and Ha'man went in to feast with Queen Esther. [2]And on the second day, as they were drinking wine, the king again said to Esther, "What is your petition, Queen Esther? It shall be granted you. And what is your request? Even to the half of my kingdom, it shall be fulfilled." [3]Then Queen Esther answered, "If I have found favor in your sight, O king, and if it please the king, let my life be given me at my petition, and my people at my request. [4]For we are sold, I and my people, to be destroyed, to be slain, and to be annihilated. If we had been sold merely as slaves, men and women, I would have held my peace; for our affliction is not to be compared with the loss to the king." [5]Then King Ahas'u-e'rus said to Queen Esther, "Who is he, and where is he, that would presume to do this?" [6]And Esther said, "A foe and enemy! This wicked Ha'-man!" Then Ha'man was in terror before the king and the queen. [7]And the king rose from the feast in wrath and went into the palace garden; but Ha'man stayed to beg his life from Queen Esther, for he saw that evil was determined against him by the king. [8]And the king returned from the palace garden to the place where they were drinking wine, as Ha'-man was falling on the couch where Esther was; and the king said, "Will he even assault the queen in my presence, in my own house?" As the words left the mouth of the king, they covered Haman's face. [9]Then said Harbo'na, one of the eunuchs in attendance on the king, "Moreover, the gallows which Ha'man has prepared for Mor'decai, whose word saved the king, is standing in Haman's house, fifty cubits high." [10]And the king said, "Hang him on that." So they hanged Ha'man on the gallows which he had prepared for Mor'decai. Then the anger of the king abated.

8 On that day King Ahas'u-e'rus gave to Queen Esther the house of Ha'man, the enemy of the Jews. And Mor'decai came before the king, for

---

7:2: Mk 6:23.

6:8 a royal crown: Persian art depicts horses wearing crowns, making this an authentic historical detail.

6:9 robes ... horse ... proclaiming: Similar to the stately honors bestowed on Joseph as the vizier or prime minister of Egypt in Gen 41:42–43.

6:10 Mordecai the Jew: The statement shows that Ahasuerus/Xerxes is uninformed about the personal quarrel between Haman and Mordecai and further suggests that he remains uncertain about which people Haman's edict dooms to destruction. **Leave out nothing:** It is a bitter but fitting irony that Mordecai refused to honor Haman (3:2) and now Haman is forced to honor Mordecai (6:11).

6:13 you ... will surely fall before him: The Greek version concludes this sentence with the words: "because the living God is with him".

7:1–10 The tension and suspense of earlier chapters finally eases as the queen reveals her ethnic identity (a Jewess, 7:4), exposes the plot to massacre her people (the Jews, 7:4), and unmasks the evil mastermind behind it (Haman, 7:6).

7:2 the second day: The day after Esther hosted her first dinner for the king and Haman (5:4–8). **drinking wine:** Recalls the earlier drinking scene where Queen Vashti aroused the king's wrath (1:10–12). The parallel is not lost on the narrator, who follows the deposition of Vashti and the execution of Haman with a notice that the anger of the king "abated" (2:1; 7:10).

7:4 to be destroyed ... slain ... annihilated: See note on 3:13. **the loss:** Perhaps financial loss is meant.

7:6 This wicked Haman: Exposed as the real enemy of the king.

7:7 went into the palace garden: No reason is given for the king's sudden exit. Perhaps he wished to compose himself or to consider how he should respond to Esther's accusation.

7:8 the couch: A floor cushion used for dining in a reclined position around a short table. **assault the queen:** The king mistakes Haman's pleading for an act of sexual aggression against his wife. **covered Haman's face:** A poetic description of Haman's expression when he realizes he is a condemned man.

7:10 prepared for Mordecai: In a twist of poetic justice, the villain is summarily executed, impaled on the deathtrap of his own making. The gibbet was constructed on the advice of Haman's wife (5:14).

8:1 the house: Haman's estate is turned over to Esther, who entrusts it to Mordecai (8:2). In ancient Persia, the property of a traitor was taken over by the government. **what he was to her:** The king is only now informed that Esther and Mordecai are relatives (2:7).

---

[e] Heb *them*.

Esther had told what he was to her; ²and the king took off his signet ring, which he had taken from Ha′man, and gave it to Mor′decai. And Esther set Mordecai over the house of Haman.

Esther Saves the Jews

3 Then Esther spoke again to the king; she fell at his feet and besought him with tears to avert the evil design of Ha′man the Ag′agite and the plot which he had devised against the Jews. ⁴And the king held out the golden scepter to Esther, ⁵and Esther rose and stood before the king. And she said, "If it please the king, and if I have found favor in his sight, and if the thing seem right before the king, and I be pleasing in his eyes, let an order be written to revoke the letters devised by Ha′man the Ag′agite, the son of Hammeda′tha, which he wrote to destroy the Jews who are in all the provinces of the king. ⁶For how can I endure to see the calamity that is coming to my people? Or how can I endure to see the destruction of my kindred?" ⁷Then King Ahas′u-e′rus said to Queen Esther and to Mor′decai the Jew, "Behold, I have given Esther the house of Ha′man, and they have hanged him on the gallows, because he would lay hands on the Jews. ⁸And you may write as you please with regard to the Jews, in the name of the king, and seal it with the king's ring; for an edict written in the name of the king and sealed with the king's ring cannot be revoked."

9 The king's secretaries were summoned at that time, in the third month, which is the month of Si′van, on the twenty-third day; and an edict was written according to all that Mor′decai commanded concerning the Jews to the satraps and the governors and the princes of the provinces from India to Ethiopia, a hundred and twenty-seven provinces, to every province in its own script and to every people in its own language, and also to the Jews in their script and their language. ¹⁰The writing was in the name of King Ahas′u-e′rus and sealed with the king's ring, and letters were sent by mounted couriers riding on swift horses that were used in the king's service, bred from the royal stud. ¹¹By these the king allowed the Jews who were in every city to gather and defend their lives, to destroy, to slay, and to annihilate any armed force of any people or province that might attack them, with their children and women, and to plunder their goods, ¹²upon one day throughout all the provinces of King Ahas′u-e′rus, on the thirteenth day of the twelfth month, which is the month of Adar′.

The King's Edict

16 *The following is a copy of this letter:*

"The Great King, Artaxerxes, to the rulers of the provinces from India to Ethiopia, one hundred and twenty-seven satrapies, and to those who are loyal to our government, greeting.

2 "The more often they are honored by the too great kindness of their benefactors, the more proud do many men become. ³They not only seek to injure our subjects, but in their inability to stand prosperity they even undertake to scheme against their own benefactors. ⁴They not only take away thankfulness from among men, but, carried away by the boasts of those who know nothing of goodness, they suppose that they will escape the evil-hating justice of God, who always sees everything. ⁵And often many of those who are set in places of authority have been made in part responsible for the shedding of innocent blood, and have been involved in irremediable calamities, by the persuasion of friends who have been entrusted with the administration of public affairs, ⁶when these men by the false trickery of their evil natures beguile the sincere good will of their sovereigns.

7 "What has been wickedly accomplished through the pestilent behavior of those who exercise authority unworthily, can be seen not so much from the more

---

8:2 signet ring: Placed on Mordecai's finger, making him the new prime minister of Persia in place of Haman (3:1, 10). The ring was used to seal official state documents in the name of the king (8:8). Other symbols of his new authority are mentioned in 8:15.

8:4 the golden scepter: May imply that Esther is making a second, uninvited appearance before the king (4:11). Her first audience, though stressful, was successful (15:1–16).

8:6 calamity that is coming: The king's edict of genocide is still in force against the Jewish population of Persia at this point in the story (13:1–7).

8:8 you may write: The "you" is plural in Hebrew, referring to Esther and Mordecai. Once again, the king is content to delegate his responsibility to others for the implementation of government policies (as in 3:10–11). **cannot be revoked:** A decree that is ratified by royal authority becomes a "law of the Medes and the Persians" that cannot be repealed, as stated also in Dan 6:8, 12, 15. This being so, Ahasuerus/Xerxes can do no better than promulgate a second edict to neutralize the effect of the earlier one issued by Haman. Note that the new edict counteracts the old one point for point (compare 8:11–12 with 3:13).

8:9 month of Sivan: Corresponds to May–June.

8:10 mounted couriers: Postmen on horseback made for swift mail delivery. See note on 3:13.

8:11 allowed the Jews: In the Greek version the king permitted the Jews, not only to act in self-defense, but "to observe their own laws".

16:1–24 Also known as Addition E:1–24, which is inserted between 8:12 and 8:13 of the Hebrew account. It purports to be a copy of the government edict that counteracts the prior edict issued by Haman in 13:1–7. Unlike the first letter, which contends that Jews pose a serious danger to the civil and social order, the second extols the benefits that the Jewish community brings to society.

16:1 our: The king speaks throughout the letter in the first person plural, an idiom known as "the royal we".

16:2–6 Power easily corrupts persons in high position, so that they take advantage of their subordinates and sometimes even their superiors. Ahasuerus/Xerxes learns this the hard way: no sooner does he promote Haman to the office of prime minister (3:1) than he is deceived and manipulated by him (3:8–11).

16:6 trickery: The king's attempt to duck responsibility for the planned massacre of Jews.

16:7 ancient records: Accounts of court intrigue fill the annals of Near Eastern history.

ancient records which we hand on as from investigation of matters close at hand. [8]For the future we will take care to render our kingdom quiet and peaceable for all men, [9]by changing our methods and always judging what comes before our eyes with more equitable consideration. [10]For Haman, the son of Hammedatha, a Macedonian (really an alien to the Persian blood, and quite devoid of our kindliness), having become our guest, [11]so far enjoyed the good will that we have for every nation that he was called our father and was continually bowed down to by all as the person second to the royal throne. [12]But, unable to restrain his arrogance, he undertook to deprive us of our kingdom and our life, [13]and with intricate craft and deceit asked for the destruction of Mordecai, our savior and perpetual benefactor, and of Esther, the blameless partner of our kingdom, together with their whole nation. [14]He thought that in this way he would find us undefended and would transfer the kingdom of the Persians to the Macedonians.

15 "But we find that the Jews, who were consigned to annihilation by this thrice accursed man, are not evildoers but are governed by most righteous laws [16]and are sons of the Most High, the most mighty living God, who has directed the kingdom both for us and for our fathers in the most excellent order.

17 "You will therefore do well not to put in execution the letters sent by Haman the son of Hammedatha, [18]because the man himself who did these things has been hanged at the gate of Susa, with all his household. For God, who rules over all things, has speedily inflicted on him the punishment he deserved.

19 "Therefore post a copy of this letter publicly in every place, and permit the Jews to live under their own laws. [20]And give them reinforcements, so that on the thirteenth day of the twelfth month, Adar, on that very day they may defend themselves against those who attack them at the time of their affliction. [21]For God, who rules over all things, has made this day to be a joy to his chosen people instead of a day of destruction for them.

22 "Therefore you shall observe this with all good cheer as a notable day among your commemorative festivals, [23]so that both now and hereafter it may mean salvation for us and the loyal Persians, but that for those who plot against us it may be a reminder of destruction.

24 "Every city and country, without exception, which does not act accordingly, shall be destroyed in wrath with spear and fire. It shall be made not only impassable for men, but also most hateful for all time to beasts and birds."

[13]A copy of what was written was to be issued as a decree in every province, and by proclamation to all peoples, and the Jews were to be ready on that day to avenge themselves upon their enemies. [14]So the couriers, mounted on their swift horses that were used in the king's service, rode out in haste, urged by the king's command; and the decree was issued in Susa the capital.

15 Then Mor'decai went out from the presence of the king in royal robes of blue and white, with a great golden crown and a mantle of fine linen and purple, while the city of Susa shouted and rejoiced. [16]The Jews had light and gladness and joy and honor. [17]And in every province and in every city, wherever the king's command and his edict came, there was gladness and joy among the Jews, a feast and a holiday. And many from the peoples of the country declared themselves Jews, for the fear of the Jews had fallen upon them.

The Destruction of the Enemies of the Jews

9 Now in the twelfth month, which is the month of Adar', on the thirteenth day of the same, when the king's command and edict were about to be

---

16:9 changing our methods: In view of Haman's treachery, the king resolves to exercise tighter control over Persian policy making in the future.

16:10 Macedonian: A derogatory slur. The Macedonians lived in northern Greece and were the hated enemies of the Persians. Ironically, the Persians not only failed to subjugate the Greeks in the early fifth century B.C., but the Greeks succeeded the Persians as rulers of the eastern Mediterranean in the fourth century B.C. with the conquests of Alexander the Great, history's most famous Macedonian.

16:11 father ... second: The title and position of the Persian prime minister (3:1).

16:13 our savior: Twice we are told that Mordecai saved the king from a plot against his life, once in *12:1-6* and again in *2:19-23*.

16:15 most righteous laws: The commandments of the Torah (Deut 4:5-8; CCC 1963).

16:16 sons of the Most High: The children of Israel are the children of God by virtue of the Mosaic covenant (Deut 14:1). See essay: *What Is a Covenant?* at Deut 5. **mighty living God:** Ahasuerus/Xerxes is not the first Gentile king to acknowledge the God of Israel (see Ezra 1:2; Dan 2:47; 3:28-29).

16:17 not to put in execution: The king cannot revoke his previous decree (8:8), but he can discourage his subjects from implementing it and allow the Jews to defend themselves.

16:20 reinforcements: Local officials are asked to aid and equip the Jewish people in their fight for survival (9:3). **the thirteenth day:** The day that Haman's edict for the empire-wide massacre of the Jews goes into effect (3:13). **Adar:** Corresponds to February–March.

16:22 a notable day: The king hopes that Adar 13 will become, not only a religious holiday among the Jews, but also a civil holiday celebrated by "loyal Persians" (16:23).

8:15 royal robes: Mordecai is dressed as the new prime minister (8:2). His clothing has similarities to the vestments worn by Israel's high priest (Ex 28:4-39). The blue and white robes, mantle of fine linen and purple wool evoke the king's lavish décor in 1:6.

8:17 declared themselves Jews: The Greek version is more explicit, stating that "many of the Gentiles were circumcised and adopted a Jewish way of life."

9:1-15 On the 13th of Adar, the day scheduled for doom, the Jewish people of Persia turn the tables on their enemies. This is the final and climactic reversal of the storyline: just as the de-crowning of Vashti made way for the coronation

executed, on the very day when the enemies of the Jews hoped to get the mastery over them, but which had been changed to a day when the Jews should get the mastery over their foes, ²the Jews gathered in their cities throughout all the provinces of King Ahas′u-e′rus to lay hands on such as sought their hurt. And no one could make a stand against them, for the fear of them had fallen upon all peoples. ³All the princes of the provinces and the satraps and the governors and the royal officials also helped the Jews, for the fear of Mor′decai had fallen upon them. ⁴For Mor′decai was great in the king's house, and his fame spread throughout all the provinces; for the man Mordecai grew more and more powerful. ⁵So the Jews struck all their enemies with the sword, slaughtering, and destroying them, and did as they pleased to those who hated them. ⁶In Susa the capital itself the Jews slew and destroyed five hundred men, ⁷and also slew Par-shan-da′tha and Dalphon and Aspa′tha ⁸and Pora′tha and Ada′lia and Arida′tha ⁹and Parmash′ta and Ar′isai and Ar′-idai and Vaiza′tha, ¹⁰the ten sons of Ha′man the son of Hammeda′tha, the enemy of the Jews; but they laid no hand on the plunder.

11 That very day the number of those slain in Susa the capital was reported to the king. ¹²And the king said to Queen Esther, "In Susa the capital the Jews have slain five hundred men and also the ten sons of Ha′man. What then have they done in the rest of the king's provinces! Now what is your petition? It shall be granted you. And what further is your request? It shall be fulfilled." ¹³And Esther said, "If it please the king, let the Jews who are in Susa be allowed tomorrow also to do according to this day's edict. And let the ten sons of Ha′man be hanged on the gallows." ¹⁴So the king commanded this to be done; a decree was issued in Susa, and the ten sons of Ha′man were hanged. ¹⁵The Jews who were in Susa gathered also on the fourteenth day of the month of Adar′ and they slew three hundred men in Susa; but they laid no hands on the plunder.

The Feast of Purim Inaugurated

16 Now the other Jews who were in the king's provinces also gathered to defend their lives, and got relief from their enemies, and slew seventy-five thousand of those who hated them; but they laid no hands on the plunder. ¹⁷This was on the thirteenth day of the month of Adar′, and on the fourteenth day they rested and made that a day of feasting and gladness. ¹⁸But the Jews who were in Susa gathered on the thirteenth day and on the fourteenth, and rested on the fifteenth day, making that a day of feasting and gladness. ¹⁹Therefore the Jews of the villages, who live in the open towns, hold the fourteenth day of the month of Adar′ as a day for gladness and feasting and holiday-making, and a day on which they send choice portions to one another.

20 And Mor′decai recorded these things, and sent letters to all the Jews who were in all the provinces of King Ahas′u-e′rus, both near and far, ²¹enjoining them that they should keep the fourteenth day of the month Adar′ and also the fifteenth day of the same, year by year, ²²as the days on which the Jews got relief from their enemies, and as the month that had been turned for them from sorrow into gladness and from mourning into a holiday; that they should make them days of feasting and gladness, days for sending choice portions to one another and gifts to the poor.

23 So the Jews undertook to do as they had begun, and as Mor′decai had written to them. ²⁴For Ha′man the Ag′agite, the son of Hammeda′tha, the enemy of all the Jews, had plotted against the Jews to destroy them, and had cast Pur, that is the lot, to crush and destroy them; ²⁵but when Esther came before the king, he gave orders in writing that his wicked plot which he had devised against the Jews should come upon his own head, and that he and his sons should be hanged on the gallows. ²⁶Therefore they called these days Purim, after the term Pur. And therefore, because of all that was written in this letter, and of what they had faced in this matter, and of what had befallen them, ²⁷the Jews ordained and took it upon

of Esther and the fall of Haman prepared for the rise of Mordecai, so the defeat of anti-Jewish Gentiles leads to the founding of a new Jewish holiday. • When the whole of Israel was about to perish, the blessed Esther prevailed over the anger of the tyrant by fasting and praying. By faith, she turned her people's ruin into feast days for Israel, for they used to celebrate a feast when an enemy was slain and Israel was delivered from conspiracy. Now [= at Easter] the devil is slain, that tyrant who opposes the whole world, and so our feast relates not merely to history but to eternity. It is not merely a shadow or a type but the reality (St. Athanasius, *Festal Letters* 4).

9:3 princes ... satraps ... governors ... officials: Help comes to the Jews of Persia even from government authorities.

9:10 ten sons of Haman: The elimination of Haman's legacy is complete with the death of his male offspring. **plunder:** Permission was given the Jewish fighters to seize the goods of the slain (8:11), but they refrained (9:15–16). For a possible explanation, see note on 3:1.

9:13 tomorrow also: Extending the conflict in the capital for a second day explains why the Feast of Purim became a two-day event (9:21). **hanged:** A public impalement of the corpses is meant. See note on 2:23.

9:16–28 The Feast of Purim is established as a holiday celebrated by feasting, exchanging gifts, and giving alms to the poor (9:19, 22). No prayers or liturgical rites are prescribed in the story, although eventually God's deliverance of the Jews came to be celebrated by the annual reading of the Book of Esther in the synagogue. Fixing the precise dates of the feast (Adar 14th and 15th) and making their observance mandatory mean that Purim is being added to the Mosaic festal calendar delineated in Lev 23:4–44. In later Judaism, extending into modern times, the festival came to involve heavy drinking (Babylonian Talmud, *Megillah* 7b).

9:16 seventy-five thousand: The Greek version gives the number of the slain as 15,000.

9:20 sent letters: Mordecai mandates the celebration of Purim. Perhaps this explains why the first day of the feast was known in ancient times as "Mordecai's day" (2 Mac 15:36).

9:27 all who joined them: Converts to Judaism are invited to participate in the festivities of Purim (8:17).

themselves and their descendants and all who joined them, that without fail they would keep these two days according to what was written and at the time appointed every year, ²⁸that these days should be remembered and kept throughout every generation, in every family, province, and city, and that these days of Purim should never fall into disuse among the Jews, nor should the commemoration of these days cease among their descendants.

29 Then Queen Esther, the daughter of Ab'ihail, and Mor'decai the Jew gave full written authority, confirming this second letter about Purim. ³⁰Letters were sent to all the Jews, to the hundred and twenty-seven provinces of the kingdom of Ahas'u-e'rus, in words of peace and truth, ³¹that these days of Purim should be observed at their appointed seasons, as Mor'decai the Jew and Queen Esther enjoined upon the Jews, and as they had laid down for themselves and for their descendants, with regard to their fasts and their lamenting. ³²The command of Queen Esther fixed these practices of Purim, and it was recorded in writing.

Mordecai's Dream Fulfilled

10 King Ahas'u-e'rus laid tribute on the land and on the coastlands of the sea. ²And all the acts of his power and might, and the full account of the high honor of Mor'decai, to which the king advanced him, are they not written in the Book of the Chronicles of the kings of Med'ia and Persia?

³For Mor'decai the Jew was next in rank to King Ahas'u-e'rus, and he was great among the Jews and popular with the multitude of his brethren, for he sought the welfare of his people and spoke peace to all his people.

10 ⁴And Mordecai said, "These things have come from God. ⁵For I remember the dream that I had concerning these matters, and none of them has failed to be fulfilled. ⁶The tiny spring which became a river, and there was light and the sun and abundant water—the river is Esther, whom the king married and made queen. ⁷The two dragons are Haman and myself. ⁸The nations are those that gathered to destroy the name of the Jews. ⁹And my nation, this is Israel, who cried out to God and were saved. The Lord has saved his people; the Lord has delivered us from all these evils; God has done great signs and wonders, which have not occurred among the nations. ¹⁰For this purpose he made two lots, one for the people of God and one for all the nations. ¹¹And these two lots came to the hour and moment and day of decision before God and among all the nations. ¹²And God remembered his people and vindicated his inheritance. ¹³So they will observe these days in the month of Adar, on the fourteenth and fifteenth of that month, with an assembly and joy and gladness before God, from generation to generation for ever among his people Israel."

9:31 fasts: The Hebrew is open to interpretation. The text may be referring to other Jewish feast days that involve fasting; or it may mean that fasting is made part of the observance of Purim itself. In later Judaism, a fast came to be observed on Adar 13th, the day *before* the Feast of Purim; it is known today as "the Fast of Esther".

10:2 Book of the Chronicles: It was common practice in Near Eastern kingdoms to keep an official record of events, dates, and statistics related to the administration of the empire (cf. 2:23; 6:1; 1 Kings 14:19; 2 Chron 25:26). The author here claims that a government logbook was kept in Persia that gave a more complete account of Ahasuerus/Xerxes' kingship as well as Mordecai's tenure as prime minister. If historical, the registry has not survived.

10:3 all his people: The final words of the Hebrew version of Esther.

10:4—11:1 Also known as Addition F:1–11. Structurally, Mordecai's dream constitutes the outer frame of the Esther story, serving as its introduction and conclusion.

10:4–12 Mordecai's dream in *11:2–12* is interpreted as a prophecy now fulfilled. He learns that God is primarily responsible for orchestrating the successful outcome of the Esther story. The belief that Israel is a nation set apart for God's purposes and placed under his protection is likewise reinforced.

10:9 signs and wonders: An expression used often in the Bible to describe the miracles of the Exodus (Ex 7:3; Deut 6:22; 26:8).

WORD STUDY

Pur (9:24)

pur (Heb.): represents the word *pūru*, meaning "lot" in the Babylonian dialect of Akkadian. The author of Esther gives its Hebrew equivalent as *haggoral*, which translates "the lot" (9:24). In Babylon as in Israel, a lot was a marked object that was cast like a die to make decisions on important matters (Prov 18:18; Is 34:17; Jon 1:7). In the Book of Esther, Haman casts a lot to determine when the Jews of the empire are to be slaughtered (Esther 3:7). Because the Jewish people became victors rather than victims on this fateful day, they commemorated it as the Feast of Purim or "Lots" (9:26). The Greek version of Esther adds another layer of significance to the feast. In addition to the lot cast by Haman, which determined the day of the massacre, Mordecai learned in a dream that the Lord made two lots, one for the Jews and another for the Gentiles, and these determined in advance that God would deliver his covenant people from Haman's decree of destruction (Esther *10:9–13*).

Postscript

11 [1]*In the fourth year of the reign of Ptolemy and Cleopatra, Dositheus, who said that he was a priest and a Levite,* [e] *and Ptolemy his son brought to Egypt* [f] *the preceding Letter of Purim, which they said was genuine and had been translated by Lysimachus the son of Ptolemy, one of the residents of Jerusalem.*

11:1 The final verse is a librarian's note, known as a colophon, that identifies (1) when the Greek version of Esther came to Egypt (**the fourth year ... of Ptolemy**), (2) the person who brought it there (**Dositheus**), and (3) the person who translated it in Israel (**Lysimachus ... of Jerusalem**). Establishing the date of the colophon, however, depends on the identity of the royal couple in question. This is not easily determined, as several kings named Ptolemy ruled in Hellenistic Egypt and had wives named Cleopatra (e.g., Ptolemy VIII, whose fourth year was ca. 114 B.C.; Ptolemy XII, whose fourth year was ca. 77 B.C.; and Ptolemy XIV, whose fourth year was ca. 48 B.C.).

---

[e] Or *priest, and Levitas.*
[f] Cn: Gk *brought in.*

Study Questions
Esther

Chapters 11–12 (italic)

For understanding
1. ***11:2.*** Around which year does the narrative begin? Which month of ancient Israel's liturgical calendar is Nisan, and to what does it correspond? Who is Mordecai? From what is his name derived? Why was he perhaps given this non-Jewish name?
2. ***11:3.*** What was Susa? Where was the city built? What other OT figure also served at the court in Susa?
3. ***11:4.*** If the expression "one of the captives" refers to Mordecai himself, when was he exiled from Israel, and what difficulty does it create for the story? On the other hand, how would the problem of chronology be resolved? What is Mordecai's dream? In what form will the story unfold? According to what order does the dream and its interpretation stand at both ends of the story as prologue and epilogue?

For application
1. ***11:5–11.*** How well do you remember your dreams? What importance do you give them, or what meaning have they had for you?
2. ***11:12.*** What, if anything, have your dreams revealed to you about yourself? Do you think any of them may have come from God? If so, for what purpose?
3. ***12:2.*** Some crimes, such as child abuse, legally oblige others to report them to the authorities; other acts of wrongdoing are left to the conscience of the witness. If you were aware of either type of wrong, what considerations would lead you to reveal it to an authority? What fears might prevent you from reporting it?

Chapter 1

For understanding
1. **Word Study: Ahasuerus (1:1).** What is the name of the Persian king in the Hebrew text of Esther, and what Old Persian term does it render? How do Greek writers reproduce both the Hebrew and the Persian name? Who is the king in question? In the Greek version of Esther, how is his name given, and with which Persian kings must he not be confused? Outside the Bible, how is Ahasuerus/Xerxes described?
2. **1:1.** Who achieved the vast dimensions of the Persian Empire? Into how many administrative districts were Persian lands divided, and what were they called? Why is the number 127 not necessarily in conflict with this fact?
3. **1:9.** Where outside the Bible is Vashti mentioned? Who does the Greek historian Herodotus name as Xerxes' wife? Why might the discrepancy between Herodotus and the Bible not be irreconcilable?
4. **1:12.** What does Queen Vashti refuse to do? What did court etiquette normally dictate about royal women? Beyond that, why may Vashti have refused to come? What does one Jewish tradition speculate about her motive?

For application
1. **1:7–8.** Have you ever been invited to a party at which you were "expected" to be present? What moral difficulty if any did this expectation create for you? What did you decide to do, and how did you feel about it afterward?
2. **1:10–12.** The note for v. 12 gives some reasons why Queen Vashti refused to come at the king's command. What choice would she normally have had when the king summoned her? What consideration have you given to the way our society treats women? How have the Church's attitudes toward women changed over the centuries?
3. **1:16–22.** St. Paul's description of the relations between husband and wife in Eph 5:21–30 has provoked much discussion in our era. How do you understand the passage? What is the Church's interpretation of it (CCC 1612–16, 2204–6)? If you are married, how does it apply to your marriage?

Chapter 2

For understanding
1. **2:7.** What is Esther's birth name, and what does it mean in Hebrew? From what is the name Esther likely derived? As a Jewess, to which tribe does she belong? Who is Esther's father?
2. **2:16.** To what does the month of Tebeth correspond? When is the "seventh year"? What explains the prolonged delay?
3. **2:17.** During what period does Esther become the queen and principal wife of Ahasuerus/Xerxes? Though Herodotus makes no mention of Esther, when does his account of Xerxes' reign break off?
4. **2:23.** To what practice does the term "hanged" refer? Of what was it an early form, and for what was it used? What is the Book of the Chronicles?

For application
1. **2:1–4.** What are your standards of beauty in a person of the other sex? What should physical beauty suggest to you about the quality of the person? How do you ordinarily assess the moral attributes of someone you have just met?
2. **2:7.** If you have ever named a person, on what basis did you choose the name (or names)? What did the name mean to you? What do you think the name means to God, since he knows that person by name (cf. Ex 33:17; Is 45:4; 2 Tim 2:19)?
3. **2:10.** At certain times in history, concealing one's ethnic identity has been a matter of life and death. If you or an ancestor changed your surname, what was the reason for the change? Of what in your ethnic background are you most ashamed? Of what are you most proud?
4. **2:18.** Read the note for this verse. What is it about a banquet that would suggest a comparison with heaven? How might you relate that comparison with your experience of the Mass?

Chapter 3

For understanding
1. **3:1.** How is Haman branded, and when was he introduced into the story? What is an Agagite? How is this detail highly significant from the standpoint of biblical history, as it refers both to King Saul and to Mordecai and Esther? What is Haman's position in the empire?
2. **3:2.** What does the Torah say about acts of homage such as bowing? What are two possible explanations for Mordecai's conduct? According to one Jewish tradition, why did Mordecai refuse to bow?
3. **3:6.** What does Haman do with a personal insult? What does the fact that his thirst for vengeance is far out of proportion to the perceived crime indicate?
4. **3:8.** How does Haman misrepresent the Jews so as to recommend their elimination? How does the king show himself irresponsible and naïve?

For application
1. **3:2.** Among the ecclesial, military, corporate, or other groups with whom you associate, what are the protocols or standards of etiquette for greeting or addressing leaders such as clergy, officers, or executives? Do you know anyone who resists them, and, if so, why do they? How do you explain your own conformity or dissent?
2. **3:5.** How strict are the protocols mentioned in the previous question? How are violations of the protocols treated? How do you want others, such as children or strangers, to address you in public? How would you take it if they ignored your wish?
3. **3:7.** What is stereotyping? How would you recognize it if someone held a stereotypical view of certain ethnic or racial groups? What stereotypes do you acknowledge having about any such groups?
4. **3:8–13.** Over the history of your country, when has the government taken steps to relocate, remove, or eliminate an ethnic group? What were some of the official reasons given for these actions? How are such actions viewed today? What attempts, if any, has the government taken to remedy or provide reparation for them?

Chapter 13 (italic)

For understanding
1. *13:1–7.* What does this addition purport to be? How does Haman, the architect behind the letter, paint the Jews? For what does the edict call, and to what does it give voice?
2. *13:6.* Why are the Jews not named in the decree? Why does the Greek version of Esther put the extermination date one day after the Hebrew version of 3:13? In any case, how are both the 13th and 14th of Adar remembered among the Jews?

For application
1. *13:1–7.* The note for these verses uses the term "ethnic cleansing". As a euphemism, what does it really mean? What instances of ethnic cleansing can you recall from recent world history?
2. *13:4–7.* What is an innuendo? What advantage does the government see in not naming the group being targeted? Considering the size of the empire (India to Ethiopia), what guarantee is there that only Jews would be targeted? Given the vagueness of the decree, how likely is the desired outcome in v. 7 to be realized?

Chapters 3–4

For understanding
1. **4:1–17.** What does Mordecai plead with Esther to do? How is pressure applied to her?
2. **4:11.** Why did no one dare to make an uninvited appearance before the king? At his discretion, however, what could the king do? Who does Josephus say stood around the royal throne? What does the fact that Esther has not been summoned by Ahasuerus/Xerxes for an entire month suggest?
3. **4:14.** Although God is not explicitly mentioned, what is implicit? What does Mordecai invite Esther to see about the hand of God in her unique situation?
4. **4:16.** Of what is fasting a form? When does the heroic moment come for Esther? What do bravery and a spirit of self-sacrifice combine to make her? According to St. Clement of Rome, what quality in her soul prompted God to respond to Esther's fasting and humiliation?

For application
1. **3:15.** Why would the king and his prime minister relax at this point? On the other hand, why is the capital "perplexed"?
2. **4:1–7.** What sorts of opposition to the practice of their faith do Christians face today, both globally and in your locality? In what degree of danger do you think Christians stand?
3. **4:13.** Assuming you are committed to your faith, how comfortable do you feel with the times in which you live? Why do you think God may have placed you where you are?
4. **4:16.** What is the purpose of religious fasting? Why does the Church require periods of fasting, such as during Lent? What is your own personal practice?

Chapter 13–14 (italic)

For understanding
1. *13:8–17.* By what divine role does Mordecai appeal to God? On what does his hope for salvation rest? According to St. Aphrahat, how are Mordecai's and Jesus' prayer and penance similar?
2. *14:1–19.* How does the prayer of Esther mirror the prayer of Mordecai? What does she ask for herself? To the prayers of what other biblical characters does her prayer show many similarities? According to St. Clement of Alexandria, how did Esther deliver Israel from the power of the king and the cruelty of his vizier?

3. **14:9.** On what grounds does Esther appeal to God? In what would destruction of the covenant people result?
4. **14:17.** What is the "wine of the libations"? What is Esther careful to avoid?

For application
1. **13:9–11.** When you petition the Lord for something, how do you begin your prayer? What makes praise of God an act of humility? How is it appropriate as part of a prayer of petition?
2. **13:13–14.** Mordecai claims in prayer that his refusal to bow to Haman is not done out of pride. As one of the "capital sins", how harmful to human relationships is personal pride? At what point does confidence in your own position or accomplishments turn to arrogance?
3. **14:1–3.** Esther tries to humble herself through dramatic expressions of self-abnegation. If you were in dire circumstances like Esther's, what outward manifestations of self-denial would you consider to emphasize the seriousness of your prayer? Why does Jesus recommend hiding the fact that you are fasting at all (cf. Mt 6:16–18)?
4. **14:8–11.** What reasons does Esther give for why God should act on Israel's behalf? When you pray for a certain outcome, what reasons do you sometimes give why God should act? What are some similarities and differences between her approach to prayer and yours?

Chapter 15 (italic)

For understanding
1. **15:7.** What does the king's fierce anger hint that Esther has done? Why does the queen faint?
2. **15:8.** Who is in control of the situation? What theology is implicit here?

For application
1. **15:1–5.** Think of a time in your life when you had to prepare yourself for a task you were terrified to perform. How did you prepare yourself for it, both inwardly and outwardly? What was the contrast between your appearance and the way you felt? What part did prayer play in your preparation?
2. **15:13–14.** How do you evaluate the honesty of Esther's reply to the king? If the person you most dread to approach were to try to allay your fears as the king did, how might you assure him that you were really not afraid?

Chapter 5

For understanding
1. **5:3.** What kind of expression is the king's offer of "half of my kingdom"? How many more times is this offer made in Esther, and when? When does Herod Antipas echo these words? What is ironical in the comparison between Esther and Herodias?
2. **5:8.** What does the pair of feasts mirror at the beginning of the book, and what does it anticipate at the end of the book?
3. **5:14.** How high is "fifty cubits"? What can be concluded from the height of the gibbet? For what did the Persians use gallows?

For application
1. **5:4–8.** Read the note for v. 4. Given the extremity of Esther's fear and the king's concern for her, why do you think she delays making her true request known to him?
2. **5:9–12.** Why does it often happen that pride really does go before a fall? Have you, like Haman, ever congratulated yourself on your worth? How premature was your self-congratulation? Describe a fall or a "comeuppance" that followed.

Chapter 6

For understanding
1. **6:1.** What orchestrates the king's insomnia? What does the Greek version of Esther say explicitly? What is the "book of memorable deeds", and what does it say about Mordecai?
2. **6:8.** How does Persian art depict horses?
3. **6:10.** What does the king's statement show that he is uninformed about, and what does it further suggest? What is the bitter but fitting irony here?

For application
1. **6:3.** In our culture, what kinds of honors do we bestow on others, and for what do we typically honor them? Within your own social circle, including your family, how do you honor others, and for what? Have you ever been honored, and, if so, how was that honor shown?
2. **6:6–9.** Haman plans a grandiose procession, presuming the honor is for himself. If you wanted to honor a family member for any reason, such as an important anniversary, how would you plan for it? What would you consider doing?
3. **6:13.** The Psalms frequently pray that those who plan a trap for the innocent will fall into it themselves (e.g., Ps 141:9–10). Do the Psalms pray for justice or for vengeance? What is the difference? Why does God reserve vengeance to himself?

Chapter 7

For understanding
1. **7:1–10.** How do the tension and suspense of earlier chapters finally ease?
2. **7:2.** What is "the second day"? What does mention of drinking wine recall? How do we know that the parallel is not lost on the narrator?
3. **7:7.** What reason is given for the king's sudden exit? What does he perhaps wish to do?

4. **7:8.** What is the couch referred to here? For what does the king mistake Haman's pleading? What does the poetic description of Haman's expression mean?

For application
1. **7:2.** Why is wine often served at occasions like fundraisers? Why is the drinking of wine a significant detail in the Esther narrative? How might serving wine help Esther's cause?
2. **7:4.** Notice the sequence of verbs in the first sentence of this verse (repeated in the same sequence in 3:13). For the reader, how does the sequence intensify the doom planned for Esther and her people? What would happen to the meaning if you reversed the order?
3. **7:8.** The RSV translation describes Haman's facial expression this way: "as the words left the mouth of the king, they covered Haman's face" ; the NABRE renders it: "the face of Haman was covered over." Which is more poetic? Which is clearer? How would you describe his expression in your own words? What artistic renderings of such facial expressions have you seen, and in what context?

Chapter 8

For understanding
1. **8:1.** What is given to Esther, and what does she do with it? In ancient Persia, what happened to the property of a traitor? Of what is the king only now informed?
2. **8:2.** What does placing a signet ring on Mordecai's finger signify? For what was the ring used?
3. **8:8.** Once again, what is the king content to do regarding government policies? What happens to a decree that is ratified by royal authority? This being so, what can Ahasuerus/Xerxes do? What is the reader to note about the edict?

For application
1. **8:8.** The note for this verse explains what happens in Persia to a decree that is ratified by royal authority. In your society, how are laws enacted? Once a bad law is put into effect, why is it so difficult to repeal it? Rather than repeal the law outright, what mechanisms are available in your government to work around or neutralize it?
2. **8:11.** Read the note for this verse. Is there any group within your country that is entitled to observe its own laws? How is that group free to govern itself while remaining subject to the laws of the nation at large?

Chapter 16 (italic)

For understanding
1. **16:1–24.** What does Addition E:1–24 purport to be? What did the first letter contend? How does the second contrast with it?
2. **16:2–6.** How does power corrupt persons in high positions? What does Ahasuerus/Xerxes learn the hard way?
3. **16:10.** What is the term "Macedonian", used to describe Haman? Where did Macedonians live, and what was their relationship to the Persians? What ironically happened to the Persians in the early fifth century B.C.?
4. **16:17.** Since the king cannot revoke his previous decree, what can he do?

For application
1. **16:5–6.** When a crime is committed, how guilty under the law is a person who is unwittingly an accomplice to it? Is the accomplice *morally* guilty of either formal (intentional) or material (physical) cooperation in the crime? How responsible is the king for what would have happened to the Jews under Haman's decree?
2. **16:15.** The note for this verse cites CCC 1963, which describes the role of the Law of Moses. How does that paragraph explain the special function of the Law according to St. Paul? How is the Mosaic Law the "first stage on the way to the kingdom"?
3. **16:16.** Does your country publicly acknowledge the role of God in its affairs? If so, how is that acknowledgment demonstrated? Of what does God's role consist?

Chapters 8–9

For understanding
1. **9:1–15.** On the 13th of Adar, the day scheduled for doom, what do the Jewish people of Persia do? How is this the final and climactic reversal of the storyline? According to St. Athanasius, how did the blessed Esther prevail over the anger of the tyrant, and what does it have to do with the defeat of the devil?
2. **9:16–28.** How is the Feast of Purim celebrated? Though no prayers or liturgical rites are prescribed in the story, how did God's deliverance of the Jews eventually come to be celebrated in the synagogue? What do fixing the precise dates of the feast (Adar 14th and 15th) and making their observance mandatory mean? In later Judaism, extending into modern times, what did the festival come to involve?
3. **Word Study: Pur (9:24).** What is the origin of the Hebrew word *pur*? In Babylon, as in Israel, what kind of object was a lot? In the Book of Esther, how does Haman use it? Because the Jewish people became victors rather than victims on this fateful day, how do they commemorate it? Beyond this, what additional layer of significance does the Greek version of Esther give the feast?
4. **9:31.** How is the Hebrew reference to fasts in this verse open to interpretation? In later Judaism, when did a fast come to be observed?

For application
1. **8:17.** When Christianity became legal in the fourth century, many pagans soon became Christians. What are some of the reasons why they converted? How would bishops determine whether a conversion was genuine?

2. **9:5.** According to the letter from the king (*16:20*), was the battle fought by the Jews against their enemies a defensive or offensive engagement? In the Christian dispensation, what four conditions for defense by military force would make a defensive war legitimate (CCC 2309)? Should a nation accumulate arms to deter potential adversaries from war (CCC 2315)?
3. **9:6–10.** Read Ezek 18:1–20. How would you evaluate the morality of eliminating all of Haman's male line for the crime of their father? In modern times, what should happen to the family of someone convicted of a notorious crime such as mass murder?
4. **9:20–28.** What historical events have occasioned an annual celebration within the Catholic Church? How, for example, does the Church commemorate the victory of the Battle of Lepanto? Can you think of any other examples?

Chapters 10 and 11 (italic)

For understanding
1. **10:2.** What documents was it common practice in Near Eastern kingdoms to keep? What does the author here claim?
2. *10:4–12.* How is Mordecai's dream in *11:2–12* interpreted? For what does he learn that God is primarily responsible? What belief is likewise reinforced?
3. *11:1.* What type of note is the final verse, and what does it identify? However, on what does establishing the date of the note depend? Why is this not easily determined?

For application
1. *10:5.* Does any given prophecy have only one fulfillment, or may it have more than one? Can you think of an example to support your answer? If more than one, which is the "definitive" fulfillment?
2. *10:9.* Read the note for this verse. Where else in the Bible is this expression used? With what is it connected?

BOOKS OF THE BIBLE

THE OLD TESTAMENT (OT)

Gen	Genesis
Ex	Exodus
Lev	Leviticus
Num	Numbers
Deut	Deuteronomy
Josh	Joshua
Judg	Judges
Ruth	Ruth
1 Sam	1 Samuel
2 Sam	2 Samuel
1 Kings	1 Kings
2 Kings	2 Kings
1 Chron	1 Chronicles
2 Chron	2 Chronicles
Ezra	Ezra
Neh	Nehemiah
Tob	Tobit
Jud	Judith
Esther	Esther
Job	Job
Ps	Psalms
Prov	Proverbs
Eccles	Ecclesiastes
Song	Song of Solomon
Wis	Wisdom
Sir	Sirach (Ecclesiasticus)
Is	Isaiah
Jer	Jeremiah
Lam	Lamentations
Bar	Baruch
Ezek	Ezekiel
Dan	Daniel
Hos	Hosea
Joel	Joel
Amos	Amos
Obad	Obadiah
Jon	Jonah
Mic	Micah
Nahum	Nahum
Hab	Habakkuk
Zeph	Zephaniah
Hag	Haggai
Zech	Zechariah
Mal	Malachi
1 Mac	1 Maccabees
2 Mac	2 Maccabees

THE NEW TESTAMENT (NT)

Mt	Matthew
Mk	Mark
Lk	Luke
Jn	John
Acts	Acts of the Apostles
Rom	Romans
1 Cor	1 Corinthians
2 Cor	2 Corinthians
Gal	Galatians
Eph	Ephesians
Phil	Philippians
Col	Colossians
1 Thess	1 Thessalonians
2 Thess	2 Thessalonians
1 Tim	1 Timothy
2 Tim	2 Timothy
Tit	Titus
Philem	Philemon
Heb	Hebrews
Jas	James
1 Pet	1 Peter
2 Pet	2 Peter
1 Jn	1 John
2 Jn	2 John
3 Jn	3 John
Jude	Jude
Rev	Revelation (Apocalypse)